PRINCIPLED REASONING IN HUMAN RIGHTS ADJUDICATION

Implied constitutional principles form part of the landscape of the development of fundamental rights in common law jurisdictions, affecting issues ranging from the remuneration of judges to the appropriation of property by the state. *Principled Reasoning in Human Rights Adjudication* offers thematic analysis of the use of the implied constitutional principles of the rule of law and separation of powers in human rights cases. The book examines the functions played by those principles in rights adjudication in Australia, Canada, the Commonwealth Caribbean and the United Kingdom. It argues that a complete understanding of implied constitutional principles requires thoroughgoing analysis of the sources and methods of implication and of the specific roles played by such principles in the adjudicative process. By disaggregating particular functions and placing those functions within their respective institutional contexts, this book develops an understanding of the features of cases in which implied constitutional principles are invoked and the work done by those principles.

Volume 15 in the series Hart Studies in Comparative Public Law

Hart Studies in Comparative Public Law
Recent titles in this series:

Constitutionalising Secession
David Haljan

Parliaments and Human Rights
Redressing the Democratic Deficit
Edited by Murray Hunt, Hayley Hooper and Paul Yowell

The Right to Freedom of Assembly
A Comparative Study
Orsolya Salát

An Inquiry into the Existence of Global Values
Through the Lens of Comparative Constitutional Law
Edited by Dennis Davis, Alan Richter and Cheryl Saunders

The Scope and Intensity of Substantive Review
Traversing Taggart's Rainbow
Edited by Hanna Wilberg and Mark Elliott

Entick v Carrington
250 Years of the Rule of Law
Edited by Adam Tomkins and Paul Scott

Administrative Law and Judicial Deference
Matthew Lewans

Soft Law and Public Authorities
Remedies and Reform
Greg Weeks

Legitimate Expectations in the Common Law World
Edited by Matthew Groves and Greg Weeks

The Dynamics of Exclusionary Constitutionalism
Mazen Masri

Constitutional Courts, Gay Rights and Sexual Orientation Equality
Angioletta Sperti

Principled Reasoning in Human Rights Adjudication

Se-shauna Wheatle

•HART•
OXFORD • LONDON • NEW YORK • NEW DELHI • SYDNEY

HART PUBLISHING
Bloomsbury Publishing Plc
Kemp House, Chawley Park, Cumnor Hill, Oxford, OX2 9PH, UK

First published in hardback, 2017
Paperback edition, 2019

A catalogue record for this book is available from the British Library.

Library of Congress Cataloging-in-Publication data

ISBN: HB: 978-1-78225-981-7
PB: 978-1-50993-132-3
ePDF: 978-1-78225-983-1
ePub: 978-1-78225-982-4

Typeset by Compuscript Ltd, Shannon

Acknowledgements

I am grateful to Professor Christopher McCrudden for the skilful supervision he provided during the course of the thesis that preceded this book. Special gratitude is also extended to the community at Exeter College, Oxford, and Durham Law School, where I taught while completing my doctorate and the book manuscript, respectively. The students and staff at both institutions, particularly Professors Jonathan Herring and Roger Masterman, provided ideas, a listening ear, and a congenial, supportive atmosphere. I also thank Nicholas Barber and Professor David Feldman for providing useful suggestions during the final *viva voce* and to anonymous reviewers who provided thoughtful comments on the draft manuscript. I am grateful to the Rhodes Trust for the financial support necessary for me to embark on my academic journey and to the staff at Rhodes House for providing logistical, pastoral, and other forms of support during my postgraduate studies. Thanks also extend to the staff at the University of the West Indies, particularly to those influential lecturers who stimulated my interest in the law and encouraged me to pursue further studies. Above all, I am grateful to my parents, Alethia and Junior Wheatle, to my siblings, Rochey and Junior, to my partner Ben, my niece Maya and to my dear friends, for their patience, hugs, and laughter.

Table of Contents

Part II: Functions Played by the Implied Constitutional Principles of the Rule of Law and Separation of Powers

Table of Abbreviations

AG	Attorney General
CA	Court of Appeal
CCJ	Caribbean Court of Justice
CRA	Constitutional Reform Act
Cth	Commonwealth (of Australia)
DPP	Director of Public Prosecutions
ECHR	European Convention for the Protection of Human Rights and Fundamental Freedoms (European Convention on Human Rights)
ECtHR	European Court of Human Rights
HC	High Court
HL	House of Lords
HRA	Human Rights Act
SC	Supreme Court
SSHD	Secretary of State for the Home Department
UKSC	United Kingdom Supreme Court

Table of Cases

COMMONWEALTH CARIBBEAN

UNITED KINGDOM

OTHER

1

Introduction: The Doctrinal and Institutional Context

IMPLIED CONSTITUTIONAL PRINCIPLES form part of the landscape of the development of fundamental rights in common law jurisdictions. The significance of constitutional principles in the common law world has been underscored by the United Kingdom Supreme Court's recent endorsement of fundamental principles 'recognised at common law' which, along with constitutional instruments, are norms of special constitutional importance.[1] This book examines the phenomenon of the use of implied constitutional principles in *judicial* decision-making in fundamental rights cases. The significance of this judicial practice is evident in the broad influence of reasoning by implied principles in cases considering issues ranging from the remuneration of judges,[2] to the appropriation of property by the state.[3] Its importance to constitutional study is also attributable to the fact that such principles can serve as a ground for invalidating legislation, as has been held by the Judicial Committee of the Privy Council.[4]

The book centres on the constitutional principles of the separation of powers and the rule of law, as these principles, which feature prominently in judicial decisions, are foundational to our very understanding of the constitutional democracies in which our courts function. Thus, Donald Lutz, writing of principles of constitutional design, and Trevor Allan, expounding on constitutional justice, maintain that constitutionalism implies the presence of the principles of the separation of powers and the rule of law.[5] Frequently, these principles are implied rather than expressly stated in constitutional

[1] *R (on the application of Buckinghamshire CC) v Secretary of State for Transport* [2014] UKSC 3, [2014] 1 WLR 324 (SC) (*HS2* case) [207]; Paul Craig, 'Constitutionalising Constitutional Law: HS2' [2014] *Public Law* 373, 382–87.

[2] *Reference Re Remuneration of Judges of the Provincial Court of Prince Edward Island* [1997] 3 SCR 3 (SC, Canada) (*Provincial Judges Reference* or *Remuneration Reference*).

[3] *Toussaint v Attorney General of St Vincent* [2007] UKPC 48, (2007) 70 WIR 167 (Judicial Committee of the Privy Council (JCPC), St Vincent and the Grenadines).

[4] *DPP of Jamaica v Mollison* (2003) 64 WIR 140 (JCPC, Jamaica).

[5] TRS Allan, *Constitutional Justice: A Liberal Theory of the Rule of Law* (Oxford, Oxford University Press, 2001) 1–5; Donald Lutz, *Principles of Constitutional Design* (Cambridge University Press, 2006) x, 3, 5.

documents. There is abundant theoretical debate over the meaning of each principle, as well as scholarly literature addressing the normative question of the legitimacy of judicial use of implied constitutional principles.[6] For instance, Mark Walters has written in defence of the invocation of implied constitutional principles, partly by identifying a connection between this practice and the use of *lex non scripta* (law which does not derive its normative status from encapsulation in written form).[7] The legitimacy of recourse to implied principles in cases involving challenges to the constitutionality of governmental and legislative acts has been most extensively questioned in Canadian commentary owing to a series of influential Canadian Supreme Court cases which conferred renewed prominence on constitutional principles in Canadian constitutionalism.[8]

This book aims to enhance the existing scholarly literature in two critical respects. Current scholarship is primarily augmented by providing a more pragmatic analysis of the meaning and use of implied constitutional principles through the lens of case law. The term 'pragmatic' is used to signal attention to the use and application of these principles in opposition to a purely theoretical approach.[9] Secondly, the book engages in thematic analysis of the functions played by such principles in judicial decision-making. The objective is not to propose a normative argument regarding the use of implied constitutional principles or particular conceptions of such principles. Rather, by critical thematic examination of case law, I discuss the ways in which these principles are used as a means of legitimating judicial decisions in rights cases, and the conceptual and constitutional difficulties that arise from this practice. This analysis presents a necessary companion to the existing normative discourse of invoking implied constitutional principles in rights cases.

Several terminological issues affect the issues in this book, one such issue being the understanding of the term 'fundamental rights adjudication'. In

[6] See, eg, Jean Leclair, 'Canada's Unfathomable Unwritten Constitutional Principles' (2002) 27 Queen's Law Journal 389; FC DeCoste, 'Smoked: Tradition and the Rule of Law in *British Columbia v Imperial Tobacco Canada Ltd*' (2006) *Windsor Yearbook of Access to Justice* 328; Jeffrey Goldsworthy, 'Unwritten Constitutional Principles' in Grant Huscroft (ed), *Expounding the Constitution: Essays in Constitutional Theory* (Cambridge University Press, 2008); Mark Walters, 'Written Constitutions and Unwritten Constitutionalism' in Grant Huscroft (ed), *Expounding the Constitution: Essays in Constitutional Theory* (Cambridge University Press, 2008).

[7] Walters, 'Unwritten Constitutionalism' (ibid).

[8] See eg *Remuneration Reference* (n 2 above); *Reference re Secession of Quebec* [1998] 2 SCR 217 (SC, Canada) (*Secession Reference*).

[9] The term 'pragmatic' is therefore not used as part of the debate between pragmatic constitutional development versus an ideological approach to constitutional development. On this debate, see, eg, Ivor Jennings, *The Law and the Constitution*, 5th edn (University of London Press, 1963) especially 8–9, 157; Christopher McCrudden, 'Northern Ireland, and the British Constitution' in Jeffrey Jowell and Dawn Oliver (eds), *The Changing Constitution*, 6th edn (Oxford University Press, 2007) 228–31.

this book, that term is used to refer to cases in which it is alleged that the act or omission of a governmental organ violates an individual's liberty. Liberty is understood as inclusive of both positive and negative conceptions of liberty and is not limited to liberties expressed in a constitutional or rights instrument.[10] Further, while there is academic debate on the correct adjectival terminology to attach to rights, such as 'human rights', 'constitutional rights', or 'fundamental rights', the analysis undertaken here does not hinge on a choice between these terms and accordingly, this book does not join that debate.[11]

The vast majority of the adjudication cited throughout the book is comprised of appellate judgments from the common law jurisdictions selected. This includes analysis of constitutional case law in which fundamental rights are both directly and indirectly in issue, as decisions that indirectly raise rights issues can illuminate the content or applications of the implied constitutional principles, and can contain relevant *obiter dicta* on the rights implications of the court's reasoning or decision. Further, though this is a study on the implementation of these principles in constitutional cases, reference will also be made to administrative law cases in addition to constitutional and human rights judgments, in recognition that administrative law at times forms the ground of implementation of constitutional principles such as the rule of law.[12]

The research presented in this book is conducted through the use of comparative methodology, allowing a more complete and more nuanced picture of the workings of implied constitutional principles.[13] The jurisdictions examined are Canada, the Commonwealth Caribbean, Australia, and the United Kingdom, which all possess fundamental similarities such as a common law tradition and a 'Westminster-style' parliamentary democracy.[14]

[10] Christopher McCrudden and Gerald Chambers, 'Introduction: Human Rights in British Law' in Christopher McCrudden and Gerald Chambers (eds), *Individual Rights and the Law in Britain* (Clarendon Press, 1994) 9.

[11] On some of the arguments in this debate, see, eg, Joseph Raz, 'Human Rights Without Foundations' in Samantha Besson and John Tasioulas (eds), *The Philosophy of International Law* (Oxford University Press, 2010) 328–29, 336–37; Jeremy Waldron, 'Human Rights: A Critique of the Raz/Rawls Approach' in Adam Etinson, *Human Rights: Moral or Political?* (Oxford University Press, forthcoming). On 'fundamental rights', see Tom Hickman, *Public Law after the Human Rights Act* (Hart Publishing, 2010) 17–21.

[12] Jeffrey Jowell, 'The Rule of Law Today' in Jeffrey Jowell and Dawn Oliver, *The Changing Constitution* (Oxford University Press, 1994) 73; Mark Elliott, *The Constitutional Foundations of Judicial Review* (Hart Publishing, 2001) 251.

[13] Ran Hirschl, 'On the Blurred Methodological Matrix' in Sujit Choudry, *The Migration of Constitutional Ideas* (Cambridge University Press, 2006) 45–46.

[14] Vivek Krishnamurthy, 'Colonial Cousins: Explaining India and Canada's Unwritten Constitutional Principles' (2009) 34 *Yale Journal of International Law* 207, 211; David Erdos, *Delegating Rights Protection: The Rise of Bills of Rights in the Westminster World* (Oxford University Press, 2010) 5–6; Vicki C Jackson, 'Comparative Constitutional Law: Methodologies' in Michel Rosenfeld and András Sajó (eds), *The Oxford Handbook of Comparative Constitutional Law* (Oxford University Press, 2012) 1168–69.

The label 'Westminster-style' or 'Westminster model' constitutional system describes a constitutional design that incorporates an executive selected largely from, and responsible to, a legislature (that is, a system of responsible government).[15] I have therefore adopted the 'most similar case' research design to focus on factors that are common to analogous jurisdictions, to identify the relevant distinctions that arise and to control for variables that are not central to the purposes of this research.[16]

This methodological design permits the testing of theories regarding the functions played by the implied principles across four common law jurisdictions. In particular, the book adds to the current literature by including detailed, contextual analysis of case law from the Commonwealth Caribbean, a jurisdiction that is largely ignored in the existing literature. Inclusion of Caribbean case law in the discourse on implied constitutional principles brings the post-colonial element of the law in newly independent states into sharp relief. Thus, the methodological choices made also present the opportunity to examine the case law within a post-colonial context, taking account of historical factors and the tensions between nationalistic inclinations and foreign influences in Constitution-building. These aspects of the historical and socio-political context are raised throughout the book, showing the role of implied principles against that contextual background.

The methodological approach adopted in carrying out this comparative study is simultaneously functional and contextual. It is functional in its attempt to discover why particular constitutional principles are utilised, the functions for which they are employed, and how these functions operate in the institutional contexts identified in this book.[17] The case material is also examined in its historical context, seeking to gain an understanding of the impact of social and political history. Specifically, subsequent chapters take account of the impact of history on the aspirations of the institutional apparatus of the state, and how these aspirations are reflected in the citation of constitutional principles.[18] There is also some classificatory work, particularly with respect to the rule of law, in an attempt to monitor trends in the understanding of the rule of law in common law jurisdictions.[19] This classificatory approach is an important precursor to developing our understanding of judges' engagements with differing rule of law conceptions.

[15] *R v Kirby, ex p Boilermakers' Society of Australia* (1956) 94 CLR 254 (HC, Australia) 275; Peter Gerangelos, *The Separation of Powers and Legislative Interference in Judicial Process: Constitutional Principles and Limitations* (Hart Publishing, 2009) 35.

[16] Hirschl (n 13 above) 48.

[17] On functional comparative work, see Jackson (n 14 above) 62–63.

[18] See Jackson (n 14 above) 67.

[19] See Jackson (n 14 above) 57–58.

I. MAP OF THE BOOK

The book proceeds by progressing from a critical analysis of the concept of implied principles, the rule of law and separation of powers to a proposal of the functions that these principles seek to perform in cases raising rights questions. Part I (comprising chapters two–four) first engages with conceptual debates surrounding the contestable concept of 'principles'; it also considers the key question of what constitutes 'implying' a norm primarily into constitutional or other legislation protecting rights, and explains the selection of the rule of law and separation of powers as the principles forming the primary areas of study. Part I also outlines the content of each principle to be subjected to thematic analysis. This is an essential prior issue that allows us to clarify what meanings are attributed to the rule of law and separation of powers as used by judges in the jurisdictions examined. Part II of the book (comprising chapters five–eight) identifies the functions played by implied principles in rights adjudication and the factors that contribute to each function. The Conclusion summarises the main themes explored in the book and the main findings that emerged from the research. The remainder of this Introduction briefly outlines the main issues considered in each chapter of the book.

Chapter two constructs a conceptual understanding of 'implied constitutional principles'. Part II of the chapter analyses the term 'implied principles' by first explaining the meaning ascribed to the term 'implied' in the book and classifying the methods of implication utilised by judges in the jurisdictions examined. This is followed by analysis of the meaning of the term 'principles', drawing on the theories of Ronald Dworkin and Robert Alexy to distinguish principles from other norms.[20] I draw on Alexy's conceptual apparatus despite the fact that he writes within the context of the civil law system in Germany. The differences that arise between the civil and common law in this area are differences in application and institutional apparatus, which do not undermine the relevance of Alexy's conceptual ideas. Part III of the second chapter seeks to demonstrate the significance of the separation of powers and rule of law in the discourse on the use of implied principles in fundamental rights adjudication. It is argued that the centrality of the rule of law and the separation of powers to constitutionalism is a critical aspect of the appeal of these principles in resolving rights issues. While there are other implied constitutional principles that may merit further study, there are features that distinguish the rule of law and separation of powers from other principles. First, the rule of law and separation of powers

[20] Ronald Dworkin, *Taking Rights Seriously* (Harvard University Press, 1978) ch 2; Robert Alexy, *A Theory of Constitutional Rights* (Julian Rivers tr, Oxford University Press, 2002) ch 3.

are interrelated foundational principles of constitutional democracies[21] and are inextricably bound to the substantive and organisational imperatives of constitutionalism.[22] Secondly, these principles are part of the unwritten English Constitution, which were subsequently incorporated in the constitutional arrangements of the other Commonwealth jurisdictions. In this chapter, there is discussion of some elements of the historical and institutional contexts of the case law that will be considered in detail subsequently. For instance, there is brief discussion of the role of parliamentary supremacy in constitutional and rights development in the respective jurisdictions.

In chapter three, on Judicial Conceptions of the Rule of Law, I seek to understand and categorise what is meant when judges refer to the 'rule of law' and, generally, what judicial decisions reveal about the meaning of the concept. There is much theorising about the appropriate conception of the rule of law, as expressed in the writings of Joseph Raz and Ronald Dworkin as well as in more recent analyses.[23] In a more pragmatic study, Jeffrey Jowell has written on the conceptions of the rule of law reflected in UK case law.[24] However, there is a dearth of academic literature conducting comparative analysis of where the case law in the respective jurisdictions rests along the spectrum of conceptions of the rule of law. This chapter adopts Jowell's pragmatic approach but uses comparative methodology to test the theories. First, the theoretical discourse is briefly outlined; then there is a focus on thematic analysis of the case law. I do not contend that there is one conception of the rule of law that is reflected in the jurisdictions examined, but rather, analyse what judicial decisions reveal about the specific applications of the rule of law by judges.

Chapter four applies the same pragmatic approach to the separation of powers principle. Part II of the chapter outlines the relevant theoretical framework of the separation of powers[25] while Part III discusses the content of the 'Westminster model' of separation of powers as revealed through case

[21] Allan, *Constitutional Justice: A Liberal Theory of the Rule of Law* (n 5 above); Lutz (n 5 above).

[22] Martin Loughlin and Neil Walker, 'Introduction' in Martin Loughlin and Neil Walker, *The Paradox of Constitutionalism: Constituent Power and Constitutional Form* (Oxford University Press, 2008) 1–2; Aoife O'Donoghue, *Constitutionalism in Global Constitutionalisation* (Cambridge University Press, 2014) 19–20.

[23] See, eg, NW Barber, 'Must Legalistic Conceptions of the Rule of Law Have a Social Dimension?' (2004) 17 *Ratio Juris* 474.

[24] Jeffrey Jowell, 'The Rule of Law and Its Underlying Values' in Jeffrey L Jowell and Dawn Oliver (eds), *The Changing Constitution*, 7th edn (Oxford University Press, 2011). See also Alison L Young, 'The Rule of Law in the United Kingdom: Formal or Substantive?' (2012) 6 *Vienna Journal on International Constitutional Law* 259.

[25] The most recent contributions to the theoretical discussions include Eoin Carolan, *The New Separation of Powers: A Theory for the Modern State* (Oxford University Press, 2009) and Christoph Möllers, *The Three Branches: A Comparative Model of Separation of Powers* (Oxford University Press, 2013).

law. It is argued that in the context of 'Westminster style' systems, the term 'separation of powers' is often used as an equivalent of the concept of 'judicial independence'. Part IV of the chapter situates the separation of powers principle within the context of rights adjudication, discussing the use of the principle in the resolution of rights issues. Finally, Part V addresses the impact of the Constitutional Reform Act 2005 (UK) and the Human Rights Act 1998 (UK) on the application of the separation of powers in the UK, as evidenced through judicial decisions.[26] This discussion reveals a complex picture regarding the court's role as a check on other organs of state and the tension between judicial supervision and judicial restraint in fundamental rights adjudication.[27] In exploring the literature and case law on applications of the rule of law and separation of powers principles, it will be argued that while there is no unity of definition of the two principles, in that they are by no means identical, there is some overlap in the ways in which they are applied by courts. Notably, they are both often applied as expressions of judicial independence.

With that, the book moves to Part II, in which the functions played by implied constitutional principles are considered. In chapter five, I examine the use of implied principles as aids in the interpretation of statutory text. This chapter examines the reasons for the appeal to these principles by the judiciary and the interpretative functions played by the usage of such principles. Part II of the chapter proposes that implied constitutional principles are employed as 'distancing devices'[28] in hard cases, which includes cases in which fundamental rights are implicated. Part III explains how the nature of principles permits their use as common grounds in normative conflict, providing a broad base of agreement on which to proceed to the resolution of complex rights issues. In Part IV of the chapter, there is analysis of implied principles as tools for maintaining institutional respect, particularly in disputes regarding the limits of the courts' intervention in fundamental rights issues. The chapter uses the debate over privative clauses to reveal the operation of constitutional principles as bases of argumentation in dialogue over the boundaries of judicial review of administrative action and adjudication of allegations of rights violations.[29]

[26] See Vernon Bognador, *The New British Constitution* (Hart Publishing, 2009) 287–89; Roger Masterman, *The Separation of Powers in the Contemporary Constitution: Judicial Competence and Independence in the United Kingdom* (Cambridge University Press, 2011).

[27] See, eg, *R v Lichniak* [2002] UKHL 47, [2003] 1 AC 903 [14] (HL); Aileen Kavanagh, 'Defending Deference in Public Law and Constitutional Theory' [2010] *Law Quarterly Review* 222.

[28] Joseph Raz, 'On the Authority and Interpretation of Constitutions' in Larry Alexander (ed) *Constitutionalism: Philosophical Foundations* (Cambridge University Press, 1998) 190.

[29] The term 'privative clause' is used in reference to a clause that purports to oust judicial review. The terms 'privative clause' and 'ouster clause' are used interchangeably.

Chapter six then examines the phenomenon whereby judges hold (or state in *obiter dicta*) that implied constitutional principles can serve as independent grounds for invalidating legislation. Part II of the chapter proposes that there are three circumstances in which judges adopt this course of action. The first occurs where there is a gap in the Bill of Rights with respect to the fundamental right that is engaged in the case before the court. The second occurs where there is a gap in the power granted to the court to invalidate legislation by the text of the Constitution or Bill of Rights and the third arises where legislation challenges the court's power to review governmental action that affects individual rights. In examining such cases, it will be argued in Part III of this chapter that two trends are evident. First, where judges have determined that legislation may be invalidated on the ground of an implied principle, they have placed reliance on an application of the principle that protects jurisdictional boundaries. Thus, in these cases, either the separation of powers was the implied principle on which the decision was based or, if the rule of law was used, it was an application of the conception of the rule of law that mandates separation of organs of state. Within this larger trend, there is a second trend whereby courts are most protective of the borders of the judicial sphere, thereby ascribing greater normative force to principles in defence of judicial power.

Connections between reasoning by implied principles and judicial engagement with comparative legal analysis are explored in chapter seven, which begins by proposing reasons why judges cite foreign judgments and arguing that the appeal of comparative law intersects with the appeal of implied principles in rights adjudication.[30] This analysis highlights the centrality of the legitimation of institutions, institutional processes, and the state. A dominant theme in this discussion is the reputational currency of implied principles used in conjunction with foreign legal analysis. Part III of this chapter discusses ways in which implied principles function as gateways to foreign judgments, arguing that the practice appears directed towards the reinforcement of the legitimacy of the court as an institution.[31] Against this background of legitimacy reinforcement, Part IV contends with the colonial legacy reflected in and channelled through reliance on unwritten principles in former British colonies. Parts V and VI of the chapter then discuss the extent to which courts are developing common approaches to common problems, and the scope and impact of the exchange of ideas and methodology across the jurisdictions considered in this book.

[30] See, eg, Gary Jacobsohn, 'Constitutional Values and Principles' in Michel Rosenfeld and András Sajó (eds), *The Oxford Handbook of Comparative Constitutional Law* (Oxford University Press, 2012).

[31] This discussion is influenced by ideas from Anne-Marie Slaughter, 'Judicial Globalization' (1999–2000) 40 *Virginia Journal of International Law* 1103 and Christopher McCrudden, Human Rights and Judicial Use of Comparative Law, in Esin Örücü (ed), *Judicial Comparativism in Human Rights* (Martinus Nijhoff Publishers, 2004).

The final substantive chapter, chapter eight, adds to the current literature by drawing on the analysis in previous sections of the book to demonstrate the preliminary work to be undertaken as a prolegomenon to a normative analysis. It presents four main factors that influence the normative issue of the legitimacy of the use of implied constitutional principles in adjudication, the first being the method by which the principle is implied. Analysis of the first factor incorporates discourse on the nature and purpose of interpretation, adopting Raz's argument that interpretation is both forward and backward looking.[32] The second factor discussed is the specific use for which an implied constitutional principle is employed, that is, whether it is used as an interpretive aid, a gateway to foreign law, or a ground for invalidating legislation. This discussion is connected to the issue of the institutional legitimacy of the courts and to the question whether the use of implied principles leads to the displacement of bills of rights. The level of determinacy of the constitutional principle in question—which addresses the charge that the content of principles is unacceptably vague—is acknowledged as the third factor, but I argue that considerations of determinacy are significantly less relevant than the first two factors.[33] Finally, the chapter considers the degree of similarity between reasoning by implied principles and adopting doctrines that permit judicial invalidation of enacted constitutional amendments.[34] Ultimately, while the textual and institutional implications of defeat of constitutional amendments through implied principles would be momentous, it would be premature (and exaggerative) to conclude that reasoning by implied principles inevitably leads to a doctrine of unconstitutional constitutional amendments.

II. RECURRING THEMES

There are several recurring themes that emerge throughout the book, particularly in Part II's study of the functions played by the rule of law and separation of powers. One theme that is apparent in the analysis of the functions served by implied constitutional principles is the theme of legitimisation. This includes the quest to legitimise arguments, reasoning, institutions of state (particularly the courts), institutional processes, and ultimately, the

[32] Aileen Kavanagh, 'The Elusive Divide between Interpretation and Legislation under the Human Rights Act 1998' (2004) 24 *Oxford Journal of Legal Studies* 259; Joseph Raz, *Between Authority and Interpretation: On the Theory of Law and Practical Reason* (Oxford University Press, 2009).

[33] The discourse on indeterminacy includes Joseph Raz, *The Authority of Law: Essays on Law and Morality* (Clarendon Press, 1979) 70–72, 181–82; Timothy Endicott, 'Linguistic Indeterminacy' (1996) 16 *Oxford Journal of Legal Studies* 667, 669; Kavanagh 'Elusive Divide' (ibid).

[34] See Gary J Jacobsohn, *Constitutional Identity* (Harvard University Press, 2010) 34–83.

legitimisation of the state *qua* state. Another significant theme that emerges is that of institutional self-protection, which highlights the attempt of state institutions—particularly courts—to protect their jurisdictional sphere against interference and diminution by other organs of the state. The legacy of Empire is also a critical element in the proceeding discussions. It will be argued that the desire to preserve a British legacy of the rule of law and democratic institutions impacted and continues to influence constitutional development in the former colonies of Canada, Australia, and the Commonwealth Caribbean.[35] It becomes apparent that the perception and use of language occupies a place in the legacy of Empire and the delivery of legal judgments. In these respective realms, language performs both a binding function (a connector that continues to tie the old Empire and the new Commonwealth) and a freeing function (that maintains flexibility in legal judgments and permits fluidity in the development and application of legal norms).

Throughout the case law examined in the course of this book, there is a strong sense of the connections between the laws and institutions of the past and those of the present, as well as an attempt to reconcile the demands of changing circumstances with tradition. It is partly this sense of time, and the tension between continuity and change, that permeates much of the use of the rule of law and the separation of powers by common law courts. It is partly this sense of time that also contributes to the legitimisation of state institutions through appeal to implied constitutional principles, either as representations of continuity between the laws and institutions of the former imperial ruler or as indications of fidelity to precedent and to the very foundations of democratic constitutionalism. There is also a distinct spatial element to the use of the implied principles, as there is an appeal to these principles as an attempt to distance judges from the perception that they are making moral or political decisions. The spatial element is also manifest in a quite different sense, in that the use of the rule of law and separation of powers filters across the geographical boundaries of common law jurisdictions, contributing to similarities of language and of decision-making methodology.

Thus, this book seeks to explore the use of the rule of law and the separation of powers as legal principles by judges, and to show the connections between such usage and the broader development of rights adjudication both within and across the jurisdictions in question. This analysis can then help to further inform more normatively driven scholarship on the use of these principles in general and the legitimacy of courts' use of such principles in particular. These issues form part of a larger narrative arc of constitutionalism in general and the intersection between comparative constitutionalism and common law constitutionalism in particular.

[35] See, eg, David Brooke, 'The Rule of Law and the British Empire—Part II' (2013) 8 *Irish Law Times* 121, 122–23.

Part I

The Conceptual Context and the Meanings of the Implied Constitutional Principles

2

Implied Principles and Constitutionalism

I. INTRODUCTION

RELIANCE ON THE principles of separation of powers and rule of law speaks to the very bedrock of constitutional values and the fundamental ordering of both the institutional apparatus of the state and the norms binding those institutions. Concrete and contextual examination of the judicial use of these principles in fundamental rights adjudication must be underpinned by conceptual understanding of 'implied principles', and their place within constitutional democracy and adjudication. The task of laying that basic conceptual groundwork is undertaken in this chapter, beginning with analytical discourse of the term 'implied principles'.[1] This analysis is pursued by first explaining the meaning ascribed to the term 'implied' in the context of this study and identifying the methods of implication utilised by judges in the jurisdictions under review. Next, drawing on legal and constitutional theory, the concept of 'principles' is explored, situating principles within the scheme of legal norms and constitutional development. The chapter then demonstrates the significance of the separation of powers and the rule of law in discourse on the use of implied principles in constitutional and fundamental rights adjudication. The pivotal argument is the centrality of the rule of law and separation of powers to constitutionalism, which, as argued below, is a key aspect of the appeal of these principles in resolving constitutional and fundamental rights issues.

II. ON IMPLIED PRINCIPLES

Disaggregating the words in the term 'implied principles' serves to inject greater conceptual clarity into the discourse, by more vividly identifying methods or sources of implication and delineating the concept of principles.

[1] The terms 'unwritten principles' and 'implied principles' are used interchangeably throughout this book.

The conceptual analysis is in large part an exercise in distinction—distinguishing the implied from the expressed and principles from rules. Turning to the first of these distinctions, the principles discussed here are 'implied' or 'unwritten' in the sense that they do not appear in the substantive text of the written Constitutions or Bills of Rights of the jurisdictions in question. Consistent with the prevailing treatment of preambles in statutory interpretation treatises, the substantive text is understood to exclude the preamble; as such, principles that are referenced only in the preamble are treated as implied.[2] This approach is also consistent with the manner in which courts have characterised references to principles in the preamble. For instance, in a foundational judgment on the use of implied principles in Canadian constitutional law, *Reference re Manitoba Language Rights*, the Supreme Court of Canada noted that the reference to the rule of law in the preamble to the Constitution Act 1982 (Canada) reflected an 'unwritten postulate', which is part of 'the very foundation of the Constitution of Canada'.[3] A similar understanding was ascribed to the term 'unwritten' by Chief Justice Lamer of the Canadian Supreme Court in *Reference re Remuneration of Judges of the Provincial Court (Remuneration Reference)*, who cast judicial independence as 'at root an unwritten constitutional principle, in the sense that it is exterior to the particular sections of the *Constitution Acts*'.[4]

Nonetheless, preambles are often fertile ground for references to implied constitutional principles. A preamble in a Constitution or Bill of Rights is the introductory statement to the instrument, which may bear the title 'Preamble' but may also bear another or no title.[5] In Australia, the relevant preamble appears in the opening sentences of the Commonwealth of Australia Constitution Act 1900 (Constitution of the Commonwealth of Australia 1900). The preamble often invoked in Canadian cases is the opening sentence of the British North America Act 1867 (now referred to as the Constitution Act 1867). The Constitutions of the Commonwealth Caribbean include opening sentences to their fundamental rights chapters, and those introductory clauses have been designated preambles by the courts.[6]

[2] FAR Bennion, *Bennion on Statutory Interpretation: A Code*, 5th edn (LexisNexis, 2008) 731–33; Daniel Greenberg (ed) *Craies on Legislation: A Practitioners' Guide to the Nature, Process, Effect and Interpretation of Legislation*, 10th edn (Sweet & Maxwell, 2012) paras 2.5.10 and 26.1.2–26.1.4.

[3] Reference re Language Rights Under s 23 of the Manitoba Act 1870 and s 133 of the Constitution Act 1867 (*Manitoba Language Rights Reference* or *Reference re Manitoba Language Rights*) [1985] 1 SCR 721 [70].

[4] *Reference Re Remuneration of Judges of the Provincial Court of Prince Edward Island* [1997] 3 SCR 3 (SC, Canada) [83].

[5] Liav Orgad, 'The Preamble in Constitutional Interpretation' (2010) 8 *International Journal of Constitutional Law* 714, 715–16; Anne Twomey, 'Constitutional Recognition of Indigenous Australians in a Preamble' (Constitutional Reform Unit, Sydney Law School 2011) 16.

[6] *Lewis v AG* [2001] 2 AC 50 (JCPC, Jamaica); *AG v Joseph and Boyce* (2006) 69 WIR 104 (Caribbean Court of Justice (CCJ), Barbados).

Two complementary inquiries help to illustrate the functions played by preambles in constitutional and fundamental rights law. The first is to discover the main roles played by the preamble, as apparent on the face of the Constitution or Bill of Rights, and secondly, to have regard to the legal status of preambles as determined by judicial usage.[7] Within the instrument, the preamble's roles range from explanatory, exhortatory, and formative to symbolic. In its explanatory role, the preamble informs the reader of the relevant factual background of the Constitution, including references to consultations preceding the enactment of the document.[8] It may also be explanatory in a purposive sense, by outlining the animating objectives and goals behind the document. Thus, in this role, it 'serves to specify the reasons for the Constitution's enactment, its *raison d'être* and eternal ideals.'[9] The formative function of the preamble consists of describing and consolidating the national identity of the state.[10] As an exhortatory statement, it encourages respect for—and obedience to—the law. A venerated expression of this role of preambles is found in Plato's work *The Laws*. For Plato, a preamble should encourage free compliance with the law on the basis that the law is virtuous, rather than through the threat of sanctions.[11] Finally, the preamble may play a symbolic role, sometimes manifested in its recognition of past offences of the state, an attempt to assuage concerns of groups that have been historically aggrieved by the state, and intentionality for a new national direction.

Turning to judicial treatment of preambles, these clauses play a meaningful assistive role in constitutional and rights adjudication. Liav Orgad provides a tripartite typology of preambles, which largely derives from the ways in which courts marshal preambles in adjudication: the ceremonial-symbolic preamble, the interpretive preamble and the substantive preamble. Ceremonial-symbolic preambles are viewed as educative and exhortatory but 'are not regarded as [an] integral part of the law and do not create any rights or have binding interpretative power.'[12] Interpretive and substantive preambles, as the names suggest, are accorded greater legal normative import. The interpretive role may fit two potential models, either with use of the preamble restricted to cases of ambiguity or, alternatively, generally available as an aid to construction regardless of ambiguous language.[13]

[7] Orgad (n 5 above) 722.

[8] Twomey (n 5 above) 16.

[9] Orgad (n 5 above) 722. See also Eric Voegelin, *Published Essays*, 1934–1939, vol 9 of *The Collected Works of Eric Voegelin* (University of Missouri Press, 2001) 32.

[10] Orgad (n 5 above) 722.

[11] The reader may observe that the explanatory and the hortatory roles may also serve an educative function. Both those roles may include information that assists members of the general populace to obtain an understanding of the constitution and its history.

[12] Orgad (n 5 above) 722.

[13] Mark McKenna, Amelia Simpson and George Williams, 'First Words: The Preamble to the Australian Constitution' (2001) 24 *UNSWLJ* 382, 387; Twomey (n 5 above).

The use of preambles to resolve ambiguities in the body of a statute is of historic vintage, and was supported in *Blackstone's Commentaries on the Laws of England*.[14] Of course, it is highly debatable what constitutes ambiguity in a statutory term or section and it has rightly been observed that Constitutions and Bills of Rights are drafted using vague, open-ended terms, which may give rise to frequent characterisations of ambiguity.[15] However, it is far from a settled question whether the legal role of preambles must be limited to resolving ambiguity. Therefore, an alternative formulation of the role of preambles in constitutional or rights interpretation maintains that the preamble is generally relevant in construing the instrument as a whole.[16]

The preambles in the Constitutions of Australia,[17] Canada,[18] and Commonwealth Caribbean states[19] have been given interpretive force by superior courts in those jurisdictions. This interpretive force has been used to support the court's use of implied principles in adjudication.[20] The Canadian Supreme Court adopted this approach to the preamble to the Constitution Act 1867 in *Reference re Secession of Quebec*. Having identified the relevance and importance of constitutional principles in the Canadian constitutional framework, the Court proceeded:

> In the *Provincial Judges Reference* we cautioned that the recognition of these constitutional principles ... could not be taken as an invitation to dispense with the written text of the Constitution ... However, we also observed in the *Provincial Judges Reference* that the effect of the preamble to the Constitution Act, 1867 was to incorporate certain constitutional principles by reference ... we determined that the preamble 'invites the courts to turn those principles into the premises of a constitutional argument that culminates in the filling of gaps in the express terms of the constitutional text.'[21]

Returning to Orgad's classification, the preamble is given substantive force where it operates as an independent source of rights or obligations. While courts in Australia, Canada, and the Caribbean generally give interpretive force to the preamble, in the latter two jurisdictions, judges have at times treated the preamble as somewhere along the boundary between interpretive and substantive. Hence, in the *Remuneration Reference*, La Forest JA (who dissented in part) complained that Lamer CJ had essentially—and illegitimately—given substantive force to the preamble. La Forest JA commented, 'I take issue, however, with the Chief Justice's view that the

[14] McKenna (ibid) 723–24.
[15] Twomey (n 5 above).
[16] Twomey (n 5 above) 20.
[17] Twomey (n 5 above) 42–44. *Cf* McKenna (n 13 above) 386–93.
[18] Twomey (n 5 above) 29–33.
[19] *Lewis* (n 6 above); *Natalie Campbell-Rodriquez* [2007] UKPC 65, [2008] 4 LRC 526 (JCPC, Jamaica) 533.
[20] There are, of course, also ample examples in civil law systems: Orgad (n 5 above).
[21] *Reference re Secession of Quebec* [1998] 2 SCR 217 (SC, Canada) [53] (citations omitted).

preamble to the Constitution Act, 1867 is a source of constitutional limitations on the power of legislatures to interfere with judicial independence',[22] indicating La Forest JA's clear perception that Lamer CJ's use of the preamble extended beyond interpretation and entered the realm of substantive force. In the Caribbean as well, both the Privy Council and the Caribbean Court of Justice[23] have given indications of the substantive force of the preamble. In *Lewis v AG of Jamaica*, the Privy Council found that the term 'protection of the law' used in the preamble to the Bill of Rights in the Constitution of Jamaica 1962 invokes the concept of the rule of law and was violated by the decision of the executive to execute prisoners on death row before the determination of their petitions by an international human rights body.[24] The case law therefore reinforces the definition of 'implied' articulated at the beginning of this chapter as principles which do not appear in substantive sections of written Constitutions or Bills of Rights. Thus, while preambles play a critical role in the judicial discourse on implied principles, judicial invocation of principles referred to in preambles remain characterised as a use of implied principles.

With this understanding of implication as a launching pad, we can itemise the processes of implication in five categories: (1) there are terms in the text that may be interpreted as synonyms for the implied principle in question (the equivalence method); (2) there are terms or rights in the text—such as the right to equality—which are characterised as particular applications of the principle in question (the application method); (3) the principles are implied by the structure of the text (the structural method); (4) the principles are not referred to in the substantive provisions of the Constitution or Bill of Rights, but are referred to in parts of the Constitution such as the preamble, which are not expressly justiciable (the preambular method); (5) the principles are said to emanate from the unwritten British Constitution from which the Constitutions in question derive much of their inspiration (the historical method).[25] These methods of implication are not mutually exclusive so some overlap should be expected between the categories in practice.

[22] *Remuneration Reference* (n 4 above) [304].

[23] The Judicial Committee of the Privy Council is the final appellate body for the Commonwealth Caribbean states Antigua and Barbuda, Bahamas, Grenada, Jamaica, St Christopher and Nevis, Saint Lucia, Saint Vincent and the Grenadines, and Trinidad and Tobago but the newly established Caribbean Court of Justice is the final appellate tribunal for Barbados, Belize, Dominica, and Guyana.

[24] *Lewis* (n 6 above) 85.

[25] See a similar categorisation of the basis of judicial restraint of state power in John Basten, 'The supervisory jurisdiction of the Supreme Courts' (2011) 85 *Australian Law Journal* 273, 278–79. In jurisdictions that fall outside the purview of this study, such as the Republic of India and the Republic of Ireland, principles are also derived from the 'Directive Principles' outlined in the respective Constitutions. These 'Directive Principles' are in the body of the text but are directed at the legislature rather than the courts and are expressed to be non-justiciable.

In the first form of implication—the equivalence method—a term used in the text is viewed as synonymous with the constitutional principle. It is this technique that led the Privy Council in *Thomas v Baptiste* to find that the term 'due process' incorporates the notion of the rule of law, and therefore, to take the term 'due process' beyond procedural requirements regarding the conduct of a criminal trial and incorporate 'standards of justice' observed by those jurisdictions which respect [or purport to respect] the rule of law.[26] The application method is a more common implication technique, whereby rights or duties referred to in the text are said to represent applications of a constitutional principle. This reasoning has been used to justify incorporation of the rule of law into the court's reasoning, as well as to determine the content of the rule of law. For instance, in *Plaintiff S/157/2002 v Commonwealth* the High Court of Australia interpreted section 75(v) of the Constitution of the Commonwealth of Australia 1900, which confers on the High Court original jurisdiction to hear matters in which the remedies of mandamus, prohibition or injunction are sought against an officer of the Commonwealth, as an entrenchment of what the court referred to as a 'minimum provision of judicial review'. The Court proceeded to find that this section 'constitutes a textual reinforcement' of the rule of law as an assumption of the Australian Constitution.[27]

The third—structural—method of implication has been particularly instrumental in the implication of the separation of powers principle into Constitutions. *Hinds v R*, in which the Privy Council held that the separation of powers was an underlying principle of the Constitution, is a useful example. Lord Diplock, delivering the opinion of the Board, reasoned as follows:

> *All Constitutions on the Westminster model deal under separate Chapter headings with the legislature, the executive and the judicature* ... the legislature, in the exercise of its power to make laws for the 'peace, order and good government' of the state, may provide for the establishment of new courts and for the transfer to them of the whole or part of the jurisdiction previously exercisable by an existing court. What, however, is implicit in *the very structure of a Constitution on the Westminster model* is that judicial power, however it be distributed from time to time between various courts, is to continue to be vested in persons appointed to hold judicial office in the manner and on the terms laid down in the

[26] *Thomas v Baptiste* [2000] 2 AC 1 (*JCPC, Trinidad and Tobago)* 22. Indeed, there does exist historical evidence that the idea of due process was meant to evoke the rule of law. See Frederick Mark Gedicks, 'An Originalist Defence of Substantive Due Process: Magna Carta, Higher Law Constitutionalism and the Fifth Amendment' (2009) 58 *Emory Law Journal* 585.

[27] *Plaintiff S157/2002 v Commonwealth of Australia* (2003) 211 CLR 476 (HC, Australia) [5], [103].

> Chapter dealing with the judicature, even though this is not expressly stated in the Constitution.[28]

The fourth method of implication occurs where the principle is referred to in a preambular constitutional provision but where the principle is not expressly included in the substantive text of the Constitution. Two examples of this are the Constitution of Barbados 1966 and the Constitution Act 1982 (Canada). The opening paragraphs of the Constitution of Barbados include the following words:

> Now, therefore, the people of Barbados-
>
> ...
>
> b. affirm their belief that men and institutions remain free only when freedom is founded upon respect for moral and spiritual values and the rule of law...

The Constitution Act 1982 opens with the words '[w]hereas Canada is founded upon principles that recognise the supremacy of God and the rule of law' and the Constitution Act Canada 1867 refers to Canada having 'a Constitution similar in Principle to that of the United Kingdom.' The Canadian Supreme Court has invoked the preambles of the Constitution Acts in support of both the identification and use by the courts of implied constitutional principles. In the view of the Court, as expressed in *Reference re Manitoba Language Rights*, the rule of law 'becomes a postulate of our own Constitutional order by way of preamble to the Constitution Act, 1982, and its implicit inclusion in the preamble to the Constitution Act, 1867, by virtue of the words "with a Constitution similar in Principle to that of the United Kingdom".'[29] In that case, the fifth method of implication was also evident in the Court's account of the longstanding position of the rule of law in the 'English Constitution':

> The rule of law has always been understood as the very basis of the English Constitution characterising the political institutions of England from the time of the Norman Conquest (AV Dicey, *The Law of the Constitution* (10th ed 1959), at p 183). It becomes a postulate of our own constitutional order by way of the preamble to the *Constitution Act, 1982*, and its implicit inclusion in the preamble to the *Constitution Act, 1867* by virtue of the words 'with a Constitution similar in principle to that of the United Kingdom'.[30]

This outline of the methods of implication of constitutional principles invites reflection on the related question of the sources of these principles, as

[28] *Hinds v R* [1977] AC 195 (JCPC, Jamaica) 213 (emphases added; citations omitted). See also *New South Wales v Commonwealth of Australia* (1915) 20 CLR 54 (HC, Australia) (*Wheat* case) 90–93.

[29] *Reference re Manitoba Language Rights* (n 3 above) [63].

[30] ibid.

indicated in case law. From the five methods of implication we can identify four sources: substantive provisions in the Constitution and/or Bill of Rights (used in the equivalence and application methods of implication), the preamble to the Constitution and/or Bill of Rights (central to the preambular method), the 'unwritten' English Constitution (which is used in the historical method of implication), and the structure of the Constitution (used in the structural method). There is some opacity regarding what is referred to as the 'structure' of the Constitution, as it can be predicated on three possible meanings of 'structure'. On one level, the term 'structure' can refer to the arrangement of the constitutional document, which is the meaning suggested by Lord Diplock's references in *Hinds* to the chapters and drafting style of the new Constitutions of former British colonies. Diplock addressed the 'structure' of 'Westminster Constitutions' by referring to the Constitutions' practice of dealing 'under separate chapter headings with the legislature, the executive and the judicature.'[31] On a second level, the structure of the Constitution invokes the arrangement of the organs or institutions of state, particularly in relation to each other. This is the meaning ascribed to 'structural argumentation' by Philip Bobbitt, who characterised 'structural arguments' as those based on 'inferences from the existence of constitutional structures and the relationships which the Constitution ordains among these structures' and as dependent on an assessment of 'the entire Constitutional text as a whole'.[32] Finally, the third sense in which the term 'structure' may be used, is the expression of the structure of the Constitution as the 'fundamental structure', a term which was used by Isaacs J of the Australian High Court in *New South Wales v Commonwealth* (the *Wheat* case).[33] This third meaning evokes the image of the Constitution as resting on a foundational (and fundamental) unwritten structure, of which implied constitutional principles form part. The description of that structure as fundamental brings squarely to mind the question—which remains unanswered in case law—whether the structure shares with the written Constitution the status of fundamental law, or constitutes a higher order law to which even the written Constitution is subordinated.

The methods of implication using the sources outlined are embedded in the interpretive process. The extent to which these methods and the use of these sources comport with the nature and objectives of interpretation in rights cases is a necessary step towards determining whether judges *should* use these methods and sources. This evaluation is undertaken in chapter eight in the discussion of the legitimacy of courts' use of implied constitutional principles in rights adjudication.

[31] *Hinds* (n 28 above) 213.

[32] Philip Bobbitt, *Constitutional Fate: Theory of the Constitution* (Oxford University Press, 1982) 74; Robin Elliot, 'References, Structural Argumentation and the Organizing Principles of Canada's Constitution' (2001) 80 *Canadian Bar Review* 67, 74.

[33] *Wheat* case (*n 28* above) 93.

Shifting focus to the latter concept in the term 'implied principles', guidance in elucidating the concept of a principle is sought from the theories of Ronald Dworkin and Robert Alexy. Emerging from both bodies of work is an understanding that a principle is a norm that is distinguishable from rules with respect to their operation in cases of conflict with other norms and their respective mode of application.[34] In *Taking Rights Seriously*, Dworkin uses the term 'principle' to denote a standard that exists alongside rules to comprise the body of the law. He argues that '[r]ules are applicable in an all-or-nothing fashion'[35] whereas where two principles conflict, they can be accorded varying weight by judges, with the principle surviving even if it does not prevail.[36] Alongside Dowrkin, Alexy describes a norm as either a rule or a principle and advances a qualitative distinction between rules and principles.[37]

The distinction between the two writers lies in the detail and specificity Alexy brings to his distinction between principles and rules and his characterisation of principles. Alexy views principles as 'optimisation requirements', as norms which require that a particular objective be achieved 'to the greatest extent legally and factually possible.'[38] Accordingly, while a rule is either always fulfilled or not, a principle can be fulfilled to varying degrees and the level of fulfilment of a principle does not affect the validity of the principle.[39] Alexy criticises Dworkin's characterisation that rules apply in an 'all-or-nothing' fashion, while principles only contain reasons pointing in a certain direction but not requiring a specific decision.[40] He objects that Dworkin's characterisation is too simplistic and that a proper explanation of the mode of application of rules requires more nuanced treatment if it is to account for exceptions to rules—some of which cannot be identified until they are created in a particular case—and if it is to account for burdens of argumentation in favour of certain principles over others.[41] For Alexy, the possibility of exceptions to a rule that cannot be exhaustively enumerated in advance changes the nature of the rule to such an extent that it does not apply in the strictly definitive way that Dworkin proposes.[42] Yet, Alexy is quick to indicate that while the possibility of exceptions to rules weakens their definitive character, it does not weaken their definitive

[34] Humberto Avila, *Theory of Legal Principles (Law and Philosophy Library)* (Springer Publishing, 2007) 11–20.

[35] Ronald Dworkin, *Taking Rights Seriously* (Harvard University Press, 1978) 24.

[36] ibid 35.

[37] Robert Alexy, *A Theory of Constitutional Rights* (Julian Rivers tr, Oxford University Press, 2002) 48.

[38] ibid 57.

[39] ibid 50.

[40] ibid 57–59.

[41] ibid.

[42] Alexy (n 37 above) 58.

character to such a degree that it gives rules the same *prima facie* characteristics as principles. The obligatory nature of rules remains stronger than that of principles, owing to the existence and operation of those principles in the legal system that urge obedience to established rules.[43] Such principles (which Alexy designates 'formal principles') might outweigh principles that argue in favour of upholding exceptions to rules.[44]

Alexy also indicates that there may be burdens of argumentation that favour one principle over another.[45] Using the example of a conflict between a principle requiring respect for an individual constitutional right and a principle requiring the pursuit of common interests, Alexy explains that there could be an onus favouring the former over the latter. Again, however, he maintains that this does not eliminate the distinction between principles and rules; burdens of argumentation favouring one principle over another do not strengthen the *prima facie* character of principles to such an extent that they eliminate the need to 'weigh' principles against each other to establish which principle takes precedence in a given case.[46] Ultimately, then, Alexy's conclusion is that the development of this more nuanced model does not undermine the argument that the prima facie character of rules and principles are fundamentally different.[47]

A further possible distinction between the two theorists lies in a comparison of Dworkin's classification of principles as standards with Alexy's position that principles are 'optimisation requirements'. For Alexy, optimisation means 'realizing to the greatest extent possible'.[48] However, despite some differences in expression, Dworkin's and Alexy's characterisations of principles are fundamentally compatible. In describing principles as optimisation requirements, Alexy merely expounds on his understanding of the way in which standards work and why they are distinct from rules. If this explanation of principles as optimisation requirements is applied, it is possible to view the same principle as both a standard and an ideal. For instance, the rule of law can be seen as an ideal which ought to be satisfied to varying degrees.[49] This does not mean it is impossible to characterise it as a standard. As a standard, it is a norm that can be considered and applied by the court and though it may not be completely fulfilled in a given case, it can be respected to a certain degree.

[43] Compare Kai Möller, 'Balancing and the Structure of Constitutional Rights' (2007) 5 *International Journal of Constitutional Law* 453, 459.

[44] Alexy (n 37 above) 58. However, it could be argued that the exception is really integrated within the rule, which would render this line of argument unnecessary.

[45] ibid 58–59.

[46] ibid.

[47] ibid 59.

[48] ibid 47.

[49] Richard Fallon, 'The "Rule of Law" as a Concept in Constitutional Discourse' (1997) 97 *Columbia Law Review* 1.

Alexy builds on this characterisation of rules and principles by arguing that most constitutional rights norms are principles which are subject to balancing whenever there is a conflict between them.[50] Kai Möller objects to Alexy's argument that, since a principle is an optimisation requirement, in order to realise a principle to the greatest extent possible, conflicts between principles must be subject to a balancing exercise. Importantly, Alexy advocates this balancing of principles even where one principle is of a constitutional nature related to individual rights while the other is based on a collective interest.[51] For Alexy, principles representing collective interests include those featured in limitation clauses, 'institutional interpretations' of constitutional rights, and non-rights constitutional provisions.[52] Here, Dworkin and Alexy diverge because Dworkin classifies some collective goals as policies and advances an important distinction between principles and policies, observing that principles are justified by arguments based on requirements of justice or rights while policies are concerned with the fulfilment of community goals such as collective economic or social objectives.[53] The Dworkinian definition of policies would include some collective goals that Alexy may classify as principles, most notably goals used as limitations on rights. Further, Dworkin argues that while judges are entitled to arrive at their decisions by reasoning on grounds of principles and rules, judges should not (and do not) base their decisions on policy considerations. Moreover, Dworkin views rights as 'trumps' so when a right conflicts with normal policy concerns, the right trumps these concerns and will usually win.[54]

This chapter is not concerned with the legitimacy of balancing principles as this question has no bearing on the understanding of the concept of implied principles. Accordingly, balancing will not be discussed in any detail here except to note that Möller identifies this as an additional point of distinction between Alexy and Dworkin. While Alexy advocates the balancing of constitutional rights (which he considers principles) against each other and against principles that represent collective interests, Dworkin opposes the balancing of constitutional rights against policy concerns, arguing that rights are trumps.[55] Accordingly, Möller argues, if Dworkin were to accept that rights are principles, he would reject the notion that they should be balanced against normal policy concerns. Möller also maintains that Dworkin does not, like Alexy, immediately turn to balancing where there are competing rights. He correctly states that Dworkin would require a moral

[50] Alexy (n 37 above) 65, 80–86.
[51] ibid 81.
[52] Alexy (n 37 above) 80–81.
[53] Dworkin, *Taking Rights Seriously* (n 35 above) 90–93.
[54] Ronald Dworkin, 'Rights as Trumps' in Jeremy Waldron (ed), *Theories of Rights* (Oxford University Press, 1984) 152; Möller (n 43 above) 460.
[55] Möller (n 43 above) 460; Dworkin, 'Rights at Trumps' (ibid) 153.

argument to determine which takes priority. Ultimately, however, Möller does not attack the notion of principles as optimisation requirements; what he attacks is Alexy's reasoning that 'when something is a principle understood as an optimisation requirement, it "logically" follows that it is subject to balancing'.[56] That argument is not material for our purposes and more importantly, if we accept Möller's contention that describing principles as optimisation requirements does not automatically require resolution of conflicts through balancing, it is possible to accept Alexy's description of principles as optimisation requirements, while avoiding the controversial notion of balancing constitutional rights norms. Finally, the basic distinctions between norms as articulated by Dworkin and Alexy are so compelling that they have penetrated beyond academic commentary and are reflected in case law.[57] The Canadian Supreme Court has characterised the Canadian Constitution as a web of principles and rules, in terms that echo the Dworkinian analysis:

> These supporting principles and rules, which include constitutional conventions and the workings of Parliament, are a necessary part of our Constitution because problems or situations may arise which are not expressly dealt with by the text of the Constitution. In order to endure over time, a constitution must contain a comprehensive set of rules and principles which are capable of providing an exhaustive legal framework for our system of government.[58]

Adoption of a normative schema that acknowledges and incorporates principles requires attention to the question of source—the (elusive) origins of constitutional principles. Again, Dworkin provides ideas that are useful in examining judicial derivation of the content of principles.[59] In arguing for the recognition of principles, Dworkin suggests citing judicial and legislative practice as well as citing other general principles that support the principle at issue, arguing that:

> It is true that generally we cannot demonstrate the authority or weight of a particular principle as we can sometimes demonstrate the validity of a rule by locating it in an act of Congress or in the opinion of an authoritative court. Instead, we make a case for a principle, and for its weight, by appealing to an amalgam of practice and other principles in which the legislative and judicial history figure along with appeals to community practices and understandings. There is no litmus paper for

[56] Möller (n 43 above) 461.

[57] The cases show that the courts acknowledge the distinction. This does not assume that they generally accept Dworkin's argument that policies should not influence judges in adjudication and there is much debate on that point in the scholarly literature. See, eg, EW Thomas, *The Judicial Process: Realism, Pragmatism, Practical Reasoning and Principles* (Cambridge University Press, 2005) 197–200.

[58] *Secession Reference* (n 21 above) [32].

[59] Dworkin, *Taking Rights Seriously* (n 35 above) 36–41.

> testing the soundness of such a case-it is a matter of judgment, and reasonable men may disagree.[60]

Dworkin further explains that the origin of legal principles lies 'in a sense of appropriateness developed in the profession and the public over time'.[61] If this sense of appropriateness fades, the principle is eroded. One question that he fails to address is, if the sense of appropriateness derives in part from 'the public', how does Dworkin and how do judges account for this factor in legal decision-making? If judges take account of the sense of appropriateness in the public, are they involved in judging public consensus? It would be constitutionally problematic to propose that such assessment forms part of the proper province of judges. One solution could be that the sense of appropriateness that is felt within the public over time filters into the profession, and by extension, the judiciary. In keeping with the pragmatic outlook of this study, it is best to take account of the principles identified and developed in the laws of the state, specifically, in judicial decisions.[62]

Dworkin's account of the development of principles is echoed by Alexy's explanation that principles 'can be derived from a tradition of detailed norm-creation and judicial decision-taking which are often the expression of widespread understanding of what the law ought to be.'[63] With specific reference to principles relevant to constitutional adjudication, Alexy has indicated that such principles include those that are related to individual rights as well as those related to 'collective interests.'[64] Principles relating to individual rights are said to be easily stated as, wherever a constitutional provision protects an individual right, there is at least one such principle behind it.[65] As noted above, for Alexy, principles related to collective interests can be derived from limitation clauses, 'an institutional interpretation of constitutional rights as part of their scope of protection', and non-rights constitutional provisions from which principles such as democracy and the social state are derived.[66]

The separation of powers principle fits most comfortably within Alexy's third category of derivation as it is primarily related to collective interests, and is in part derived from constitutional provisions which are not individual rights provisions.[67] This is consistent with the justification given

[60] ibid 36.

[61] ibid 40.

[62] ibid 41.

[63] Alexy (n 37 above) 61.

[64] ibid 80.

[65] ibid; Gustavo Zagrebelsky, 'Ronald Dworkin's principle based constitutionalism: An Italian point of view' (2003) 1 *International Journal of Constitutional Law* 621.

[66] Alexy (n 37 above) 80–81. Article 20 of the Basic Law for the Federal Republic of Germany 1949 states that the Republic is a democratic and social federal state.

[67] See analysis of the content of the separation of powers in Westminster style Constitutions in ch 4.

by courts for their recognition of the separation of powers principle in constitutional cases. For instance, in *Hinds*, the separation of powers was said to be evident throughout the structure of the Constitution of Jamaica 1962, and in particular, the provisions that address the powers and duties of each branch of government under separate chapter headings, labelled 'legislature', 'executive', and 'judiciary'.[68] The rule of law is more complex as it can be related to both individual rights and collective interests. Accordingly, the rule of law can be partly derived from rights provisions such as the right to equality[69] and the rights to protection of the law or due process.[70] It can also be derived from non-rights provisions such as the reference to the rule of law in section 1 of the Constitutional Reform Act 2005 (UK).

III. SEPARATION OF POWERS AND THE RULE OF LAW IN CONSTITUTIONALISM

Though there are other implied constitutional principles that may merit further study, there are features that distinguish the rule of law and separation of powers from such other principles.[71] Most fundamental is that the rule of law and separation of powers are inherent foundational principles of democratic constitutionalism.[72] As Donald Lutz argues, 'constitutionalism implies ... popular sovereignty, which in turn implies at least some minimum separation of powers' and the 'rule of law and popular sovereignty virtually define constitutional democracy'.[73] Further, from a historical perspective, the rule of law and separation of powers were part of the unwritten English constitution and were subsequently incorporated in the constitutional arrangements of Commonwealth jurisdictions. Principles such as constitutional supremacy or parliamentary supremacy, for instance, assume a particular hierarchy of sources of law and institutions of state, a hierarchy

[68] *Hinds* (n 28 above) 213.

[69] See, eg, *Ghaidan v Godin-Mendoza* [2004] UKHL 30, [2004] 2 AC 557 (HL) [9].

[70] See, eg, *Joseph and Boyce* (n 6 above) [60]–[64].

[71] There is abundant literature on the principles that may qualify as implied constitutional principles. On equality, see Jeffrey Jowell, 'Is Equality a Constitutional Principle' (1994) 47 *Current Legal Problems* 1; Wojciech Sadurski, *Equality and Legitimacy* (Oxford University Press, 2008); Fabienne Peter, *Democratic Legitimacy* (Routledge, 2011). For case law invoking the principle of equality as a fundamental principle, see, eg *R v Keegstra* [1990] 3 SCR 697 (SC, Canada) [49], [60], [80]; *Matadeen v Pointu* [1999] 1 AC 98 (JCPC, Mauritius) [109]; *R (Rotherham Metropolitan Borough Council) v Secretary of State for Business, Innovation and Skills* [2015] UKSC 6.

[72] TRS Allan, *Constitutional Justice: A liberal Theory of the Rule of Law* (Oxford University Press, 2001) 1–5; Donald Lutz, *Principles of Constitutional Design* (Cambridge University Press, 2006) x, 3, 5.

[73] Lutz (ibid). See also Deiter Grimm, 'The Achievement of Constitutionalism and its Prospects in a Changed World' in Petra Dobner and Martin Loughlin, *The Twilight of Constitutionalism* (Oxford University Press, 2010) 8.

which varies across democratic constitutional states.[74] Whereas principles such as equality—to the extent that they are accepted as elements of a state's Constitution—may flow from the foundational principles of rule of law and separation of powers, so the separation of powers and rule of law remain the concomitants of constitutionalism, which act as fountainheads for other important principles in the modern constitutional state.[75]

As the rule of law and the separation of powers are said to be bound up with the notion of constitutionalism, clarification of the concept of constitutionalism is requisite. While it is notoriously difficult to reduce constitutionalism to a single definition, it includes conditions for the creation, organisation, and regulation of governmental power as well as the resolution of political conflict. The pivotal themes within constitutionalism are constituting and limiting governmental power, thereby encompassing norms relating to 'the exercise of public power and the procedures through which such power is exercised.'[76] Thus, beyond the establishment of the state and its governing institutions, constitutionalism's ethos centres on regulation and limitation. It is in this vein that Peter Russell describes constitutionalism as 'a political condition in which the constitution functions as an effective and significant limit on government'.[77] So understood, constitutionalism is not prescriptive about the form of constitutional norms (whether written or unwritten, political or legal). Accordingly, judicial authority to review and invalidate legislation is not a prerequisite, neither is an entrenched codified Constitution or a written Bill of Rights.[78] Thus the crucial notion in constitutionalism is 'limited government', where the constitution functions as a limitation that may occur in the form of judicial restraints as well as political restraints and culture, and may be represented by written and unwritten norms.

While seeking to regulate and even limit the exercise of governmental power, constitutionalism does not mandate that there should be *minimal* government; rather, as Bellamy explains, constitutional limits are animated by the need to prevent arbitrary rule.[79] In similar fashion to Russell, Bellamy indicates that prevention of arbitrary government may be

[74] Stephen Gardbaum, *The New Commonwealth Model of Constitutionalism: Theory and Practice* (Cambridge University Press, 2013) 21–25.
[75] ibid.
[76] Martin Loughlin, 'What is Constitutionalisation?' in Petra Dobner and Martin Loughlin, *The Twilight of Constitutionalism?* (Oxford University Press, 2010) 55.
[77] Peter Russell, 'Constitutionalism' in Adam Kuper and Jessica Kuper, *The Social Science Encyclopedia*, 3rd edn (Routledge, 2008) 166; *cf* Cass Sunstein, 'Constitutionalism after the New Deal' (1987) 101 *Harvard Law Review* 421, 434–36. See also Suri Ratnapala and Jonathan Crowe, *Australian Constitutional Law: Foundations and Theory*, 3rd edn (Oxford University Press, 2012) 14.
[78] Peter Russell, 'Constitutionalism' (ibid) 167.
[79] Richard Bellamy, *Political Constitutionalism: A Republican Defence of the Constitutionality of Democracy* (Cambridge University Press, 2007) 8.

achieved through political mechanisms (political constitutionalism) as well as through judicially enforced individual rights (legal constitutionalism).[80] The theme of constitutionalism as a restraint on government is reflected in Francis Wormuth's 'The Origins of Modern Constitutionalism', which relates constitutionalism to the use of devices to define and constrain government, and identified two devices that are employed to do so. The first he describes as checks and balances and the second as the notion that law is general and prospective, which in Wormuth's view, is implemented by the separation of powers.[81] Despite deep, enduring contestation over the requirements of the rule of law, it is a generally accepted core precept of the rule of law that laws ought to be general and prospective. Wormuth's vision of constitutionalism therefore embodies restraints on government which are associated with both the rule of law and the separation of governmental powers.[82] These constitutional devices are said to be marshalled in order to protect 'substantial interests' such as property, freedom of conscience, and fair trial rights. There is therefore an abiding relationship between the rule of law and the separation of powers on the one hand, and rights protection on the other.[83] This relationship which is identified in the nature of constitutionalism is reflected through case law and sheds some light on courts' resort to inherent principles of constitutionalism in their reasoning in human rights cases.

There remains deep scepticism about the utility and necessity of constitutionalism in general, and legal constitutionalism in particular. Such scepticism is in large part fuelled by a perception that legal constitutionalism has come to dominate constitutionalist theory, language and practice.[84] Yet, rumours of the death of political constitutionalism have been exaggerated and it continues to hold sway in rights protection frameworks, most notably in the UK and Australia, where there is, respectively, no written Constitution and no national Bill of Rights.[85] Moreover, it is unnecessary for current purposes join the debate whether constitutionalism is essential for civil governance or which form (political or legal) ought to be preferred; the empirical fact of observance of constitutionalism by the common law

[80] ibid 1–14. *cf* Jeremy Waldron's view that modern constitutionalism is synonymous with legal constitutionalism in 'Constitutionalism—A Sceptical View' (2012) *NYU School of Law, Public Law Research Paper* No. 10-87, http://ssrn.com/abstract=1722771, 36–40.

[81] Francis D Wormuth, *The Origins of Modern Constitutionalism* (Harper & Brothers, 1949) 3–4.

[82] ibid.

[83] ibid 4.

[84] See Waldron, 'Constitutionalism—A Sceptical View' (n 80 above); Bellamy (n 79 above) 1–14; Ran Hirschl, 'The New Constitutionalism and the Judicialization of Pure Politics Worldwide' (2006) 75 *Fordham Law* Review 721.

[85] Stephen Gardbaum, *The New Commonwealth Model of Constitutionalism* (n 74 above) 234–38.

jurisdictions examined in this study and the recognition of rule of law and separation of powers as inherent within constitutionalism is paramount. Ultimately, awareness that constitutions 'increasingly seem to acquire legitimacy only to the extent that they measure up to the norms of constitutionalism' signals the 'triumph of constitutionalism', and of its substantive and procedural mandates.[86]

A. Legacy of Common Law Constitutionalism

An additional layer to understanding the constitutionalist context in which the separation of powers and rule of law are used in adjudication is the construct of common law constitutionalism. The use of implied principles has been appropriately located within the tradition of 'common law constitutionalism', where 'common law constitutionalism' is understood as the notion of an unwritten fundamental law.[87] Mark Walters describes the connection between references to unwritten principles and common law constitutionalism by indicating that the notion of *lex non scripta* refers to law that is unwritten in that its normative force is not fully explicable by its written form, and that unwritten law and common law were traditionally regarded as encompassing the same type of laws.[88]

The significance of *lex non scripta* has re-emerged with renewed importance in the form of the theory and practice of common law constitutionalism. Common law constitutionalism incorporates a series of broad themes, including a substantive conception of the rule of law, 'reliance on fundamental values which gives rise to constitutional rights', the belief that it is the common law that justifies judicial review, and that the principles of judicial review are derived from the common law.[89] The field of common law constitutionalists includes Trevor Allan, Paul Craig, Dawn Oliver, Sir John Laws, and Jeffrey Jowell.[90] In Walters' view, common law constitutionalism

[86] See Loughlin, 'What is Constitutionalisation?' (n 76 above) 55.

[87] See Mark Walters, 'The Common Law Constitution in Canada: The Return of Lex Non Scripta as Fundamental Law' (2001) 51 *University of Toronto Law Journal* 91.

[88] ibid 95.

[89] Justin Leslie, 'Vindicating Common Law Constitutionalism' (2010) 30 *Legal Studies* 301, 305. See also Paul Craig, 'Public Law, Political Theory and Legal Theory' [2000] *Public Law* 211; Paul Craig, *Administrative Law*, 7th edn (Sweet & Maxwell, 2012) 17–18; WJ Waluchow, *A Common Law Theory of Judicial Review: The Living Tree* (Cambridge University Press, 2007). On the criticism of common law constitutionalism, see JAG Griffith, 'The Brave New World of Sir John Laws' (2000) 63 *Modern Law Review* 159; JAG Griffith, 'The Common Law and the Political Constitution (2001) 117 *Law Quarterly Review* 42; Thomas Poole, 'Dogmatic Liberalism? TRS Allan and the Common Law Constitution' (2002) 65 *Modern Law Review* 463.

[90] TRS Allan, 'Questions of legality and legitimacy: Form and substance in British constitutionalism' (2011) *International Journal of Constitutional Law* 155; Paul Craig, 'Public Law, Political Theory' (ibid); Paul Craig, *Administrative Law* (ibid) 22–27; Dawn Oliver,

not only posits that there are common law principles that are 'unwritten' in the sense that they do not derive their normative force by written form, and that they are legal norms that bind governments. For Walters, common law constitutionalism also connotes that these 'unwritten principles' are fundamental in the sense that they are superior to other laws.[91] Thomas Poole has penned a critique of common law constitutionalism in which he maintains that common law constitutionalists conceive of public law as a set of higher order values that are set above political decision-making.[92] Yet, in forceful and convincing responses, Paul Craig and Justin Leslie have demonstrated that this description of common law constitutionalism mischaracterises the views of its adherents. For most—if not all—of its adherents, common law constitutionalism may accommodate parliamentary supremacy.[93] For Craig, common law constitutionalism 'does not "make the case" for US style constitutional review, whereby courts can invalidate legislation'.[94] What can fairly be said is that 'strong form' common law constitutionalism may create space for an argument that courts possess the power to invalidate legislation; this is the position taken by Sir John Laws who argues, extra-judicially, that common law principles form a 'higher-order law'. For Laws, then, '[t]he constitution, not the Parliament, is in this sense sovereign'.[95] In Laws' view, a higher order law confers power upon Parliament and 'must of necessity limit it.'[96]

However, 'weak form' common law constitutionalism, such as that advocated by Dawn Oliver, takes a more moderate position. Thus, Oliver is of the view that parliamentary supremacy is 'necessary for the maintenance of good relations between the courts and the other branches of government.'[97] A middle ground is occupied by Allan and Craig who advocate the concept of dual sovereignty whereby Parliament and the judiciary are each supreme in their own constitutional sphere.[98] Further, even within this framework of dual sovereignty, Craig remains adamant that under current constitutional

'Is the Ultra vires Doctrine the Basis of Judicial Review?' (1987) *Public Law* 543; Sir John Laws, 'Law and Democracy' [1995] *Public Law* 72; Jeffrey Jowell, 'Of Vires and Vacuums: The Constitutional Context of Judicial Review' in Christopher Forsyth (ed) *Judicial Review and the Constitution* (Hart Publishing, 2000).

91 Walters, 'Common Law Constitution in Canada' (n 87 above); Thomas Poole, 'Back to the Future? Unearthing the Theory of Common Law Constitutionalism' (2003) *Oxford Journal of Legal Studies* 435, 439 et seq.

92 Poole, 'Back to the Future' (ibid).

93 Leslie (n 89 above) 305.

94 Paul Craig, *Administrative Law*, 6th edn (Sweet & Maxwell, 2008) 23.

95 Laws (n 90 above).

96 ibid 87.

97 Dawn Oliver, *Constitutional Reform in the UK* (Oxford University Press, 2003) 354.

98 TRS Allan, 'Constitutional Dialogue and the Justification of Judicial Review' (2003) 23 *Oxford Journal Legal Studies* 563, 578; Paul Craig, 'Constitutional Foundations, the Rule of Law and Supremacy' [2003] *Public Law* 92, 109.

doctrine, Parliament has 'the last clear and unequivocal word.'[99] The concept of dual sovereignty brings the notion of a separation of state powers into the common law constitutionalism dialogue. In the framework of dual sovereignty, therefore, courts are required to protect the rule of law and the legislature is required to respect the separation of powers by recognising and respecting the courts' role as rule of law-protector.[100]

Common law constitutionalism is reflected in case law as the idea that implied principles derived from the common law share supremacy with the constitutional text. The location of courts' references to implied principles within the literature on unwritten fundamental law receives some support from judicial statements that the constitutional framework includes principles which are 'vital un-stated assumptions'[101] and that Westminster model constitutions leave a great deal to 'necessary implication'.[102] A further potential implication of common law constitutionalism for the discourse on implied constitutional principles is that the emphasis in common law constitutionalism on normative common law justifications for the content and scope of judicial review may enable courts to look beyond the constitutional text or even defy such text in order to review executive or legislative action for compliance with fundamental constitutional principles. It may even provide an avenue for courts to assert the supremacy of unwritten principles over the written Constitution. In this vein, Walters has suggested that in the *Secession Reference* judgment, the court perceived unwritten principles as antecedent to, and in a sense supreme over, the constitutional text.[103] Again, this is not a necessary or foregone conclusion of common law constitutionalism but the common law constitutionalist framework may create the conceptual space for such reasoning.

Common law constitutionalism was originally presented as an alternative to political constitutionalism, but important research from Walters and Tracy Robinson, writing in the context of Canada and the Commonwealth Caribbean, respectively, reveal that constitutionalist discourse must now include a more complete set of alternatives in order to fully appreciate the terms and potential consequences of the debate. In that broader conversation, there is a wider set of ideas for regulating or restraining government, ranging from political constitutionalism to common law constitutionalism, and codified (or written) to unwritten constitutionalism. States in which there is a codified constitution which confers on courts the jurisdiction to

[99] Craig, 'Constitutional Foundations' (ibid) 109; Craig, *Administrative Law* (n 89 above) 17, 27–28.

[100] Allan, 'Constitutional Dialogue' (n 98 above) 580–81.

[101] *Secession Reference* (n 21 above) [49].

[102] *Hinds* (n 28 above) 211; Tracy Robinson, 'Gender, Nation and the Common Law Constitution' (2008) 28 *Oxford Journal Law Studies* 735, 742.

[103] Walters, 'Common Law Constitution in Canada' (n 87 above).

invalidate legislation have arguably left political constitutionalism behind and embraced legal constitutionalism. Also, since the constitutions are written, one would expect that common law constitutionalism has also been left behind. Yet, Walters and Robinson suggest, rightly, that such states still retain a legacy of common law constitutionalism that continues to impact their decisions in constitutional cases. In states where there is a codified constitution, discourse on the use of constitutional principles by courts evokes questions regarding the interaction between common law constitutionalism and codified constitutionalism. As will become evident in subsequent chapters, this interaction influences the functions of implied constitutional principles as well as the legitimacy of the use of such principles.

Along with the range of ideas for restraining government—including common law constitutionalism and written constitutionalism—there is also a spectrum that flows from parliamentary supremacy to constitutional (or judicial) supremacy. Within the UK, the doctrine of parliamentary supremacy has particular strength. Pressure has undoubtedly been building on the traditionally understood doctrine of parliamentary supremacy through recent constitutional developments, including the European Communities Act 1972 (UK) (ECA 1972)—enacted to give further effect to the UK's obligations under the European Community (now European Union) treaties—and the Human Rights Act 1998 (UK) (HRA 1998)—enacted to give further effect to the UK's obligations under the Convention for the Protection of Human Rights and Fundamental Freedoms (ECHR).[104] Under section 2 (4) of the ECA 1972 all primary legislation whether enacted prior or subsequent to the ECA 1972 must take effect subject to the Act, and the courts have interpreted this section as a mandate to 'disapply' legislation that is inconsistent with EC (now EU) law.[105] With respect to the HRA 1998, section 3(1) requires judges to interpret legislation so far as possible, in a manner consistent with the ECHR rights scheduled to the Act, and section 4(2) empowers judges to make declarations of incompatibility in respect of legislation that is incompatible with the ECHR. Nonetheless, it remains the orthodox view that the Westminster Parliament remains supreme, a view supported by the absence of substantive limitations on legislation by a written constitution, and, secondly, from the institutional

[104] Michael Akehurst, 'Parliamentary Sovereignty and the Supremacy of Community Law' (1989) 60 *British Yearbook of International Law* 351; TRS Allan, 'Parliamentary Sovereignty: Law, Politics, and Revolution' (1997) 113 *Law Quarterly Review* 443; Jeffrey Jowell, 'Parliamentary Sovereignty under the New Hypothesis' [2006] *Public Law* 562; Aileen Kavanagh, 'Constitutional Review under the UK Human Rights' (Cambridge University Press, 2009) 411–15.

[105] *R v Secretary of State for Transport, ex p Factortame (No 2)* [1991] 1 AC 603 (HL); *R v Secretary of State for Transport, ex p Equal Opportunities Commission* [1995] 1 AC 1 (HL).

point of view, the decision to withhold from courts the power to invalidate legislation.[106]

Parliamentary supremacy also remains a recognised principle of the Constitution of Australia. While judicial review of legislation of the Commonwealth Parliament occurs as a result of the implied power of judicial review as a necessary tool for enforcement of the Commonwealth Constitution, the Commonwealth Constitution does not include a Bill of Rights that confers jurisdiction on the courts to review primary legislation for rights consistency. However, as Julie Taylor has observed, the fact that there is a written Constitution for Australia, which has been interpreted by the High Court to permit the judicial invalidation of legislation, distinguishes it from the UK.[107] Thus, while parliamentary supremacy continues to play an important role in constitutional and rights development in Australia, it does not operate with the same vigour as it does in the UK.[108]

Constitutions in the Commonwealth Caribbean displace parliamentary supremacy in favour of constitutional supremacy by expressly declaring the Constitution the supreme law and conferring wide powers on the courts to provide redress for violations of fundamental rights recognised in the Constitution.[109] With respect to Canada, in current discourse on Canadian constitutional law, there are two frameworks for characterising the current constitutional structure. Stephen Gardbaum characterises the current Canadian constitutional framework as part of a 'new Commonwealth model of constitutionalism' which, in Gardbaum's words, rejects both 'legislative supremacy' and 'judicial or constitutional supremacy', preferring a model that 'treats legislatures and courts as joint or supplementary, rather than alternative, exclusive protectors and promoters of rights and decouples the power of judicial review of legislation from judicial supremacy or finality.'[110] Canada is also often described as possessing a dialogic model, which eschews the practice of giving judges the 'final word' on rights issues and instead fosters dialogue between the courts and the legislature. Peter

[106] Alison Young, *Parliamentary Sovereignty and the Human Rights Act* (Hart Publishing, 2009) ch 2; Tom Hickman, *Public Law after the Human Rights Act* (Hart Publishing, 2010) 24–25; 46–49; See also Nicholas Bamforth, 'Parliamentary Sovereignty and the Human Rights Act 1998' [1998] *Public Law* 572; Lord Irvine of Lairg QC, 'The Impact of the Human Rights Act: Parliament, the Courts and the Executive' [2003] *Public Law* 308.

[107] Julie Taylor, 'Human Rights Protection in Australia: Interpretation Provisions and Parliamentary Supremacy' (2004) 32 *Federal Law Review* 57.

[108] ibid 60.

[109] See, eg, the Constitution of Barbados 1966, s 1 of which states that the Constitution 'is the supreme law' and s 24 of which confers wide powers on the court to provide redress for violations of the Constitution's fundamental rights provisions. Section 2 of the Constitution of Jamaica 1962 does not expressly state that the Constitution is the 'supreme law' but is to the same effect, providing that 'if any other law is inconsistent with this Constitution, this Constitution shall prevail and the other law shall, to the extent of the inconsistency, be void.'

[110] Gardbaum (n 74 above) 2.

Hogg and Alison Bushell were largely responsible for the popularisation of 'dialogue' discourse,[111] using the term 'dialogue' to refer to 'cases in which a judicial decision striking down a law on Charter grounds is followed by some action by the competent legislative body'.[112] In a subsequent article by Hogg, Thornton, and White, 'dialogue' was also applied to the fact that such judicial decisions 'usually leave room for a legislative response, and usually receive a legislative response'.[113]

These median theories on the nature of Canadian constitutional law are strongly supported by Canada's Constitution. Canadian courts have the power to invalidate laws, despite the absence of an express provision in the Charter of Rights and Freedoms 1982, granting such power. This power is understood to be the effect of the clause asserting the supremacy of the Constitution (section 52(1) of the Constitution Act 1982) and the clause requiring the enforcement of the Charter (section 24(1), Constitution Act 1982), and the courts have acted accordingly.[114] However, while the Canadian Supreme Court is empowered to invalidate legislation that violates Charter rights, the 'notwithstanding' clause in section 33 of the Charter confers an override power on Parliament, permitting it to enact legislation 'notwithstanding a provision included in section 2 or sections 7 to 15' of the Charter. Thus Canada lies along the middle of the spectrum between constitutional supremacy and parliamentary supremacy.

Accompanying the common law constitutionalist context of the use of implied constitutional principles is the question whether natural law theories are part of the relevant historical and conceptual framework. Both in respect of the development of common law and the development of constitutionalism, the argument may be made that there is some (unarticulated) bond between the concept of implied constitutional principles and natural law. Chief Justice McLachlin of the Supreme Court of Canada, in extrajudicial remarks, has drawn a connection between the practice of reasoning by implied principles and the concept of natural law, writing that:

> The contemporary concept of unwritten constitutional principles can be seen as a modern reincarnation of the ancient doctrines of natural law. Like those conceptions of justice, the identification of these principles seems to presuppose the existence of some kind of natural order. Unlike them, however, it does not fasten on theology as the source of unwritten principles that transcend the exercise of

[111] Peter Hogg and Allison Bushell, 'The Charter Dialogue between Courts and Legislatures' (Or Perhaps the Charter of Rights Isn't Such a Bad Thing After All)' (1997) 35 *Osgoode Hall Law Journal* 75. The language of 'dialogue' has since spread throughout other states, including other parts of the Commonwealth and the UK.

[112] ibid 82.

[113] Peter Hogg, Allison Bushell Thornton, and Wade Wright, 'Charter Dialogue Revisited—or "Much Ado About Metaphors"' (2007) 45 *Osgoode Hall Law Journal* 1, 4.

[114] Gardbaum (n 74 above) 100–01.

> state power. It is derived from the history, values and culture of the nation, viewed in its constitutional context.[115]

Similarly, it has been argued that the concept of 'unwritten fundamental law' is rooted in ancient common law traditions which have been influenced by concepts of natural law or 'right reason'.[116] The notion that the development of fundamental norms as an element of constitutionalism has some affinity with natural law theories is not novel. Such connections have been drawn, for instance by James Stoner and Paul DeHart.[117] Allan has also argued that the idea of a state's constitution connotes more than a written constitution (if one exists for the state in question) and that it is allied with a concept of law which is 'intimately connected with our pursuit of justice.'[118] Allan does not necessarily embrace a natural law basis for constitutionalism and constitutional law adjudication, but he does reject a strictly positivist approach by insisting that an account of constitutionalism must begin within an understanding of law as a pursuit of justice.

Regarding the common law, it has been convincingly argued that Coke—whose writings were foundational to the development of common law and judicial review—and his contemporaries, perceived a harmonious connection between natural law and common law.[119] Of course, those that see implied constitutional principles as linked to historical natural law doctrines do not perceive a unified source for these two concepts. McLachlin CJ argues, along this vein, that implied constitutional principles are usually based on 'the history, values and culture of the nation' as opposed to theology or divinity. Phrased in other terms, while there may be parallels with the old common law respect for natural law, the use of implied principles is not founded on a vague notion of 'pre-political natural rights', but on a particular conception of what law is and what pursuits it serves in the society in question.[120]

[115] Beverly McLachlin, 'Unwritten Constitutional Principles: What is Going On?' (2006) 4 *New Zealand Journal of Public & International Law* 147, 149.

[116] Walters, 'Common Law Constitution in Canada' (n 87 above) 136; McLachlin (ibid).

[117] James R Stoner, 'Natural Law, Common Law and the Constitution' in Douglas E Edlin (ed) *Common Law Theory* (Cambridge University Press, 2007); Paul DeHart, *Uncovering the Constitution's Moral Design* (University of Missouri Press, 2007) esp 4–10. See also Aileen Kavanagh, 'The Irish Constitution at 75 Years: Natural law, Christian Values and The Ideal of Justice' (2012) 48 *Irish Jurist* 71.

[118] TRS Allan, 'Constitutional Justice and the Concept of Law' in Grant Huscroft (ed) *Expounding the Constitution: Essays in Constitutional Theory* (Cambridge University Press, 2008) 221–23.

[119] RH Helmholz, 'Bonham's Case, Judicial Review, and the Law of Nature' (2009) 1 *Journal of Legal Analysis* 332–34; Stoner, 'Natural Law, Common Law and the Constitution' (n 117 above) 171–72.

[120] Mark D Walters, 'Written Constitutions and Unwritten Constitutionalism' in Grant Huscroft (ed) *Expounding the Constitution: Essays in Constitutional Theory* (Cambridge University Press, 2008) 259.

IV. CONCLUSION

The use of implied constitutional principles in the common law jurisdictions examined in this study is firmly rooted in the concept of constitutionalism and the idea of principles as norms applicable as optimal standards in interactions between the individual and the state. The necessary discourse reaches beyond the conceptual and theoretical context and encompasses the search for legitimacy on the part of the court and the state in the application of the constitution. There is accordingly an interplay of institutional and doctrinal considerations that influence judicial reasoning by implied constitutional principles in fundamental rights cases. This interplay of factors points to the special significance of separation of powers and the rule of law as foundational constitutional principles.

The analysis in this chapter sets the stage for much of the proceeding conversation on the role of implied constitutional principles in rights adjudication. In the following chapters, issues regarding implication in interpretation, the nature of principles, and varying models of constitutionalism comprise the critical conceptual landscape. These issues therefore emerge—explicitly or implicitly—in the subsequent analysis of applications of separation of powers and rule of law, the functions played by implied constitutional principles in rights cases, and questions regarding the legitimacy of judicial invocation of constitutional principles.

3

Judicial Conceptions of the Rule of Law

I. INTRODUCTION

'IT HAS BEEN through judicial review ... that the rule of law has had its most significant recent development and where it has revealed the detail of its content.'[1] Thus, in order to determine the 'qualities' of the rule of law, we must consider the ways in which courts use the term.[2] Certainly, in expounding on the meaning of the rule of law as a legal principle, it is crucial to engage with the question of what the judiciary—collectively one of the most important legal actors in the legal system—has to say about the rule of law.

This chapter addresses the dominant judicial applications of the rule of law, as shown in judicial review cases. Here, I take Jowell's approach of seeking to examine the principles in their practical application, rather than merely focussing on the philosophical debates. There is a rousing debate among legal philosophers regarding whether the rule of law is formal or substantive in nature; Parts II and III of the chapter will first outline the contours of this theoretical debate and then demonstrate, through comparative case law, that the dominant discourse among legal philosophers is inconsistent with the dominant judicial interpretation of the principle in common law jurisdictions. These inconsistencies mainly relate to the definition and application of rule of law conceptions. Parts III and IV analyse understandings of the rule of law through the development of judicial review and through express references to the rule of law in the application of Constitutions and Bills of Rights. The persistent conflicts and tension that arise in the practical application of the rule of law in courts are considered in Part V, using the application of the rule of law as equality as a case study. As a consistently adopted attribute of the rule of law, differing interpretations of the

[1] Jeffrey Jowell, 'The Rule of Law's Long Arm: Uncommunicated Decisions' [2004] *Public Law* 246, 246.

[2] Justin Leslie, 'Vindicating Common Law Constitutionalism' (2010) 30 *Legal Studies* 301, 314; Elizabeth Carroll, '*Woolworths Ltd v Pallas Newco Pty Ltd*: A case study in the application of the rule of law in Australia' (2006) 13 *Australian Journal of Administrative Law* 87, 90.

rule of law as equality reflect continuing dissension over the meaning(s) of the principle in common law courts. Thus, designation of accepted conceptions and attributes of the rule of law is not calculated to—and cannot—accomplish erasure of contestation over the scope and application of the rule of law. Underlying the conceptualisation of the rule of law in theory and practice is the reality that this conceptualisation is 'a legitimately open-ended, evolving activity'.[3]

II. CONCEPTIONS OF THE RULE OF LAW

Grappling with the complexity of the rule of law's nature, scope and objectives results in ongoing contestation over conceptions and typologies of the rule of law. While common typologies range from thin to thick, negative to positive and formal to substantive conceptions, the consistent thread is that of expanding or narrowing the requirements imposed by the principle on the legal system and legal actors. The multiplicity of understandings has contributed to the perception that 'there are almost as many conceptions of the rule of law as there are people defending it.'[4] The formal-substantive typology has taken hold in common law legal theory; it sees the rule of law as resting within either a formal understanding that speaks to the manner of law-making or a substantive conception that prescribes requirements for the content of the law.

Craig, classifying both Dicey's and Raz's accounts as formal in this sense, helped to mainstream this typology. Dicey's inceptive exposition of the rule of law entailed, first that an individual can only be punished for breach of a law, secondly, that there is equality before the law so that all persons are subject to 'ordinary law' and 'ordinary tribunals', and thirdly, that constitutional law is the consequence of the rights of individuals as defined by the courts.[5] Raz's orthodox rule of law exposition adds more modern liberal requirements through a list of the characteristics of the rule of law, including that laws should be prospective, stable and guided by open, general, and clear rules, that there should be an independent judiciary, and

[3] Amichai Magen and Leonardo Morlino, 'Hybrid regimes, the rule of law, and external influence on domestic change' in Amichai Magen and Leonardo Morlino (eds), *International Actors, Democratization and the Rule of Law: Anchoring Democracy?* (Routledge, 2009) 8. The near ubiquity of rule of law objectives in development goals and indicators as well as among human rights and policy bodies has likely encouraged local institutional reliance on the principle while doing little to clarify the concept. For critique of international rule of law promotion, see Rosa Ehrenreich Brooks, 'The New Imperialism: Violence, Norms, and the Rule of Law' (2003) 101 *Michigan Law Review* 2275.

[4] Olufemi Taiwo, 'The Rule of Law: The New Leviathan?' (1999) 12 *Canadian Journal of Law & Jurisprudence* 151, 152

[5] Albert Venn Dicey, *Introduction to the Study of the Law of the Constitution*, 10th edn (Macmillan, 1959) 188–96.

access to the courts.[6] The overarching end of the rule of law from the perspective of formalists, is said to be the limitation of arbitrariness in the exercise of state authority.

The substantive conception, on the other hand, is said to incorporate the formal elements, but also to demand that the law fulfil other values. Most notably, the substantive conception is said to differ from formal versions by placing constraints on the substance of laws, rather than the manner in which laws are made. Dworkin is a strong proponent of this conception, arguing that, if the rule of law is to be meaningful, it must incorporate substantive requirements as to the content of the law, and that citizens have moral and political rights that ought to be enforced through positive law.[7] In line with the quest for a meaningful rule of law, Selznick warns against reducing the rule of law to merely negative aspirations, arguing that 'the larger promise of the rule of law' seeks to realise values such as 'respect for the dignity, integrity, and moral equality of persons and groups'.[8]

The accuracy of Craig's classification has been rightly challenged, paving the way for alternative and more nuanced formulations of conceptions of the rule of law.[9] For instance, contrary to Craig's categorisation, Barber convincingly argues that Raz's account of the rule of law includes considerations relating to the content of the law.[10] While Barber proposes an alternative framework of conceptions organised along the lines of legalistic and non-legalistic conceptions, the position advanced here is more moderate; what I seek to do here is adopt Barber's criticisms of the classification of Dicey's and Raz's rule of law conceptions as formal. What is relevant for the purposes of this chapter is that Barber challenges the binary division between formal and substantive conceptions and the characterisation of supposedly formal conceptions. Acceptance of Barber's alternative framework is unnecessary for acknowledgement of the wisdom of his critique of the classifications made by Craig. For instance, Barber rightly notes that the mandate

[6] Joseph Raz, 'The Rule of Law and Its Virtue' (1977) 93 *Law Quarterly Review* 195; Paul Craig, 'Formal and Substantive Conceptions of the Rule of Law: An Analytical Framework' [1997] *Public Law* 467, 469. See also Peter W Hogg and Carla F Zwibel, 'The Rule of Law in the Supreme Court of Canada' (2005) 55 *University of Toronto of Law Journal* 715.

[7] Ronald Dworkin, *A Matter of Principle* (Oxford University Press, 1985) 11–32. See also John Laws, 'The Constitution: Morals and Rights' [1996] *Public Law* 622.

[8] Philip Selznick, 'Legal Cultures and the Rule of Law' in Martin Krygier and Adam Czarnota (eds), *The Rule of Law after Communism: Problems and Prospects in East-Central Europe* (Routledge, 1999) 26.

[9] See alternative formulations in NW Barber, 'Must Legalistic Conceptions of the Rule of Law Have a Social Dimension?' (2004) 17 *Ratio Juris* 474; David Dyzenhaus, *The Constitution of Law: Legality in Times of Emergency* (Cambridge University Press, 2006) 1–16.

[10] Barber, 'Legalistic Conceptions' (ibid) 474–75. See also a more nuanced alternative to the formal-substantive formulation in Jeremy Waldron, 'The Rule of Law as a Theater of Debate' in Justine Burley (ed) *Dworkin and His Critics: With Replies by Dworkin* (Blackwell Publishing, 2004).

that laws be prospective limits the goals which a law may achieve:[11] a law does not comply with this requirement if it seeks to criminalise an act that was not criminal when it was performed. Similarly, the question whether a law satisfies the requirement of certainty will, in some cases, speak directly to the content of that law. Accordingly, strong arguments have been posed that laws such as the offence of outrage to public decency and public nuisance are uncertain in that the content and reach of the prohibition cannot be defined with certainty and that they fall foul of the requirement that the law should be prospective.[12] It is unconvincing to suggest that these arguments have no relation to the substance of the law. Since Raz's conception can affect the law in this substantive sense, it must be inaccurate to classify his conception as formal. A distinction between formal and substantive resting on whether a conception places requirements on the content of the law in insufficiently cognisant of the full implications of theories classified as 'formal' and of the interactions between the requirements of so-called formal and substantive rule of law conceptions.

This criticism of the formal and substantive dichotomy is borne out by the case law, in which three categories of applications of the rule of law can be discerned. The first is a formal conception of the rule of law as rule by law. The latter two conceptions are both substantive in the sense that they speak to the content of the law. Thus, the second is a legalistic conception that is mainly concerned with legality, and with the procedure and formulation of laws but which may affect the substance of the law. Finally, there is a more deeply valorised substantive strand that embraces wider requirements regarding the content of the law, including requirements that advance fundamental rights.

Using this rubric, Raz's theory is therefore more accurately described as legalistic.[13] Dicey's conception is more appropriately described as a valorised substantive conception.[14] This is evident from his elaborations of the elements of the rule of law. With respect to his second element—equality before the law—it is not purely a question of procedural access to courts, but also condemns status-based immunities from the application of 'ordinary law'.[15] His position that 'every man, whatever be his rank or condition, is subject to the ordinary law of the realm and amenable to the jurisdiction of the ordinary tribunals' eschews distinctions based on an

[11] Barber, 'Legalistic Conceptions' (n 9 above) 478.

[12] The Law Commission, *Simplification of Criminal Law: Public Nuisance and Outraging Public Decency* (Law Com No 193, 2010) 46–48, 52–54.

[13] Barber, 'Legalistic Conceptions' (n 9 above) 475. See also Luc Tremblay, *The Rule of Law, Justice and Interpretation* (McGill-Queen's University Press, 1997) 149–50.

[14] See Barber, 'Legalistic Conceptions' (n 9 above) 479; Jeffrey Jowell, 'The Rule of Law and Its Underlying Values' in Jeffrey Jowell and Dawn Oliver (eds), *The Changing Constitution*, 6th edn (Oxford University Press, 2007) 11.

[15] Barber (n 9 above) 480–81; Jowell, 'Underlying Values' (ibid) 11.

individual's identification as part of a particular status group. In Dicey's writings, it was therefore a requirement of the rule of law that officials, like private citizens, should be 'brought before the courts, and made, in their personal capacity, liable to punishment, or to the payment of damages, for acts done in their official character but in excess of their lawful authority.'[16] In his third element of the rule of law, Dicey contended that the rule of law pervades the constitution because the constitution is derived from individual rights as described by the courts, and that the common law was best suited for protection of these rights.[17] Craig has contended that this element should be construed as an argument that *if* it is desirous to protect individual liberties, then the common law provides a better venue than a written constitution. However, this construction seems to read down the meaning of Dicey's words. As Barber argues, Dicey proposed that a constitution infused with the rule of law provides a better tool for protection of individual liberties, and that therefore this system is to be preferred to the system of written constitutions.[18] Moreover, since Dicey's championing of the rule-of-law-infused common law was premised on the idea that the common law gives rise to individual liberties, it is hard to justify a classification of his doctrine as an articulation of a formal version of the rule of law.[19] Dicey was clearly concerned with the defence of a system of law that was well-equipped to protect (some) individual liberties; in his view, this was one of the virtues of the common law. Dicey's account of the rule of law is therefore more accurately characterised as a valorised substantive—rather than formal—conception.

In summary, it is more accurate to classify rule of law conceptions as including a formal conception of rule by law, and with substantive conceptions that range from the legalistic strand to the valorised substantive strand. Using this tripartite division of formal, legalistic, and valorised conceptions, the analysis below will show that a substantive conception is reflected in the majority of the common law jurisdictions examined. The valorised conception is reflected in decisions in the UK and the Commonwealth Caribbean, while the legalistic conception appears in decisions of the High Court of Australia, with some judges delivering dicta which embrace a valorised conception. While the late twentieth century Canadian Supreme Court articulated a version of the rule of law capable of accommodating rights protections, the new century has seen a pair of landmark judgments, one of which sought to tame the rule of law while the latter reasserted a substantive view of the rule of law in Canada. While the current picture of the rule of law in Canada is now contested, the prevailing conception at

[16] Dicey (n 5 above) 193.
[17] Dicey (n 5 above) 195–202.
[18] Barber, 'Legalistic Conceptions' (n 9 above) 480–81.
[19] TRS Allan, *Constitutional Justice: A Liberal Theory of the Rule of Law* (Oxford University Press, 2001) 18.

the apex of Canadian constitutional law is a valorised substantive version. The courts' representation of particular conceptions of the rule of law will be revealed through analysis of first, the development of heads of judicial review, particularly in the UK, secondly, the use of the principle of legality in interpretation, and thirdly, explicit references to the rule of law in applying the constitutions and bills of rights of the jurisdictions in question.

III. DEVELOPMENT OF HEADS OF JUDICIAL REVIEW

The development of heads of judicial review is largely based on the rule of law; the practice of underpinning heads of judicial review by the constitutional principle of the rule of law has been acknowledged by members of the academy and the higher judiciary. Thus, Young comments that '[t]he rule of law ... is being increasingly referred to in important judicial review decisions as a means of justifying judicial review generally, as well as underpinning specific heads of judicial review' and Jowell notes that 'the grounds of judicial review are in large part based upon the rule of law'.[20] The importance of this aspect of the discovery of rule of law applications is relevant in all common law jurisdictions but is particularly apparent in the UK, where there is no written constitution that confers the power of review on superior courts.

The three traditional grounds of judicial review—illegality, procedural impropriety, and irrationality—are all instances of the implementation of the rule of law.[21] In particular, the third ground of 'irrationality' or '*Wednesbury* unreasonableness', is partly based on a substantive conception of the rule of law.[22] The use of the ground of irrationality demonstrates that courts have sometimes been concerned not merely with administrative procedure, but also with substantive values of good administration. Thus, where judicial review includes an examination of the substance of the decision or act rather than the procedure by which the decision was made or the act taken, this reflects aspects of a substantive conception of the rule of law. Although courts often do not expressly refer to the rule of law, decisions such as *ex p Leech*[23] (holding that rules impeding the free flow of communication between a prisoner and his legal representative violate a prisoner's 'constitutional right' of access to justice) and *ex p Witham*[24] (holding that the levy of substantial court fees violate an impoverished litigant's access to

[20] Jeffrey Jowell, 'The Rule of Law: Rhetoric or Universal Principle?' (2012) 20 *Asia Pacific Law Review* 3, 6.

[21] Jowell, 'Underlying Values' (n 14 above).

[22] ibid 11. See also *R (Nadarajah) v SSHD* [2005] EWCA Civ 1363, *The Times* 14 December 2005 (CA).

[23] *R v SSHD, ex p Leech (No 2)* [1994] QB 198 (CA).

[24] *R v Lord Chancellor, ex p Witham* [1998] QB 575 (CA).

justice) reflect a substantive account of the rule of law. Despite the absence of express references to the rule of law, the judges' reasoning nonetheless reflects review of the substance of decisions, rather than merely the procedure, thereby reflecting a substantive conception of the rule of law.

Further evidence of the acceptance of the substantive concept of the rule of law is provided by common law judicial adoption of the doctrine of proportionality. As Allan argues, 'the doctrine of proportionality is clearly a feature of the ... substantive version: it entails an evaluation of public and private interests in accordance with criteria of justice and the common good.'[25] The doctrine, then, requires the court to undertake an assessment of the substantive value of proposed solutions to social problems relative to the protected interest which is affected by that proposed solution.[26] The courts have therefore accurately acknowledged that the proportionality inquiry depends on a 'value judgement' of the government initiative and the interest in question.[27]

Similar conclusions can be drawn from cases using the doctrine of legitimate expectations.[28] Craig and Schønberg have argued that protecting legitimate expectations expresses 'the requirements of predictability inherent in the rule of law.'[29] This explanation provides an account of the basis of *procedural* legitimate expectations. However, convincingly accounting for *substantive* legitimate expectations requires reference to the rule of law's substantive aims. Jowell's argument that the rule of law advances substantive aims[30] is therefore a more useful explanator for the conferral of substantive benefits under the doctrine of legitimate expectations. This is reflected in the weighing of public against private interests, which has become a feature of decisions on substantive legitimate expectations.[31]

[25] TRS Allan, 'The Rule of Law as the Rule of Reason: Consent and Constitutionalism' (1999) 115 *Law Quarterly Review* 221, 233.

[26] Aileen Kavanagh, *Constitutional Review under the UK Human Rights Act* (Cambridge University Press, 2009) 233–34.

[27] *Wilson v First County Trust* [2003] 3 WLR 568 [62]–[63] (HL) (Lord Nicholls); *R v Secretary of State for the Home Department ex p Limbuela* [2006] UKHL 66, [2006] 1 AC 396 (HL) [55] (Lord Bingham).

[28] For support for proposition that substantive legitimate expectation is based on the rule of law, see *R v Secretary of State for the Home Department, ex parte Pierson* [1997] UKHL 37, [1998] AC 539 (HL) 591 (Lord Steyn). See also TRS Allan, 'Constitutional Dialogue and the Justification of Judicial Review' (2003) 23 *Oxford Journal of Legal Studies* 563, 572–73; Allan, *Constitutional Justice: A Liberal Theory of the Rule of Law* (n 19 above) 132; Mark Elliott, *The Constitutional Foundations of Judicial Review* (Hart Publishing, 2001) 100–104; Jeffrey Jowell, 'Beyond the Rule of Law: Towards Constitutional Judicial Review' [2000] *Public Law* 671, 671–72, 674, and 678.

[29] Soren Schønberg and Paul Craig, 'Substantive Legitimate Expectations after Coughlan' [2000] *Public Law* 684, 697.

[30] Jowell, 'The Rule of Law and its Underlying Values' (n 14 above) 20–21.

[31] Allan, 'The Rule of Law as the Rule of Reason' (n 25 above) 233. See also Matthew Groves, 'Substantive Legitimate Expectations in Australian Administrative Law' (2008) 32 *Melbourne University Law Review* 470.

For instance, Lord Woolf MR, delivering the judgment of the Court in *R v North and East Devon Health Authority, ex p Coughlan*, held that the decision of the health authority to remove the applicants from a home constituted 'the unwarranted frustration of a legitimate expectation and thus … a failure of substantive fairness.'[32]

Substantive legitimate expectations have also been embraced in the Commonwealth Caribbean, having been endorsed by lower courts, the Privy Council, and the Caribbean Court of Justice. Thus, the doctrine formed the basis for the decision in *Leacock v AG of Barbados*, in which the applicant claimed a legitimate expectation—based on past practice—that having been permitted by his employers to obtain a law degree, he would be granted study leave to obtain legal professional training. Upholding his claim, the court held that Leacock had a 'legitimate expectation of a substantive benefit' which was frustrated by the employers' departure from previous practice.[33] The position of the court shows acceptance of the notion of substantive fairness as part of the framework of this ground of judicial review:

> … it can now be said with confidence that the doctrine of legitimate expectation which originated as a public law innovation to ensure procedural fairness, such as to give the right to be consulted or be heard, has now evolved and expanded to protect benefits, advantages or interests of a substantive nature which an applicant can reasonably expect to be permitted to enjoy.[34]

Similarly, substantive legitimate expectations have been protected by the two final appellate tribunals in the Commonwealth Caribbean: the Privy Council and the Caribbean Court of Justice.[35] The Caribbean Court of Justice in *AG v Joseph and Boyce* held that the appellants who had been sentenced to death had a substantive legitimate expectation that they would be allowed to complete complaint proceedings before international human rights agencies prior to the execution of their death sentence.[36] Though the expectation was one of being allowed full access to a particular process, it was substantive in the sense that what was being challenged was not a denial of the right to be heard on the change of policy, but rather, the right to have the matter considered fully and to obtain a rights body's decision (a substantive right) before execution. In an even more direct application of substantive legitimate expectations, the Privy Council held in *Paponette*

[32] [2001] QB 213 (CA) [76]. See also *Nadarajah* (n 22 above) [68].

[33] (2005) 68 WIR 181 (HC, Barbados) [49].

[34] ibid [46].

[35] *AG v Joseph and Boyce* (2006) 69 WIR 104 (CCJ, Barbados); *Paponette v Attorney General of Trinidad and Tobago* [2010] UKPC 32, [2012] 1 AC 1 (JCPC, Trinidad and Tobago). The Caribbean Court of Justice is now the final appellate court for Barbados, Belize, Dominica and Guyana. The Privy Council remains the final appellate tribunal for the other Commonwealth Caribbean jurisdictions.

[36] *Joseph and Boyce* (ibid) [125]; Albert K Fiadjoe, *Commonwealth Caribbean Public Law*, 3rd edn (Routledge-Cavendish, 2008) 218 et seq.

that in reneging on representations made to the applicants that they would be free to manage the new taxi stands from which the government required them to operate, the Government of Trinidad and Tobago frustrated the applicants' legitimate expectations and negatively affected the applicants' business.[37] There was therefore interference with the applicants' right to enjoyment of their property in section 4(a) of the Constitution of Trinidad and Tobago, and the government had failed to show that such interference was done with due process of law as it had failed to take account of the representations made to the taxi drivers.

Moreover, courts have increasingly expressly invoked a substantive conception of the rule of law in judicial review. This is represented, for instance, in cases relating to the communication of legal decisions, rules, and guidelines. Such an application was adopted in the oft-cited decision of the House of Lords in *Anufrijeva*, in which it was held that failure to communicate to the applicant a decision denying her continued income support constituted a violation of 'the constitutional principle requiring the rule of law to be observed'.[38] The majority of the Bench justified their decision on the basis that the rule of law requires legality and accountability. Notably, though the Home Secretary's decision accorded with the procedural requirements of the legislation, the Law Lords argued that to uphold the decision on this account would be 'legalism and conceptualism run riot'.[39]

The House of Lords again called upon this application of the rule of law in *R (Purdy) v Director of Public Prosecutions*.[40] It was held that the DPP had a duty to publish details of the factors he would take into consideration in deciding whether to prosecute for breach of the Suicide Act 1961 (UK). This publication was necessary to allow an individual to foresee the consequences of her actions and plan accordingly. Lord Hope cited a passage from a judgment of the ECtHR stating that:

> In matters affecting fundamental rights it would be contrary to the rule of law, one of the basic principles of a democratic society enshrined in the Convention, for a legal discretion granted to the executive to be expressed in terms of an unfettered power. Consequently, the law must indicate with sufficient clarity the scope of any such discretion conferred on the competent authorities and the manner of its exercise.[41]

This passage identifies the legalistic application of the rule of law as certainty but draws a clear and close connection between this application and 'matters affecting fundamental rights'. This tendency towards a substantive

[37] *Paponette* (n 35 above) [33]–[49].

[38] *R (Anufrijeva) v SSHD* [2003] UKHL 36, [2004] 1 AC 604 (HL) [28].

[39] ibid [32] (Lord Steyn), with whom the majority of the Law Lords agreed. Jowell, 'Underlying Values' (n 14 above) 18–21.

[40] *Regina (Purdy) v Director of Public Prosecutions* [2009] UKHL 45, [2009] 3 WLR 403 (HL).

[41] ibid [42].

conception of the rule of law and the recognition of a close connection between legalistic and valorised substantive strands is resonant in judicial review.

A. Principle of Legality

Resting between the administrative law use of the rule of law to develop heads of review and explicitly constitutionalist rule of law references, the principle of legality serves as an interpretive conduit for applying constitutional principles as a restraint on government. In constitutional and fundamental rights law in the Commonwealth, the rule of law has repeatedly been applied through the principle of legality. According to this principle, Parliament is presumed not to legislate contrary to fundamental constitutional principles and fundamental rights and freedoms.[42] Well-known expressions of the principle of legality emerge from *ex p Pierson* and *Secretary of State for the Home Department, ex p Simms.*[43] In *Pierson* Lord Steyn articulated his view of the principle of legality as a technique of statutory interpretation:

> it is to Sir Rupert Cross that I turn for the best modern explanation of 'the spirit of legality', or what has been called the principle of legality. ... The passage appears in Cross, Statutory Interpretation, 3rd ed, at 165–166, ...:
>
> "Statutes often go into considerable detail, but even so allowance must be made for the fact that they are not enacted in a vacuum. A great deal inevitably remains unsaid. Legislators and drafters assume that the courts will continue to act in accordance with well-recognised rules ... Long-standing principles of constitutional and administrative law are likewise taken for granted, or assumed by the courts to have been taken for granted, by Parliament. Examples are the principles that discretionary powers conferred in apparently absolute terms must be exercised reasonably, and that administrative tribunals and other such bodies must act in accordance with the principles of natural justice. One function of the word 'presumption' in the context of statutory interpretation is to state the result of this legislative reliance (real or assumed) on firmly established legal principles. There is a 'presumption' that mens rea is required in the case of statutory crimes, and a 'presumption' that statutory powers must be exercised reasonably. These presumptions apply although there is no question of linguistic ambiguity in the statutory wording under construction, and they may be described as 'presumptions of general application'. ... These presumptions of general application not only supplement the text, they also operate at a higher level as expressions of fundamental principles governing both civil liberties and the relations between Parliament, the

[42] *Pierson* (n 28 above) 591 (Lord Steyn); *R v Secretary of State for the Home Department, ex p Simms* [2000] 2 AC 115 (HL) 131 (Lord Hoffmann).

[43] *Simms* (ibid).

executive and the courts. They operate here as constitutional principles which are not easily displaced by a statutory text...."'

Lord Steyn then proceeded to establish a link between this principle and the rule of law, asserting that '[u]nless there is the clearest provision to the contrary, Parliament must be presumed not to legislate contrary to the rule of law. And the rule of law enforces minimum standards of fairness, both substantive and procedural.'[44] The centrality of this interpretative principle to constitutional adjudication was reaffirmed in *Evans v Attorney General*, through Lord Neuberger's ruling that an executive override of a judicial decision can only be effected through 'crystal clear' statutory wording.[45]

This vehicle for infusing legislation with the rule of law principle has been employed by other common law superior courts, including the Australian High Court. The principle of legality was utilised in *Plaintiff S157/2002*[46] and in *Al-Kateb v Godwin*.[47] The interpretative power of the rule of law was marshalled in *Al-Kateb v Godwin* as underlying the principle of legality. In *Al-Kateb* the High Court was faced with a challenge to the detention of a stateless person in an immigration detention centre, in circumstances where his removal from the centre was not reasonably practicable in the foreseeable future. This detention was made under the Migration Act 1958 (Cth) and one question argued before the court was whether, on a proper construction of the relevant sections of the Migration Act 1958, the statute authorised or required the detention of an unlawful non-citizen even if his removal from Australia was not reasonably practicable in the foreseeable future. The majority of the Court held that the statute did authorise the indefinite detention, while two dissenting judges (Justices Gleeson and Kirby) invoked the rule of law in justifying a narrower interpretation of the statute. The principle of legality was used in support of both the majority judgment and the position of the minority. Justice Gleeson explained the operation of the principle and its connection to the rule of law:

> Where what is involved is the interpretation of legislation said to confer upon the Executive a power of administrative detention that is indefinite in duration, and that may be permanent, there comes into play a principle of legality, which governs both Parliament and the courts. In exercising their judicial function, courts seek to give effect to the will of Parliament by declaring the meaning of what Parliament has enacted. Courts do not impute to the legislature an intention to abrogate or curtail certain human rights or freedoms (of which personal liberty

[44] *Pierson* (n 28 above) 591.

[45] *R (Evans) v Attorney General (Appellant)* [2015] UKSC 21 [56]–[58]; Se-shauna Wheatle and Roger Masterman, 'The 'Constitutional Aspect' in *Evans v Attorney General*' UK Const L Blog (22 Jun 2015) (available at http://ukconstitutionallaw.org). There is more fulsome analysis of the impact of *Evans* in ch 5.

[46] *Plaintiff S157/2002 v Commonwealth of Australia* (2003) 211 CLR 476 (HC, Australia).

[47] *Al-Kateb v Godwin* (2004) 219 CLR 562 (HC, Australia).

> is the most basic) unless such an intention is clearly manifested by unambiguous language, which indicates that the legislature has directed its attention to the rights or freedoms in question, and has consciously decided upon abrogation or curtailment. That principle has been re-affirmed by this Court in recent cases. It is not new. ...
>
> A statement concerning the improbability that Parliament would abrogate fundamental rights by the use of general or ambiguous words is not a factual prediction, capable of being verified or falsified by a survey of public opinion. In a free society, under the rule of law, it is an expression of a legal value, respected by the courts, and acknowledged by the courts to be respected by Parliament.[48]

For Justice Kirby, the principle of legality is a feature of constitutional and rights reasoning in the common law legal family:

> judges of our tradition incline to treat unlimited executive detention as incompatible with contemporary notions of the rule of law. Hence, judges regard such unlimited detention with vigilance and suspicion. They do what they can within their constitutional functions to limit it and to subject it to express or implied restrictions defensive of individual liberty.[49]

Justice Kirby's statement evokes the elements of tradition, history, and cross-national trends that are associated with reasoning by implied constitutional principles.[50]

The exact contours of the operation of the principle of legality as a route for applying the rule of law do, however, suffer from lack of clarity.[51] First, it is not clear what application of the rule of law will be chosen by judges, whether a substantive valorised application or a legalistic conception of the rule of law, for instance. Secondly, while the principle of legality maintains that a statute which appears to abrogate fundamental rights must be subject to 'strict construction', the standard of construction is not clearly defined. While the standard of construction is strict, it is likely that there are degrees of strictness depending on the nature of the specific fundamental right or principle in question and the nature of the interference presented by the statute in question.[52] We see the differences in application of the principle where Hayne J, who was in the majority in *Al-Kateb*, also referred to the principle of legality as a tool of construction of the statute, but took the position that the words of the statute were clear and did authorise the detention of

[48] ibid [19]–[20].

[49] ibid [161].

[50] Tracy Robinson, 'Gender, Nation and the Common Law Constitution' (2008) 28 *Oxford Journal Law Studies* 735; Mark Walters, 'The Common Law Constitution in Canada: The Return of Lex Non Scripta as Fundamental Law' (2001) 51 *University of Toronto Law Journal* 91.

[51] Hon JJ Spigelman AC, 'Principle of Legality and the Clear Statement Principle' (2005) 79 *Australian Law Journal* 769.

[52] ibid 779–80.

Al-Kateb.[53] On the other hand, Chief Justice Gleeson, dissenting, applied the principle of legality with the conclusion that the words of the statute speaking to detention were not sufficiently clear to meet the standard of construction required by the principle of legality.[54] It is revealing that while Gleeson CJ stated that the principle of legality meant that the intent to abrogate rights must be 'clearly manifested by unambiguous language', Hayne J referred to no such stringent requirement.[55] Overall, stating that 'strict construction' is required tells us something about the court's approach to interpretation but it does not tell the full story.

IV. EXPLICIT REFERENCES TO THE RULE OF LAW IN APPLYING A CONSTITUTION OR BILL OF RIGHTS

Despite the introduction of written constitutions and/or bills of rights in the jurisdictions examined, the rule of law has remained a feature of the construction and implementation of the constitutions and bills of rights. Courts have variously described the principle as 'a fundamental element of the ... legal system',[56] a 'foundational principle of the constitution',[57] and a 'fundamental—implicit feature of the Constitution.'[58] Across these jurisdictions, the rule of law is activated in a substantive sense, ranging from the legalistic conception to the valorised conception, thereby undercutting dominant theoretical conclusions about the meanings and scope of the rule of law.

The High Court of Australia has adopted a legalistic conception of the rule of law, applying the principle in support of judicial review and access to courts. This conception was evident in the foundational case on the rule of law in Australian jurisprudence—*Australian Communist Party v Commonwealth of Australia*,[59] in which the High Court of Australia was asked to determine the validity of the Communist Party Dissolution Act 1950 (Cth), which declared the Australian Communist Party an unlawful association, dissolved it, and granted the Governor General the power to dissolve organisations associated with the Australian Communist Party. The majority of the judges held that the statute was *ultra vires* the power of the Commonwealth Parliament and invalid. In arriving at this conclusion, Dixon J considered whether this Act fell within an incidental or implied

53 *Al-Kateb* (n 47 above) [241] (Hayne J).
54 ibid [19]–[22] (Gleeson CJ).
55 Spigelman (n 51 above) 781–82.
56 Carroll (n 2 above) 88.
57 *New Brunswick Broadcasting Co v Nova Scotia (Speaker of the House of Assembly)* [1993] 1 SCR 319; *Reference re Senate Reform* [2014] 1 SCR 704.
58 *Zuniga and Others v Attorney General* [2014] 5 LRC 1 (CCJ, Belize).
59 (1951) 83 CLR 1 (HC, Australia).

power of Parliament to uphold and preserve the Commonwealth and its institutions from subversion. Dixon J concluded that it did not, finding that, as the Act offers no objective test for determining when the power to dissolve a body ought to be exercised, the Act purported to make Parliament a judge in its own cause with respect to the operation of this power. In an important passage, Dixon J called in aid the rule of law:

> The power is ancillary or incidental to sustaining and carrying on government. Moreover, it is government under the Constitution and that is an instrument framed in accordance with many traditional conceptions, to some of which it gives effect, as, for example, in separating judicial power from other functions of government, others which are simply assumed. Among these I think that it may fairly be said that the rule of law forms an assumption. In such a system I think that it would be impossible to say of a law of the character described, which depends for its supposed connection with the power upon the conclusion of the legislature concerning the doings and the designs of the bodies or person to be affected and affords no objective test of the applicability of the power, that it is a law upon a matter incidental to the execution and maintenance of the Constitution and the laws of the Commonwealth. Indeed, upon the very matters upon which the question whether the bodies or persons have brought themselves within a possible exercise of the power depends, it may be said that the Act would have the effect of making the conclusion of the legislature final and so the measure of the operation of its own power.[60]

This passage evokes not only the idea that government must act under and according to law, but also, the requirement that there must be an independent judge of the extent to which the government complies with the law (in this case, the Constitution). The case thereby invokes the application of the rule of law in the legalistic sense of a requirement of adjudication by an independent judiciary.

The High Court's interpretation of a privative clause in the Migration Act 1958 (Cth) in *Plaintiff S157/2002* also depicted the legalistic conception. In determining the scope of this clause, the Court considered it alongside section 75(v) of the Constitution of the Commonwealth of Australia 1900, which grants the High Court jurisdiction to hear matters in which an order of mandamus, prohibition or injunction is sought against an officer of the Commonwealth. The Court held that section 75 (v) entrenches 'a minimum provision of judicial review', which constrains attempts to limit judicial review of federal administrative acts, a plurality of the judges arguing that by entrenching a minimum level of judicial review, section 75(v) 'constitutes a textual reinforcement' of the rule of law.[61] Gleeson CJ, concurring with the Court, also contended that the 'assumption of the rule of law'

[60] ibid 193.

[61] *Plaintiff S157* (n 46 above) [103]; Leighton McDonald, 'The entrenched minimum provision of judicial review and the rule of law' (2010) 21 *Public Law Review* 14.

was part of the context in which the case should be decided. For Gleeson, the application of the rule of law of law meant that privative clauses must be 'construed "by reference to a presumption that the legislature does not intend to deprive the citizen of access to the courts, other than to the extent expressly stated or necessarily to be implied"'.[62] Gleeson CJ thereby called upon the principle of legality as a means of applying the rule of law as against executive action and against the legislature.

A valorised substantive conception of the rule of law has found less acceptance in Australian jurisprudence. In a speech with reasoning expanding the concept of the rule of law invoked by Dixon J in the *Communist Party* case, Gummow and Hayne JJ in *Kartinyeri v Commonwealth of Australia* noted that the rule of law may be relevant in the court's interpretation of the Commonwealth Parliament's power under section 51(xxvi) of the Australian Constitution to make laws with respect to the 'people of any race'.[63] While Dixon J's reference to the rule of law fit within a legalistic conception of the rule of law, that voiced by Gummow and Hayne JJ in *Kartinyeri* suggests that the principle is relevant in determining questions of legislatively imposed race-based disadvantages. This moves beyond the legalistic substantive realm to the valorised substantive conception. Yet, such bold pronouncements which have opted for a valorised substantive application of the rule of law have been infrequent and confined to minority judgments.[64]

Nonetheless, the Australian High Court has repeatedly asserted that the rule of law is an 'underlying assumption' of the Constitution, and applied the principle in cases that call for determination of the impact of governmental action on individual rights. The High Court's pronouncements have been more opaque than those in the UK and the Commonwealth Caribbean, but Australian judicial opinion does envision a wider conception of the rule of law than the rule by law conception. Specifically, the rule of law is applied as a requirement for an independent judiciary and the exercise of supervisory jurisdiction by courts over parliamentary and executive action. There is room for further evolution of the application of the principle by the High Court, a possibility recognised by Gummow and Hayne JJ, who, noting the Court's reference to the rule of law as an assumption of the Constitution, stated that 'the occasion has yet to arise for consideration of all that may follow from [it].'[65]

The development of Caribbean fundamental rights law has also been aided by rule of law reasoning, with judicial decisions reflecting a valorised

[62] *Plaintiff S157* (n 46 above) [32], citing *Public Service Association (SA) v Federated Clerks' Union* (1991) 173 CLR 132 (HC, Australia) [160].

[63] (1998) 195 CLR 337 (HC, Australia) [88]–[89].

[64] Adrienne Stone, 'Judicial Review Without Rights: Some Problems for the Democratic Legitimacy of Structural Judicial Review' (2008) 28 *Oxford Journal Legal Studies* 1, 12–13.

[65] *Kartinyeri* (n 63 above) [381].

substantive view of the rule of law. This conception is particularly potent in the Privy Council's expansive interpretation of the terms 'protection of the law' and 'due process of law', which are used in Caribbean Bills of Rights.[66] The Privy Council has held that the term 'protection of the law'—used in the preamble to the Bill of Rights of the Constitution of Jamaica 1962—and the term 'due process of law'—which appears in the Constitution of Trinidad and Tobago 1976—bear the same meaning.[67] The Board has accorded an interpretation to these terms that seeks to further a substantive aim of justice. This interpretive course began with *Thomas v Baptiste*, in which Lord Millett, delivering the judgement of the Board, held that:

> ... 'due process of law' ... invokes the concept of the rule of law itself and the universally accepted standards of justice observed by civilised nations which observe the rule of law ... The clause thus gives constitutional protection to the concept of procedural fairness.[68]

Though Lord Millett describes the clause as an embodiment of constitutional protection of the concept of 'procedural fairness', he did not limit the scope of the clause to procedural fairness. Further, Lord Millett expressly invoked 'universally accepted standards of justice observed by civilised nations' as part of the very content of due process of law.[69]

This line of reasoning was furthered a year later in *Lewis*. The Privy Council found that the 'protection of the law' conferred in the preamble to the fundamental rights chapter of Jamaica's Constitution was violated by the decision of the Government of Jamaica to execute the appellants before the determination of their petitions before an international human rights agency.[70] Lord Slynn of Hadley, delivering the majority judgment in *Lewis*, argued that:

> In their Lordships' view when Jamaica acceded to the American Convention and to the International Covenant and allowed individual petitions the petitioner became entitled under the protection of the law provision in section 13 to complete the human rights petition procedure and to obtain the reports of the human rights bodies for the Jamaican Privy Council to consider before it dealt with the application for mercy and to the staying of the execution until those reports had been received and considered.[71]

[66] See, eg, Constitution of Barbados 1966, s 11; Constitution of Trinidad and Tobago 1976, s 4.

[67] *Thomas v Baptiste* [2000] 2 AC 1 (JCPC, Trinidad & Tobago) 21; *Lewis v AG of Jamaica* [2001] 2 AC 50 (JCPC, Jamaica) 85.

[68] *Thomas* (ibid) 22.

[69] ibid.

[70] *Lewis* (n 67 above). The preamble was replaced in the new fundamental rights chapter introduced by the Charter of Fundamental Rights and Freedoms (Constitutional Amendment) Act 2011.

[71] ibid 85.

Lord Hoffmann dissented, accusing the majority of failing to give a logical explanation for the use of due process to 'convert the ... executive action [of ratifying a human rights treaty] into the gold of legislative power'.[72] The Privy Council's decision can—at least in part—be accounted for as a move beyond a formal conception of the rule of law by finding that the principle demanded more than conformity with domestic provisions and incorporated an obligation to permit the operation of unincorporated human rights treaties. The decision that the protection of the law would be violated if the applicants were executed before a determination of their petitions, achieved through the back door a partial incorporation of human rights standards that may be higher than those prescribed in the Constitution.

The capacity of the rule of law to give substantive and remedial support to fundamental rights was further endorsed by the Caribbean Court of Justice when it assumed the Privy Council's role as final appellate tribunal for an increasing number of Caribbean jurisdictions. The Court thereby agreed in *Attorney General v Joseph and Boyce* that due process and protection of the law bear the same meaning and applied this interpretation in concluding that where the Constitution does not provide express remedy for breach of protection of the law, the Court has an inherent jurisdiction to provide such remedy.[73] In what has been fairly referred to as a 'provocative and frustratingly cryptic' passage, de la Bastide P and Saunders J found that an inherent jurisdiction must accompany the individual's right to procedural fairness which exists as part of due process of law, without clarifying the doctrinal basis of that jurisdiction, distinct from the existence of a corresponding right.[74] This line of cases that extends across the region and across the old guard (so to speak) of the Privy Council and the new guard of the Caribbean Court of Justice encapsulate Caribbean constitutional embrace of values of procedural fairness and access to courts as rule of law values that inform and reinforce constitutional rights protection.

For decades the Canadian Supreme Court interpreted the rule of law in a valorised substantive sense, as a principle that incorporates 'constitutional principles and values'.[75] In the *Patriation Reference* in which the Supreme

[72] ibid [88].

[73] *Joseph and Boyce* (n 35 above) [60]–[64].

[74] Tracy Robinson, 'Our Inherent Constitution' in Tracy Robinson and David S Berry (eds) *Transitions in Caribbean Law: Law-Making, Constitutionalism and the Convergence of National and International Law* (Ian Randle Publishers, 2013) 259.

[75] *Reference re Secession of Quebec* [1998] 2 SCR 217 (SC, Canada) [71]–[72] (the rule of law as a requirement that government action comply with the law, including the Constitution) See also *Reference re Remuneration of Judges of the Provincial Court of Prince Edward Island* [1997] 3 SCR 3 (SC, Canada) [10] (judicial independence is necessary for the maintenance of the rule of law). On the rule of law and the vagueness doctrine, see *Reference re Language Rights Under s. 23 of Manitoba Act, 1870 and s. 133 of Constitution Act, 1867* (*Manitoba Language Rights Reference or Reference re Manitoba Language Rights*) [1985] 1 SCR 721 (SC, Canada) 747–52, 749; *R v Nova Scotia Pharmaceutical Society* [1992] 2 SCR 606 (SC,

Court considered the constitutional requirements for amendment of the Canadian Constitution, it was stated:

> [t]he 'rule of law' is a highly textured expression, importing many things which are beyond the need of these reasons to explore but conveying, for example, a sense of orderliness, of subjection to known legal rules and of executive accountability to legal authority.[76]

The Court went further in the *Secession Reference*. The details of this case are explored in more detail in subsequent chapters, but at this juncture it suffices to note that the Court observed that '[a]t its most basic level, the rule of law vouchsafes to the citizens and residents of the country a stable, predictable and ordered society in which to conduct their affairs' and, additionally, that '[i]t provides a shield for individuals from arbitrary state action.'[77]

However, between 2005 and 2007 the Supreme Court applied a thinner rule of law model, holding that the rule of law, insofar as it is binding against the legislature, is limited to a requirement that laws comply with legislated manner and form requirements. This new approach was revealed in *British Columbia v Imperial Tobacco Canada Ltd*, which arose out of the British Columbia Tobacco Damages and Health Care Costs Recovery Act 2000 (British Columbia). The Act was directed at the manufacturers of tobacco products, entitling the government to make claims against the manufacturers to recover the cost of health care benefits caused wholly or partly by tobacco related wrongs. The tobacco manufacturers challenged the statute, arguing, inter alia, that the retroactivity of the statute and its targeting of a specific group of companies offended against the rule of law. The Supreme Court rejected the manufacturers' argument, stating in relation to the rule of law that:

> This Court has described the rule of law as embracing three principles. The first recognizes that 'the law is supreme over officials of the government as well as private individuals and thereby preclusive of the influence of arbitrary power': ... The second 'requires the creation and maintenance of an actual order of positive laws which preserves and embodies the more general principle of normative order': ... The third requires that 'the relationship between the state and the individual ... be regulated by law'...
>
> So understood, it is difficult to conceive of how the rule of law could be used as a basis for invalidating legislation such as the Act based on its content. That is

Canada) 643. On the rule of law as access to courts, see *BCGEU v British Columbia* (AG) [1988] 2 SCR 214 (SC, Canada) 230. See also *Roncarelli v Duplessis* [1959] SCR 121 (SC, Canada) 142; Hogg and Zwibel, 'Rule of Law' (n 6 above).

[76] *Reference re Resolution to Amend the Constitution* [1981] 1 SCR 753 (SC, Canada) (*Patriation Reference*) 805–06.

[77] *Secession Reference* (n 75 above) [70].

> because *none of the principles that the rule of law embraces speak directly to the terms of legislation.*[78]

Imperial Tobacco reflects a rule of law doctrine that, unlike the court's earlier decisions, is positivistic, relying more strictly on the text.[79] The Supreme Court reaffirmed this approach to the rule of law in *Christie v British Columbia (Attorney General)* while entering a caveat clarifying that *Imperial Tobacco* did not close the door to other principles being incorporated into the rule of law.[80] So the law in Canada on this point is not yet settled.

Despite the Supreme Court's direct engagement with the question of acceptable applications of the rule of law in Canadian constitutional law in *Imperial Tobacco*, it is difficult to extrapolate concrete reasons for the change in tide from the judgments delivered in *Imperial Tobacco* and *Christie v British Columbia*. Nonetheless, there are three possible lines of treatment of *Imperial Tobacco*. The first is that the court abandoned a substantive conception of the rule of law in favour of a more formal rule by law conception. Under this view, while there was formerly a complaint that the Court had not been explicit and clear about the tenets of the rule of law concept that it applied,[81] this judgment expressed—however briefly—the Court's rejection of a substantive doctrine. This view holds that *Imperial Tobacco* reflects a rule of law doctrine that, unlike the court's earlier decisions, is positivistic and nationalistic.[82] The second possible treatment of the judgment is that the Court was not primarily speaking to the content of the rule of law but to the scope of its normative force. This position would view the Court's judgment as a holding that to the extent that the rule of law contains substantive content, this is opposable against the executive and judiciary, but cannot be used as an independent ground to defeat legislation. This is what was arguably conveyed by paragraph 60 of the judgment, in which Major J stated:

> the government action constrained by the rule of law as understood in *Reference re Manitoba Language Rights* and *Reference re Secession of Quebec* is, by definition, usually that of the executive and judicial branches. Actions of the legislative branch are constrained too, but only in the sense that they must comply with legislated requirements as to manner and form (ie the procedures by which legislation is to be enacted, amended and repealed).[83]

[78] *British Columbia v Imperial Tobacco Canada Ltd* [2005] 2 SCR 473 (SC, Canada) [58]–[59] (emphasis added, citations omitted).

[79] Mark Carter, 'The Rule of Law, Legal Rights in the Charter and the Supreme Court's New Positivism' (2007) 33 *Queen's Law Journal* 453, 465–70, and 472. See also *Nova Scotia Pharmaceutical Society* (n 75 above) 641; Tremblay, *Rule of Law* (n 13 above) 26–27.

[80] [2007] 1 SCR 873 (SC, Canada) [21]. See also *Charkaoui v Canada (Citizenship and Immigration)* [2007] 1 SCR 350 (SC, Canada).

[81] Tremblay, *Rule of Law* (n 13 above) 25–28.

[82] Carter, 'New Positivism' (n 79 above).

[83] *Imperial Tobacco* (n 78 above) [60].

The third approach to the case is that while the *Imperial Tobacco* bench did appear to reject a substantive conception of the rule of law, this was not the final word of the Canadian Supreme Court on the rule of law. Notably, the caveat issued in the 2007 judgment in *Christie v British Columbia* clarified that 'in *Imperial Tobacco*, this Court left open the possibility that the rule of law may include additional principles'.[84] So it is quite reasonable to take the position that the Court did adopt a rule by law conception in *Imperial Tobacco* in response to the factual and institutional circumstances of that case. This reading of Canadian case law is supported if we take into account the possibility that the Court was influenced by reluctance to enhance corporate interests. In *Imperial Tobacco*, the parties who sought to rely on the rule of law were tobacco manufacturers who were attempting to limit their liability[85] and in *Christie* the Supreme Court noted that if the applicants' argument that the rule of law supported a general right to a lawyer were to succeed, this right would apply to cases where '*corporate* rights and obligations' were at issue.[86] The third approach to *Imperial Tobacco* is supported by the Supreme Court's 2014 judgment in *Trial Lawyers Association of British Columbia v British Columbia* which reaffirmed its twentieth century jurisprudence that 'access to justice is fundamental to the rule of law'.[87] Holding that hearing fees that prevented people from accessing courts infringe the core jurisdiction of the courts under both section 96 of the Constitution and the underlying principle of the rule of law, the Court maintained that '[i]n the context of legislation which effectively denies people the right to take their cases to court, concerns about the maintenance of the rule of law are not abstract or theoretical.'[88] *Trial Lawyers Association* thereby confirmed *dicta* in Christie that the Court remains free to adopt a more substantive rule of law conception in subsequent cases. The shift in the Court's approach is evident in the not altogether convincing effort to distinguish the *Christie* decision on the basis that the 7% surcharge on legal fees at issue in *Christie* 'was not shown to have a similar impact' on access to courts.[89] If hearing fees which require litigants who are not impoverished to 'sacrifice reasonable expenses' in order to access courts[90] are judged unconstitutional, it is difficult to see why a surcharge on legal aid fees—legal aid being subscribed to by low-income persons—would not similarly undermine the right to access justice. Indeed, it has been suggested that the

[84] *Christie* (n 80 above) [21]. See also *Charkaoui* (n 80 above).
[85] See Carter, 'New Positivism' (n 79 above) 470–71.
[86] *Christie* (n 80 above) [13] (emphasis added); ibid 479.
[87] *Trial Lawyers Assn. of British Columbia v British Columbia (Attorney General)* [2014] 3 SCR 31 [39] (McLachlin CJ).
[88] ibid [40] (McLachlin CJ). Section 96 empowers the federal government to appoint provincial judges.
[89] *Trial Lawyers Association* (n 87 above) [41].
[90] *Trial Lawyers Association* (n 87 above) [46].

Trial Lawyers Association decision 'may have undermined' *Christie* on the issue of access to justice.[91] Whichever of the three views is adopted, not only is there room for further movement by the Court—an indication of the ongoing nature of this discourse within the Court—but overall, the dominant interpretation of the rule of law in the Canadian Supreme Court is a substantive valorised version but one whose effect has been tamed in recent years by reference to the need to balance respect for unwritten fundamental principles with respect for the text.[92] Respect for such balance is critical in the Canadian context where implied constitutional principles arguably have less work to do on account of the combination in Canada of a modern Bill of Rights, a clear mandate for judicial enforcement—including invalidation of legislation—and a record of judicial confidence in exercising their enforcement powers.

The range of rule of law conceptions reflected in the case law refutes a binary classification. Moreover, within the jurisdictions reviewed, the dominant view that emerges from the case law is that the rule of law ideal implicates the substance of the law through either a legalistic or valorised model. What is revealed is that the dominant discourse among legal theorists is inconsistent with the dominant judicial interpretation of the principle in common law jurisdictions.

V. CONFLICTS WITHIN THE RULE OF LAW: EQUALITY AS AN APPLICATION OF THE RULE OF LAW

The overall trajectory of the application of the rule of law in the jurisdictions examined is towards adoption of a substantive conception of the rule of law (whether in its bolder valorised strain or in the moderate legalistic sense). Yet, recognition of this trajectory should not mask the uncertainties that persist with respect to the interaction of different, sometimes conflicting operations of the rule of law. Such uncertainties may, for example, be manifested in the existence of a conflict between the application of the rule of law as certainty of the law and the application of the rule of law as a requirement for equality. There may also be uncertainties in the delimitation of the boundaries of each application of the rule of law such as the exact content of the requirement of equality as an application of the rule of law. The application of the rule of law as a requirement of equality provides fertile ground for highlighting some of these uncertainties. As such, this section briefly uses this particular application of the rule of law to show

[91] Paul Vayda, 'Chipping Away at Cost Barriers: A Comment on the Supreme Court of Canada's Trial Lawyers Decision' (2015) 36 *Windsor Review of Legal and Social Issues* 207, 212.

[92] Canadian Charter of Rights and Freedoms 1982, s 24.

the variation that still exists in determining the content or boundaries of an application of the rule of law.

The jurisdictions that have adopted a substantive conception of the rule of law view equality as one of its constituent principles. This view is reflected in UK decisions prior and subsequent to the enactment of the HRA 1998 and in the former British colonies of the Commonwealth Caribbean. Lord Woolf CJ has even declared that the 'right not to be discriminated against is one of the most significant requirements of the protection provided by the rule of law'.[93] A similarly forceful argument has been made in the Caribbean by Fitzpatrick JA in the Guyanese case of *Yassin*, who stated that 'equality and arbitrariness are sworn enemies; one belongs to the Rule of Law in a republic, (while) the other, to the whim and caprice of an absolute monarch.'[94]

However, on the question of the meaning of this notion of 'equality' that forms part of the rule of law, there are divergent responses. There is a cleavage between commentators who see the rule of law requirement of equality as being restricted to equal application of laws, and those that witness a wider role for the requirement, as one that mandates that laws be equal in substance. Jowell contends that there is a principle of equality that requires not only equal application and enforcement of laws, but also equal laws. Yet, he denies that the latter is part of the rule of law.[95] On the other hand, Allan contends that Dicey's account of the rule of law may be updated to allow for a defence of equality as rationality, which is opposable against Parliament. Allan's 'substantive principle' of equality embodies equality by requiring that likes be treated alike in terms of some conception of the public good. It embraces rationality by requiring that all classifications (which depart from like treatment) 'be reasonably related to legitimate, defensible public purposes'.[96] Allan deduces that when the rule of law is expressed in these terms, it demands 'equal citizenship'. He also points to intimations of the equal citizenship principle which are evident in Dicey's second meaning of the rule of law, that is, that persons are equal before the law. Lord Bingham in 'The Rule of Law' also maintains that equal application of laws (except where differentiation is objectively and reasonably justified) is a core feature of the rule of law.[97] He goes further, arguing that one aspect of the rule of law is that the law must protect

[93] *A v Secretary of State for the Home Department* [2004] QB 335 (CA) [7], reversed on unrelated grounds: [2005] 3 All ER 169 (HL).

[94] *Yassin v Attorney of Guyana* GY 1996 CA 3, 30 August 1996 (Fitzpatrick JA), quoting Bhagwati J in *Gandhi v Union of India A.I.R.* [1978] SC 597 (SC, India).

[95] Jeffrey Jowell, 'Is Equality a Constitutional Principle' (1994) 47 *Current Legal Problems* 1.

[96] Allan, 'The Rule of Law as the Rule of Reason' (n 25 above) 231.

[97] TH Bingham, *The Rule of Law* (Allen Lane 2010) 55–59.

'fundamental human rights', with non-discrimination being included in his list of fundamental rights.[98]

In the jurisdictions under examination, there are indications that the courts embrace equality as a component of the rule of law that affects the substance of laws, and not merely the application of laws. In this sense, the value of equality that emerges from the rule of law is substantive and not merely formal. This idea is particularly strong in the UK, but there is less evidence of its acceptance in the other Commonwealth jurisdictions. The idea that equality is an aspect of the rule of law which requires that laws be substantively equal was evident in the UK before the advent of the HRA 1998 in the dissent of Ward LJ in *Fitzpatrick v Sterling Housing Association*:

> I am entitled to presume that Parliament always intends to conform to the rule of law as a constitutional principle and accordingly to respect the constitutional rights of the individual to enjoy equality under the law.[99]

Ward LJ's sentiments are now reflected in the post-HRA decision in *Ghaidan v Godin-Mendoza*. Lord Nicholls, with whom two of their Lordships agreed, held that '[d]iscriminatory law undermines the rule of law because it is the antithesis of fairness.'[100] The Court applied this understanding of the rule of law in holding that the exclusion of gay partners from secure tenancies violated the right to privacy, in conjunction with the right to non-discrimination, under the ECHR.

Recalling that judicial review exposes the content of the rule of law because the rule of law is a principled justification for review of executive action, judicial review cases also help to illuminate whether the notion of equality that forms part of the rule of law is formal or substantive in nature. The idea that discriminatory law (law that is discriminatory in content and not just application) undermines the rule of law is reflected in judicial review cases where the Court has found discriminatory decisions *ultra vires*. Accordingly, in *R v Immigration Appeal Tribunal, ex p Begum*, the Court held that an immigration rule was *ultra vires* because it effectively disqualified citizens of poorer countries while allowing dependants from wealthier countries to be considered on more sympathetic grounds.[101] Similarly, the common law principle of equality was held to invalidate a decision on

[98] For a contrary view, see Jowell, 'Equality' (n 95 above), where he argues that there is a principle of equality that requires both equal application of laws and equal laws, but denies that the latter is part of the rule of law.

[99] [1998] 2 WLR 225 (CA) 256. The decision of the majority of the Court of Appeal was reversed by the House of Lords though not for the reasons given in Ward LJ's dissent. The majority of the House of Lords found that the case was not concerned with equality or non-discrimination.

[100] [2004] UKHL 30, [2004] AC 557 (HL) [9].

[101] [1986] Imm AR 385 (QBD); Jowell, 'Equality' (n 95 above) 13.

grounds of *Wednesbury* unreasonableness in *R (Gurung) v Ministry of Defence*.[102] According to the Court, the constitutional principle of equality meant that '[e]xcept where compellingly justified, distinctions must never be made on the ground of race, colour, belief, gender or other irrational ground.'[103]

In Australia, the issue of whether discriminatory law violates the rule of law has been raised before the High Court. As stated above, in the *Kartinyeri* case, in which the Australian High Court considered the permissibility of race-based distinctions in legislation, Gummow and Hayne JJ noted that the rule of law may be relevant in determining the constitutionality of the impugned legislation.[104] However, this was the view of the minority, as the remaining judges decided the case on different grounds. Further, the judgment of Gummow and Haynes JJ is unique among Australian judgments for its engagement with equality as a direct application of the rule of law.

This 'lively question' regarding the extent to which the rule of law principle encompasses equality is likely to remain the subject of debate for many years to come. As with other applications of the rule of law, the application of the rule of law as a requirement of respect for equality continues to be developed by the courts and its exact contours remain contested. Yet, as will be discussed in chapter eight, this fact does not negate the existence of the rule of law principle as a legal norm applicable by the courts.[105]

VI. CONCLUSION

Justin Leslie has remarked that 'it would appear that a substantive rule of law operates within the courts. This conception has at its core human rights considerations and forms the intellectual basis for decisions concerning rights.'[106] Though Leslie made these comments in reference to the application of the rule of law in UK courts, his observation is equally applicable to the Commonwealth Caribbean, where Phillips JA of the Court of Appeal of Trinidad and Tobago conceived of the country's constitutional rights and freedoms as 'expressly designed to secure the continuation in the newly independent nation ... of the Rule of Law'.[107]

[102] [2002] EWHC 2463, *The Times*, 28 December 2002, QBD (Admin Ct) quoting a Lecture delivered by Lord Steyn, 18 September 2002, 18.

[103] ibid.

[104] *Kartinyeri* (n 63 above)

[105] See Jowell, 'Rhetoric or Universal Principle' (n 20 above) 5.

[106] Leslie (n 2 above) 315.

[107] *Lasalle v A-G* (1971) 18 WIR 379 (CA, Trinidad and Tobago) 383.

With Canada adopting a substantive valorised version and Australia recognising a more modest legalistic model, which nonetheless influences the content of the law, there is certainly a spectrum of rule of law conceptions reflected in the courts, the most dominant of which are substantive. It is true that for some judgments that refer to the rule of law in a substantive sense, there is no articulation of a 'guiding theory' behind the conception adopted by the court. For some judges, it must be noted, a more complete guiding theory is expressed in their extrajudicial writings, for instance, in speeches and articles by Lord Steyn and Sir John Laws.[108] Nonetheless, the absence of a guiding theory in some cases can be readily explained by noting the institutional goals of courts. One function of the court in a common law jurisdiction is to resolve the disputes that arise in the cases before it. In this sense, courts operate in a more responsive manner than theorists do. It is not at all surprising that they do not launch into lingering theoretical debates about the nature of the rule of law when resolving the dispute before them.

There is room for discussion about the exact boundaries of the substantive content of the rule of law as is revealed by analysis of the application of the rule of law as equality. Yet, those questions are outside the bounds of this study. What this chapter sought to demonstrate is that the case law in the common law jurisdictions examined runs from acceptance of a rule by law conception to acceptance of a substantive conception of the rule of law (whether in its legalistic sense or in the bolder valorised sense). Overall, the majority of jurisdictions in this study apply a substantive conception of the rule of law, though there remain areas of uncertainty regarding the precise contours of substantive applications of the rule of law principle.

[108] Sir John Laws, 'Law and Democracy' [1995] *Public Law* 72; Lord Steyn, 'Democracy, the Rule of Law and the Role of Judges' [2006] *European Human Rights Law Review* 243.

4

Applications of the Separation of Powers

I. INTRODUCTION

TO HEARKEN BACK to a theme with which we opened our examination of the implications of the rule of law and the separation of powers in fundamental rights adjudication, the separation of powers is one attempt by proponents of constitutionalism to provide a solution to the dilemma of the 'frank acknowledgement of the role of government in society, linked with the determination to bring that government under control and to place limits on the exercise of its power'.[1] The quest to define the term and delimit its application has given rise to complex and varying conceptions of the doctrine. Set against the background of this conceptual debate, this chapter will examine the content of the 'Westminster model' of separation of powers and the extent to which that model has evolved, particularly with the advent of the Human Rights Act 1998 (UK) (HRA) and the Constitutional Reform Act 2005 (UK) (CRA).[2] It will be shown that in the context of the Westminster system, or Westminster style systems,[3] the term 'separation of powers' is often used as an equivalent to—or conduit for—the assertion of judicial independence. The chapter will also address the way in which this separation of powers model informs the court's perception of its role as a check on other organs of state and the importance of exercising judicial restraint in fundamental rights adjudication.[4] It is maintained throughout this book that a significant theme that enhances our understanding of the role played by constitutional principles in rights adjudication is the

[1] MJC Vile, *Constitutionalism and the Separation of Powers*, 2nd edn (Liberty Fund, 1998) 2.

[2] See Vernon Bognador, *The New British Constitution* (Hart Publishing, 2009) 287–89; AW Bradley and KD Ewing, *Constitutional and Administrative Law*, 15th edn (Longman, 2011) 86–88.

[3] As stated in ch 1, the term 'Westminster style' is used as a reference to constitutional systems in which there is a representative democracy and an executive responsible to the legislature.

[4] See, eg, *R v Lichniak* [2002] UKHL 47, [2003] 1 AC 903 [14] (HL); Aileen Kavanagh, 'Defending Deference in Public Law and Constitutional Theory' (2010) *Law Quarterly Review* 222.

institutional element of these principles. This institutional theme is brought to the fore when evaluating the application of the separation of powers.

Part II of the chapter addresses the relevant theoretical context for a discussion of the separation of powers in the Westminster model of government. This includes analysis of the pure and partial conceptions of separation of powers, as well as the distinction between the formal and material theories. The remainder of the chapter focuses on the development of the separation of powers principle in the Westminster system through the perspective of judicial decisions. In this discussion, while there is some case law from the other common law jurisdictions, most of the material relied upon is UK-based. There are two reasons for this. First, there have been significant developments surrounding the separation of powers in the UK subsequent to the HRA 1998 and the CRA 2005 and this chapter seeks to explore these developments. Secondly, analysis of narratives of the transplantation of the Westminster model—inclusive of the separation of powers—to other jurisdictions is appropriately addressed in chapter seven, on the use of implied principles as gateways to comparative judicial analysis. Therefore, in Part III of this chapter, there is analysis of the practical application of the separation of powers in courts. This leads to discussion of the effect of separation of powers arguments on fundamental rights cases in Part IV. Part V then discusses the extent of the impact of the HRA 1998 and the CRA 2005 on the separation of powers in the UK, particularly as revealed in case law.

II. VARYING SEPARATIONS OF POWERS

Despite denunciations of the existence of separation of powers in the British Constitution, the doctrine has over time secured a place in the Constitution and even more so in the Westminster-style systems adopted in former British colonies. Refutations of the separation of powers' importance to understanding the British constitution have been direct and forceful; O Hood Phillips rejected the doctrine as a 'constitutional myth', while SA De Smith regarded it as an 'irrelevant distraction'.[5] Nonetheless, modern constitutional theory and case law refute such dismissals of the relevance of separation of powers to constitutional discourse in common law countries.[6] Further, in the process of adapting the Westminster system to 'Westminster-style' systems, post-colonial common law countries have sharpened the

[5] O Hood Phillips, 'A Constitutional Myth: Separation of Powers' (1977) 93 *Law Quarterly Review* 11; SA De Smith, 'The Separation of Powers in New Dress' (1966) 12 *McGill Law Journal* 491, 491.

[6] Roger Masterman, *The Separation of Powers in the Contemporary Constitution* (Cambridge University Press, 2011) 12–22.

distinctions among the arms of state, while securing those distinctions with higher degrees of judicial enforcement than permitted under the British constitution.

Before delving fully into an exploration of the doctrine in the Westminster system, it would be useful to consider the broader theoretical framework developed around the separation of powers. The meaning of the term 'separation of powers' has long been disputed in academic discourse and the term has been described by Geoffrey Marshall as 'one of the most confusing in the vocabulary of political and constitutional thought'.[7] Locke and Montesquieu were the first theorists to articulate modern theories of separation of powers, with Locke providing a normative justification for the separation of the powers of the state:

> It may be too great a temptation to human frailty, apt to grasp at power, for the same persons who have the power of making laws, to have also in their hands the power to execute them, whereby they may exempt themselves from obedience to the laws they make, and suit the law, both in its making and execution, to their own private advantage.[8]

Yet Locke's proposal for the division of powers is not identical to the tripartite division of powers that is commonly equated with separation of powers theory today. While calling for a separation of legislative and executive powers, he did not develop judicial power as a distinct element. This was despite the fact that he recognised the need for the independence and impartiality of the judiciary.[9] Montesquieu, on the other hand, articulated a stricter separation of powers, arguing that:

> When legislative power is united with executive power in a single person or in a single body of the magistracy, there is no liberty, because one can fear that the same monarch or senate that makes tyrannical laws will execute them tyrannically. Nor is there liberty if the power of judging is not separate from legislative power and from executive power. If it were joined to legislative power, the power over the life and liberty of the citizens would be arbitrary, for the judge would be the legislator. If it were joined to executive power, the judge could have the force of an oppressor.
>
> All would be lost if the same body of principal men, either of nobles or of the people, exercised these three powers: that of making the laws, that of executing the public resolutions and that of judging the crimes or the disputes of individuals.[10]

[7] Geoffrey Marshall, *Constitutional Theory* (Oxford University Press, 1971) 97.
[8] John Locke, Second Treatise of Civil Government, Ch XII, [143], cited in Vile (n 1 above) 62.
[9] Vile (n 1 above) 64–65.
[10] Charles de Secondat, baron de Montesquieu, *The Spirit of Laws* (Anne M Cohler, ed and tr, Cambridge University Press, 1989) 157.

The literature on the doctrine has blossomed and the theoretical framework reveals that the separation of powers doctrine can be described along several conceptual spectrums. Chief among the spectrums relevant to the Westminster context are the conceptualisation of a pure separation of powers versus a partial separation of powers, and along another axis, the classification of the separation of powers as either a formal or a material doctrine. It is along these axes that separation of powers theory will be outlined in brief. A more detailed exposition of the content of this doctrine could not be contained within the confines of this chapter; accordingly, the focus of this chapter is directed towards addressing these axes of the doctrine insofar as they may elevate our understanding of the operation of the separation of powers principle in Westminster-style systems.

On the pure-partial axis, the pure conception seeks to articulate ideas of the structure of the institutions of the state as distinct and wholly separate from each other. The 'pure doctrine' may be perceived as, in one sense, antecedent to a more practical 'partial doctrine', which takes account of competing political and legal theories and of the practical realities of the functioning of the state. The pure doctrine is described thus by Vile:

> It is essential for the establishment and maintenance of political liberty that the government be divided into three branches or departments, the legislature, the executive, and the judiciary. To each of these three branches there is a corresponding identifiable function of government, legislative, executive or judicial. Each branch of the government must be confined to the exercise of its own function and not allowed to encroach upon the functions of the other branches. Furthermore, the persons who compose these three agencies of government must be kept separate and distinct, no individual being allowed to be at the same time a member of more than one branch. In this way, each of the branches will be a check to the others and no single group of people will be able to control the machinery of the State.'[11]

The pure doctrine has been labeled 'stark',[12] 'extreme',[13] 'absolutist'[14] and impossible to achieve in practice.[15] The impracticality of this model of separation has been acknowledged by the judiciary, the Canadian Supreme Court having observed that the Constitution of Canada 'does not insist on a strict separation of powers'.[16] It is plagued by conceptual and practical difficulties, one of which is that it makes no allowance for the possibility that some governmental functions might not fit neatly into one branch to

[11] Vile (n 1 above) 14.
[12] ibid.
[13] ibid.
[14] Eoin Carolan, *The New Separation of Powers: A Theory for the Modern State* (Oxford University Press, 2009) 19.
[15] ibid 20.
[16] *Reference re Secession of Quebec* [1998] 2 SCR 217 (SC, Canada) [15].

the exclusion of others.[17] It articulates a vision whereby there is a system of negative checks and balances applied to the agencies of government. By this it is meant that no further device needs to be implemented in order to contain agencies within their proper functions and to prevent them from encroaching on the functions of other agencies.[18] Thus, the pure theory does not indicate, as a practical matter, how agencies are to be effectively restrained from appropriating the functions of other agencies. A response to this deficiency was to articulate a system of positive checks and balances and to develop a partial theory of the separation of powers which admits overlaps between the three branches.

The notion of checks and balances itself exposes a crucial fissure among separation of power theorists, which is the divide over whether the act of one branch restraining another advances, undermines, or is a justifiable departure from the separation of powers.[19] The partial theory can be accounted for as an attempt to incorporate a checks and balances model or simply an acknowledgement that a pure separation is impractical.[20]

This takes us to another axis along which the separation of powers is examined the distinction between material and formal theories. Whether the pure or the partial theory is adopted, there must be a mechanism for determining how to divide the functions of the state in order to allocate these functions to corresponding sets of state institutions. The material theory seeks to solve this difficulty by asserting an inherent difference between the nature of the legislative, judicial, and executive functions, so it seeks to define each function and then allocate them to distinct sets of institutions.[21] Thus the legislative function is described as rule-making, the judicial function as rule-adjudication, and the executive function as rule-application. The problem with this categorisation is that it is difficult, if not impossible, to identify *inherent* differences between judicial, executive, and legislative functions. Further, each organ of government engages in activities that encompass all three types of rule relationships.[22] For instance, the practice of rule-adjudicating often involves a degree of rule-making and rule-execution. Jennings criticises this flaw in the material theory in the following terms:

> It is quite impossible to draw a distinction between 'judicial' and 'administrative' functions in terms of the nature or substance of the functions actually exercised

[17] Masterman, *Separation of Powers* (n 6 above) 11.

[18] Vile (n 1 above) 12–13.

[19] Geoffrey Marshall, *Constitutional Theory* (Clarendon Press, 1980) 102–03. See also Paul R Verkuil, 'Separation of Powers, the Rule of Law and the Idea of Independence' (1989) 30 *William & Mary Law Review* 301, 310.

[20] Richard White, 'Separation of powers and legislative supremacy' (2011) 127 *Law Quarterly Review* 456, 459.

[21] ibid 459.

[22] Vile (n 1 above) 319–20.

> by the courts and the administrative authorities in this country. The most that can be said is that the courts are much more concerned with questions of law, and the administrative authorities with questions of discretion. Nor is it possible to draw a precise distinction between the functions of Parliament and of the administrative authorities, subject always to the rule that Parliament can by legislation do what it pleases, and that most of the powers of administrative authorities (like the powers of the courts) derive from legislation.[23]

The salience of this critique of the material theory does not mean that we cannot identify core or primary functions of government and assign such functions primarily to one set of institutions over others.[24] It merely questions the means by which this theory seeks to accomplish the task of allocation.

The formal theory seeks to resolve the allocative exercise through a different route. It starts where the material theory ends; under the formal theory we would examine the allocation of state powers to institutional groups within the state and only consequent upon that examination would we derive and describe the functions. The formal theory therefore differs from the material version by rejecting the idea of an inherent distinction between legislative, executive, and judicial branches. It emphasises examination of the structural and methodological features of institutions of the state, rather than an attempt to find intrinsic characteristics and differences. It has the appeal of being a more practical approach and avoids the definitional issues that plague the material theory. Yet, there is a hole left in the theory in that while it has merit as a descriptive exercise, it does not appear to provide a prescriptive standard.

Richard White has identified two ways in which formal theories seek to resolve this flaw. One is to rely on the notion of balance of power to do the prescriptive work. Under this model, once there is a distribution of power among state institutions to ensure that there is a power balance, there is no need to rely on and subscribe to distinctions between legislative, judicial, and executive functions. A second option is to rely on a normative justification for the allocation of powers, that justification being a feature other than the inherent nature of the power being exercised. For instance, it could be argued that if an elected assembly is accorded the power to make rules of general application, which may override those of a court, this is justified on the ground that the assembly is elected by popular vote and is an expression of the popular will. Similarly, it may be maintained that a particular decision-making power should be exercised by a judge because she is impartial, independent of partisan political dictates, and/or because

[23] Ivor Jennings, *The Law and the Constitution* (University of London Press, 1959) 294.
[24] ibid 361.

the decision-making procedure employed by the judge must generally be in public view.[25]

The bulk of the debate and application of separation of powers is conducted in terms of a tripartite vision of separation of powers, but this tripartite separation has itself been challenged. Most recently, Carolan has laid out two main bases for attacking the traditional trinitarian theory, whichever conception of that traditional theory is accepted.[26] The first ground of criticism is that the orthodox theory is of little prescriptive value since it fails to provide reliable guidance for institutional design and power allocation to the institutions of the state. This alleged indeterminacy is said to arise partly from the impossibility of defining concrete distinguishing characteristics of the three functions of the state.[27] Carolan also maintains that the indeterminacy is partly the result of the uncertain objectives of the separation of powers. Theorists have proposed a range of goals as the foundational objectives of the separation of powers, goals which vary from the prevention of tyranny and the maintenance of liberty, to the maintenance of a balance of power between different interest groups and, further along the spectrum, to the enhancement of efficiency in the performance state tasks.[28] The debate over the objectives of the doctrine reflects the debate regarding the conceptions of the rule of law, as acceptance of particular objectives and the ordering of those objectives affect the extent to which the doctrine is found to address the content of legislation.[29] Secondly, it is argued that the traditional theory fails to reflect the reality of modern governmental structures. With particular reference to the UK, it does not fully account for and answer the complications that arise from the growth of administrative agencies in the twentieth and twenty-first centuries. Despite these criticisms, the tripartite division continues to be orthodox, indeed almost ubiquitous, among theorists.[30] More importantly, as is revealed in the case analysis that follows this discussion, in the second part of this chapter, this division

[25] Jennings, *The Law and the Constitution* (n 23 above) 281. The distinction between material and formal theories in the UK must be distinguished from the formal-functional divide in the US discourse. Under the functionalist conception, disputes regarding the division of governmental functions should be resolved, not by adherence to fixed rules, but rather, by reference to 'an evolving standard designed to advance the ultimate purposes of a system of separation of powers'. By contrast, the formalist conception demands a textual basis in the Constitution for any exercise of governmental authority. The formalist–functionalist debate has not penetrated the discourse and judicial practice in the UK to the extent that it has animated debate on the other side of the Atlantic so it is less useful to us in our attempt to analyse the Westminster model as developed by the courts. See Thomas W Merrill, 'The Constitutional Principle of the Separation of Powers' (1991) 7 *Supreme Court Review* 225, esp 230–31.

[26] Carolan (n 14 above) 18.

[27] Carolan (n 14 above) 25–26.

[28] Carolan (n 14 above) 27–28.

[29] Carolan (n 14 above) 28.

[30] Carolan (n 14 above) 21. See Christoph Möllers, *The Three Branches: A Comparative Model of Separation of Powers* (Oxford University Press, 2013).

continues to be dominant in the courts' articulation of the separation of powers principle in constitutional and rights law. This framing is so widely accepted within the judicial and wider legal fraternity that Lord Hoffmann, one of the celebrated judges of the last century, has remarked that '[as] everyone knows, the separation of powers means that division of the executive, legislative and judicial departments of government which Montesquieu admired in the eighteenth century British Constitution and which he thought to be the foundation of English liberty.'[31]

There are thus three main ideas that emerge as points of commonality among the various theories of separation of powers. These are, first: the separation of functions of the state into usually three powers; secondly, the division of the institutions of the state into groups, each performing one of the functions of the state (though there may be overlap); and, finally, some degree of separation of state personnel according to the work they conduct. It is often the final idea that gives rise to the most serious debate about the existence and importance of the separation of powers in the Westminster system, due to the significant overlap of personnel, particularly between the executive and legislative branches. With this theoretical background, the next part of this chapter considers the practical application of the separation of powers theory in the Westminster system. The perception and use of the separation of powers by judges enables us to examine the development of the separation of powers as a *legal* doctrine in the legal system. This is not an attempt to denude the separation of powers of its political elements or to assert that there can or should be an isolation of the legal and political aspects of the separation of powers theory. Rather, this focus on the legal elements of the theory is instrumental in identifying the understanding of the separation of powers as a legal principle and in highlighting the themes that emerge when that legal principle is applied in human rights adjudication.

III. PRACTICAL APPLICATION OF THE SEPARATION OF POWERS PRINCIPLE IN COURTS IN THE WESTMINSTER-STYLE SYSTEM

A gulf exists between the theoretical discourse on the separation of powers and its practical application in case law in that while the existence and importance of the principle has been challenged or ignored by some notable commentators, eminent judges have shown firm acceptance of the principle. Case law reflects an adoption of a partial model of the separation of powers in the UK, which reveals that the close relationship between legislative and executive bodies in the UK ought to be viewed as an instance of the

[31] Lord Hoffmann, 'The COMBAR Lecture 2001: Separation of Powers' (2002) *Judicial Review* 137, 137.

practical reflection of the partial separation of powers within the constitutional context of the UK.[32] This section shows that the judges tend to paint a picture of the separation of powers as one whereby each arm of government occupies its own sphere, but where they are ultimately interdependent. The interdependence is particularly apparent in the relationship between the government and the Westminster Parliament. Part of the dynamic among the three bodies is the recognition that parliamentary supremacy means that while there is a symbiosis among the three branches, there is not equanimity: Parliament remains supreme in relation to the other two branches.

The idea of separate functions performed by the respective branches was explained by judges in the Court of Appeal and the House of Lords in *M v Secretary of State for the Home Office*. Lord Donaldson of Lymington MR in the Court of Appeal characterised the constitutional landscape in the following terms:

> Our unwritten constitution rests upon a separation of powers. It also rests upon a mutual recognition of those powers. It is for Parliament to make new laws and to amend old laws, including the common law. It is for the courts to interpret and enforce the law. It is for the government to govern within the law. Each in its own sphere is supreme.[33]

Similarly, in the House of Lords, where the Court of Appeal's decision was upheld subject to a variation of the order, Lord Templeman put the matter thus: 'My Lords, Parliament makes the law, the executive carry the law into effect and the judiciary enforce the law.'[34] Both statements are, respectfully, an oversimplification of the true position, as will be discussed below. However, they provide a useful outlay of the division as seen by the courts. In the same case Nolan LJ expressed similar thoughts with reference to the relationship between the courts and the executive, adopting the formulation of counsel for the applicant, Stephen Sedley QC:

> The proper constitutional relationship of the executive with the courts is that the courts will respect all acts of the executive within its lawful province, and that the executive will respect all decisions of the courts as to what its lawful province is.[35]

Lord Steyn has described Nolan LJ's observation as evidence of 'the constitutional principle of the separation of powers in action.'[36] The judges made clear that while it was the province of the Home Department and the Home Secretary to determine immigration policy, it was the court's province

[32] Eric Barendt, 'Separation of powers and constitutional government' [1995] *Public Law* 599.

[33] *M v Home Office* [1992] QB 270 (CA) 306.

[34] *In Re M* [1994] 1 AC 377 (HL) 395.

[35] *M v Home Office* (n 33 above) 314–15.

[36] Lord Steyn, 'Democracy through law' (2002) 6 *European Human Rights Law Review* 723, 726.

to determine the lawful limits of that immigration policy and the executive must respect that determination and respect orders of the court which seek to enforce such decisions. Consequently, where the High Court ordered the return of a deported asylum seeker, the Home Secretary was obliged to comply with that order.

It is trite that there is far greater separation between the judiciary on the one hand and the executive and legislative branches, on the other, in the Westminster system. Under the Westminster model, both in the UK and in the newer jurisdictions examined, emphasis is placed on the separation and independence of the judiciary from other branches of government. This truism is reflected in judgments from the Commonwealth Caribbean, Australia, Canada, and the UK. For instance, in a House of Lords judgment in *Anderson v SSHD*, it was stated:

> The relationship between the legislature and the executive is close. On the other hand, the separation of powers between the judiciary and the legislative and executive branches of government is a strong principle of our system of government.[37]

Similar views have been expressed in Commonwealth Caribbean case law[38] and, in Australia, the High Court has repeatedly upheld statutes granting wide powers to the executive to make delegated legislation,[39] the Court holding that 'the distribution of legislative, executive and judicial powers in the Constitution does not operate to restrain the power of the Parliament to make such a law.'[40] Such acceptance of the shared executive and legislative powers represents the impact of the Westminster design of 'responsible government' on the application of the separation of powers.

The requirement of separation of the judiciary is often expressed in case law as a requirement for 'independence of the judiciary'. This terminology reflects the degree to which the judicial branch is subject to a higher degree of separation from the other branches than the executive and legislature are in relation to each other. There are various facets of the independence of the judiciary, which have been secured to some extent by an interlocking web of statute, convention, and case law. The security of tenure of judges has been enshrined in the Act of Settlement 1701 (UK) for more than 300 years. Article 3, Clause 7 of the Act provided that 'judges' commissions be made *quamdiu se bene gesserint*, and their salaries ascertained and established but upon the address of both Houses of Parliament it may be lawful to remove them.' According to this clause, judges were to hold tenure

[37] *R (Anderson) v SSHD* [2002] UKHL 46, [2003] 1 AC 837 (HL) [39] (Lord Steyn).

[38] *DPP of Jamaica v Mollison* (2003) 64 WIR 140 (JCPC, Jamaica) [13] (Lord Bingham).

[39] *Victorian Stevedoring & General Contracting Co Pty Ltd v Dignan* (1931) 46 CLR 73 (HC, Australia) 100–01; *Giris Pty Ltd v Commissioner of Taxation (Cth)* (1969) 119 CLR 365 (HC, Australia) 373.

[40] *Victorian Stevedoring* (ibid) 101 (Dixon J).

during good behaviour and could only be removed from office upon a vote by Parliament.

The emphasis on the independence of the judiciary as an application of the separation of powers helps to highlight an overlap between the rule of law principle and the separation of powers principle; protection of judicial independence emerges as an application of both principles. This is seen in commentary, for instance, with wide acceptance by writers ranging from Raz to Dworkin to Jowell, of the presence of an independent judicial body as a core requirement of the rule of law, and with Masterman and Barendt maintaining that the separation and independence of the judiciary is a central component of the separation of powers.[41] The overlap is also evident in the case law as judicial independence and the need for adjudication by an independent and impartial tribunal have been characterised as necessary elements of both principles.[42]

Despite the emphasis on judicial independence, one can discern a separation of functions even as between the legislature and the executive. The existence of a separation of functions as between the executive and the legislature can be represented by respect for limitations on legislative power granted to the executive. In the UK, the courts are limited to enforcing these limitations only against the executive where it is shown that a member of the executive exceeds the power granted to it by Parliament and seeks to usurp Parliamentary power.

The courts have noted these limitations in cases such as *SSHD v Pankina*, in which the Court of Appeal held that immigration requirements stipulating the minimum sum of money which should be held in an applicant's bank account at the time of application for leave to work in the UK, were rules having the substance and force of law. As such, the court held that under the Immigration Act 1971 (UK) and constitutional law regarding law-making power, the rules should have been laid before Parliament.[43] In giving the judgment of the Court, Sedley LJ argued:

> the law ... cannot simply abandon a constitutional principle which for centuries has stood as a pillar of the separation of powers in what is today a democracy under the rule of law. ... ministers are expected to do what is required of them: Parliament will expect the Home Secretary to lay before it any rules by which he or she proposes to manage immigration; the courts will expect such rules, like any other source of law, to be those and only those which have Parliament's approval;

[41] Joseph Raz, 'The Rule of Law and Its Virtue' (1977) 93 *Law Quarterly Review* 195; Ronald Dworkin, *A Matter of Principle* (Clarendon Press, 1986); Barendt (n 32 above); Masterman, *Separation of Powers* (n 6 above).

[42] *Australian Communist Party v Commonwealth of Australia* (1951) 83 CLR 1 (HC, Australia) 193; *Hinds v R* [1977] AC 195 (JCPC, Jamaica) 213; *Plaintiff S157/2002 v The Commonwealth of Australia* (2003) 211 CLR 476 (HC, Australia) [32].

[43] [2011] QB 376 (CA) [20]–[21], [33]–[37].

> and appellate tribunals will expect to find in the rules the certainty which rules must have if they are to function as law.[44]

The rights element in *Pankina* arose in the court's decision that the Home Secretary was obliged to take into account the potential impact on the applicant's private and family life, as protected by Article 8 of the ECHR. This rights component may have impacted on the court's reasoning, particularly by encouraging the judges to examine the issue as a deep constitutional question, as Sedley LJ argued, and not merely as a question of ordinary statutory interpretation. There are common threads that run through *Pankina* and the *Bancoult* case, which dealt with the legality of prerogative legislation affecting inhabitants of the Chagos Islands.[45] In *Bancoult*, inhabitants of the Chagos Islands had been compulsorily removed from their homes pursuant to an Immigration Ordinance made in 1971, in order to facilitate the use of the main island as a US military base. On a judicial review application, this Ordinance was quashed in 2000. However, the government later decided that resettlement was not feasible and acted to restrict return to the Islands. To this end, Orders in Council were drafted by ministers without Parliamentary debate or approval and were then assented to as an exercise of the royal prerogative. On an application for judicial review of the Orders in Council, the issue was raised whether the Orders, as an exercise of legislative power, were amenable to judicial review. The House of Lords held that it was entitled to review the Orders in Council, drawing a distinction on democratic grounds between legislative power exercised by Parliament and legislative power exercised by the executive. Of course, *Bancoult* and *Pankina* do demonstrate the significant law-making powers possessed by the executive and, therefore, the substantial functional overlap between the different branches of government. Yet, another common theme that appears in these opinions is the courts' steps to restrain the legislative power of the executive where the measures sought to be implemented through that power have not been given the imprimatur of Parliament.[46] The *Bancoult* case again shows the interplay in the UK between the separation of powers, parliamentary supremacy and democratic ideals. It was argued on behalf of the government in *Bancoult* that 'within the traditional tripartite separation of powers' the Order was an expression of legislative sovereignty and did not involve an exercise of executive authority. This argument was rejected by the House of Lords. In expounding on the difference between legislative power exercised by the executive and that exercised by Parliament, Lord Hoffmann underscored

[44] ibid [35].

[45] *Regina (Bancoult) v Secretary of State for Foreign and Commonwealth Affairs (No 2)* [2008] UKHL 61, [2009] 1 AC 453 (HL).

[46] Masterman, *Separation of Powers* (n 6 above) 109–10.

the sovereignty of Parliament and the normative foundation of that sovereignty: representative democracy. In his words:

> the fact that such Orders in Council in certain important respects resemble Acts of Parliament does not mean that they share all their characteristics. The principle of the sovereignty of Parliament, as it has been developed by the courts over the past 350 years, is founded upon the unique authority Parliament derives from its representative character. An exercise of the prerogative lacks this quality; although it may be legislative in character, it is still an exercise of power by the executive alone.[47]

Therefore, the distinction between the character of legislative power and executive power was used to justify, and indeed explain the need for, judicial scrutiny of executive action. The ideas expressed by Lord Hoffmann in *Bancoult* mirror similar thoughts expressed in the earlier case *ex p Fire Brigades Union*.[48] The Criminal Justice Act 1988 (UK) enacted a compensation scheme for victims of violent crimes, providing that the enacted provisions were to come into force on a day appointed by the Secretary of State. Years later, the Secretary of State decided that the provisions would not be brought into force and he purported to establish a tariff scheme for compensating victims. The House of Lords held that the Secretary of State's order establishing a new tariff scheme was unlawful as it effectively frustrated the will of Parliament to establish a statutory scheme, as expressed in the statute. Lord Browne-Wilkinson asserted that there was a division of powers between Parliament and the executive, and that the supreme legislative authority of Parliament acted as a check on the prerogative power of the executive. As His Lordship put it:

> It is for Parliament, not the executive, to repeal legislation. The constitutional history of this country is the history of the prerogative powers of the Crown being made subject to the overriding powers of the democratically elected legislature as the sovereign body.[49]

This is a clear expression of the impact of separation of powers and parliamentary supremacy, or the 'hierarchical separation of powers', as it is described by Masterman. The hierarchical relationship places Parliament in a superior position to both the executive and judicial branches. With respect to the judiciary, the hierarchical relationship was put in these terms by Lord Hoffmann: 'In this open country, the relationship between the judiciary and the legislature is one of partnership, but with the judiciary acknowledging the legislature to be the senior partner.'[50]

[47] *Bancoult* (n 45 above) [35].

[48] *R v Secretary of State for the Home Department, ex parte Fire Brigades Union* [1995] 2 AC 513 (HL).

[49] ibid 552 (Lord Browne-Wilkinson).

[50] Lord Hoffmann, 'Separation of Powers' (n 31 above) 141.

As noted in chapter two, this hierarchical relationship is not duplicated throughout the other jurisdictions in this study. For instance, in the Commonwealth Caribbean where constitutional supremacy has replaced parliamentary supremacy, each branch of government has a constitutionally allocated sphere and the court has jurisdiction to review and invalidate Acts of Parliament. This important distinction between the Westminster system and its progeny was not mentioned by Lord Diplock in his reference in *Hinds v DPP* to the separation of powers underlying all 'Westminster model' constitutions.[51] As stated in the introduction to this chapter, there are important questions to explore with respect to the transplantation of the Westminster style system and the distinctions between the UK and the newly independent jurisdictions. These questions tap into the comparative methodology used by the judges and they are explored in greater detail in chapter seven's discussion of 'Implied Principles as Gateways to Comparative Law'.

IV. EFFECT OF THE SEPARATION OF POWERS ON HUMAN RIGHTS

While the separation of powers doctrine is directed at inter-institutional conduct, it has significant implications for intra-institutional behaviour and the interaction between state institutions and citizens of the state. The use of separation of powers reasoning in fundamental rights adjudication is evidence of the latter two sets of implications.

The separation of powers, with its articulation of separate judicial power, proves useful to advocates of judicial protection of fundamental rights. The proposition is that there are process values possessed by courts which are not possessed by institutions in the other two branches, in particular the position of courts as impartial arenas for the resolution of disputes over rights and obligations. Supporting this argument, Barendt has argued that 'decisions on personal rights and liberties are inherently suitable for judicial resolution, and so must be made by a court, while the distribution of other goods and benefits may be regarded as a matter for administrative decision.'[52] This view is supported by members of the judiciary such as Lord Hoffmann, who maintains that human rights questions 'are quintessentially matters for judicial decision'.[53] Of course, the contrary position has been maintained by sceptical commentators, who contend that rights claims ought to be debated in the political sphere and therefore, are suited

[51] *Hinds* (n 42 above).
[52] Barendt (n 32 above) 605.
[53] Lord Hoffmann, 'Separation of Powers' (n 31 above) 139.

to determination by the legislative branch, largely due to the substance of rights claims and the appropriate process for their resolution.[54] This naturally leads to a difference of opinion regarding which institution is best suited for resolving such claims. Judicial uses of these competing views of the impact of separation of powers doctrine in rights adjudication are explored in more detail below.

As a practical matter, the overall impact of the separation of powers on fundamental rights adjudication is perhaps most clearly witnessed in the area of criminal penalties. There are two categories of impact that are relevant in this discussion. In the first, the separation of powers is applied to derive a requirement that the determination of the length of a sentence is maintained within the judicial branch. A representative statement of this requirement was the following by Lord Diplock in *Hinds*:

> In the field of punishment for criminal offences, the application of the basic principle of separation of legislative, executive and judicial powers that is implicit in a constitution on the Westminster model makes it necessary to consider how the power to determine the length and character of a sentence which imposes restrictions on the personal liberty of the offender is distributed under these three heads of power.[55]

An element of this requirement is that individuals ought to receive the benefit of the institutional processes of the judicial branch of government. This is an understanding which is sometimes expressed implicitly, and sometimes explicitly, in the judgments. An explicit expression of this idea occurs in *Polyukhovich v Commonwealth of Australia*, where the High Court was asked to rule upon the constitutionality of the retrospective operation of section 9 of the War Crimes Act 1945 (Cth), which made it an offence for an Australian citizen to have committed war crimes in Europe during World War II. In delivering his opinion, Deane J explained his view of the objective of the separation of judicial power. It is worth quoting his explanation at length:

> The main objective of the sometimes inconvenient separation of judicial from executive and legislative powers had long been recognized at the time of the federation. It is to ensure that 'the life, liberty, and property of the subject [is not] in the hands of arbitrary judges, whose decisions [are] then regulated only by their own opinions, and not by any fundamental principles of law' (Blackstone, Commentaries, 17th ed. (1830), vol. I, p. 269; and see, to like effect, Story, Commentaries on the Constitution of the United States (1833), §1568). That objective will, of course, be achieved only by the Constitution's requirement that judicial power be vested exclusively in the courts which it designates if the judicial

[54] See, eg, Jeremy Waldron, 'The Core of the Case Against Judicial Review' (2006) 115 *Yale Law Journal* 1346.

[55] *Hinds* (n 42 above) 225 (Lord Diplock).

> power so vested is exercised by those courts in accordance with the essential attributes of the curial process (cf Re Tracey; Ex parte Ryan). Indeed, to construe Ch. III of the Constitution as being concerned only with labels and as requiring no more than that the repository of judicial power be called a court would be to convert it into a mockery, rather than a reflection, of the doctrine of separation of powers. Common sense and the provisions of Ch. III, based as they are on the assumption of traditional judicial procedures, remedies and methodology (see below), compel the conclusion that, in insisting that the judicial power of the Commonwealth be vested only in the courts designated by Ch. III, the Constitution's intent and meaning were that that judicial power would be exercised by those courts acting as courts with all that that notion essentially requires. Accordingly, the Parliament cannot, consistently with Ch. III of the Constitution, usurp the judicial power of the Commonwealth by itself purporting to exercise judicial power in the form of legislation.[56]

Here we see the elements of the protection of individual interests through the process of the courts, a process which includes the application of 'fundamental principles of law', rather than personal opinions, in the determination of disputes. This is a purposive approach to determining the implications of the separation of powers principle. Using that reasoning, Deane J issued a strong dissent in *Polyukhovich v The Commonwealth*, finding, contra the majority, that the retrospective operation of section 9 of the War Crimes Act 1945 constituted a usurpation by the legislature of the exercise of judicial power.[57]

What is also explicit in other judgments is the description of sentencing as part of the nature of the 'judicial power' or 'judicial function'. Thus, in *Anderson v SSHD*, Lord Bingham held that a decision fixing the level of punishment is a judicial function, and should, accordingly be made by judges rather than by members of the executive branch.[58] Consequently, the Home Secretary's power to set tariffs for prisoners convicted of murder violated the right to fair trial under Article 6 of the ECHR.

The second form of application of the separation of powers in the field of criminal penalties is as a requirement of due process of the law. The judgments of the High Court of Australia are particularly illuminating on the anchoring of due process protections in the separation of powers principle. In the flagship case on separation of powers in Australia—*New South Wales v Commonwealth* (*Wheat* case)—the Court referred to 'the fundamental principle of the separation of powers as marked out in the Australian Constitution',[59] deriving support for this principle from the demarcation of functions in Chapters I, II, and III of the Australian Constitution.

[56] (1991) 172 CLR 501 (HC, Australia) 606–07 (Deane J) (citations omitted).

[57] ibid 613–14 (Deane J).

[58] *Anderson* (n 37 above) [30]–[31] (Lord Bingham).

[59] *New South Wales v Commonwealth of Australia* (*Wheat Case*) (1915) 20 CLR 54 (HC, Australia) 88.

Isaacs J described the 'essential feature' of the court as its role as an 'independent and impartial tribunal'.[60] These ideas were developed in the Australian High Court's judgment in *Leeth v Commonwealth of Australia*, which is a helpful representation of the application of the separation of powers principle to provide protection for the individual in its interaction with the state.[61] The issue in the *Leeth* case was the constitutional validity of section 4(1) of the Commonwealth Prisoners Act 1967 (Cth). The section provided that, when sentencing federal offenders, judges must fix a minimum period during which the federal offender is not eligible to be released on parole, which complies with the non-parole period of the laws of the state or territory in which the offender is convicted. The section thereby sought to establish a single parole system in each state, so that there would be no difference in parole regimes between federal prisoners serving a sentence in a state or territory prison and state or territory prisoners serving a sentence in the same prison.[62] However, another result of the section would be variations in the non-parole periods of federal offenders depending on the state or territory in which they were convicted. Leeth was convicted in Queensland under the Customs Act 1901 (Cth) of the offence of importing cannabis in commercial quantities, and was sentenced to 25 years' imprisonment. He was prescribed a non-parole period of twelve and a half years in accordance with section 4, and argued before the High Court that section 4 discriminated among federal offenders by exposing some to more punitive regimes. A majority of the High Court (Mason CJ, Brennan, Dawson, and McHugh JJ) held that section 4 was constitutionally valid, while Deane, Toohey, and Gaudron JJ dissented. What is particularly compelling for the purposes of this chapter is that a majority of the Bench (Mason CJ, Dawson, McHugh, Deane, Toohey, and Gaudron JJ) found an implied protection of due process or natural justice in the Constitution, based on the separation of judicial power from other state powers.[63] Mason CJ, and Dawson and McHugh JJ referred to the requirement to act consistently with 'the rules of natural justice' while Deane and Toohey JJ referred to the 'duty to act judicially'. The latter judges expressed the connection between this requirement and the separation of judicial powers in the following terms:

> ... the doctrine of legal equality is, to a significant extent, implicit in the Constitution's separation of judicial power from legislative and executive powers and the vesting of judicial power in designated 'courts'... Thus, in Ch. III's

[60] ibid 93.

[61] *Leeth* v *Commonwealth of Australia* (1992) 174 CLR 455 (HC, Australia).

[62] ibid 478 (Brennan J).

[63] ibid 470 (Mason CJ, Dawson, and McHugh JJ), 486–87 (Deane and Toohey JJ), 502 (Gaudron J). The location of due process or natural justice requirements in Ch III was reinforced more recently in *Totani v South Australia* (2010) 242 CLR 1 [69] (French CJ); *Wainohu v New South Wales* [2011] HCA 24 (HC, Australia) [58] (French CJ and Kiefel J).

> exclusive vesting of the judicial power of the Commonwealth in the 'courts' which it designates, there is implicit a requirement that those 'courts' exhibit the essential attributes of a court and observe, in the exercise of that judicial power, the essential requirements of the curial process, including the obligation to act judicially.[64]

Three judges (Deane, Toohey, and Gaudron JJ) found that there was a doctrine of legal equality which was a necessary implication from the Constitution and derived that requirement of equality before the law from the Constitution's separation of powers.[65] In the view of Gaudron J, 'the concept of equal justice ... is fundamental to the judicial process' and '[i]t is an essential feature of the judicial power that it should be exercised in accordance with the judicial process.' Accordingly, a statutory direction 'which would require a power vested in a court to be exercised other than in accordance with that process is necessarily invalid.'[66]

The requirement of equality before the law based on the separation of powers is in one sense quite complex, and yet, in another sense, a traditional idea. It is complex in that it embodies a right that is derived from a principle that appears, at a basic level, to be organisational and directed at the institutions of state, rather than citizens of state. Yet, this is similar to the ultimate effect of the first category addressed above, that is, that criminal penalties are to be determined by the judicial branch. Though this first requirement is one that—on the surface—protects the judicial sphere within the organisation of institutional power in the state, as its application in case law shows, it is a requirement that ultimately protects an individual's right to have a criminal penalty determined by the judiciary. Thus, both the first and second requirements derive rights from an organisational principle. The equality before the law requirement is also traditional in the sense that writers as far back as Dicey maintained that equality before the law was an element of the common law constitution. In fact, the opinion delivered by Deane and Toohey JJ in *Leeth* quoted Dicey's description of equality before the law as a requirement that 'every man, whatever be his rank or condition, is subject to the ordinary law ... and amenable to the jurisdiction of the ordinary tribunals'.[67] What is particularly powerful about the modern cases deriving equality before the law from constitutional principles is that the right is characterised as fundamental and in the jurisdictions with a

[64] *Leeth* (n 61 above) 487.

[65] ibid 486–87 (Deane and Toohey JJ); 502 (Gaudron J). Brennan J based his implication on the expression in the preamble of the 'constitutional unity of the Australian people "in one indissoluble Federal Commonwealth"': ibid 475.

[66] ibid 502 (Gaudron J). There has not been universal acceptance of the equal justice requirement on the High Court. See, eg, ibid 467–68; PH Lane, 'Constitutional Implications and a Bill of Rights' (2001) 75 *Australian Law Journal* 469, 470; Fiona Wheeler, 'Due Process, Judicial Power and Chapter III in the New High Court' (2004) 32 *Federal Law Review* 205, 205–06.

[67] Albert Venn Dicey, *Introduction to the Study of the Law of the Constitution*, 10th edn (Macmillan Publishers, 1959) 193, quoted in *Leeth* (n 61 above) 485 (Deane and Toohey JJ).

written Constitution, this fundamentality carries with it the potential for the right to be applied against legislation and to defeat inconsistent statutes. Thus, despite that the majority in the *Leeth* case held that section 4(1) was constitutional, three of the judges (Deane, Toohey, and Gaudron JJ) articulated an account of equality before the law based on the separation of judicial power from the executive and legislative branches, which would permit invalidation of legislation. The three judges then concluded that the section did violate equality before the law and that the court could declare it invalid on that basis. Thus, while having a traditional foundation, the modern application provides a role for equality before the law that extends beyond Dicey's conception by potentially subverting legislative will. In this sense, the partial adoption of implied principles from traditional writings on the English constitution might lead to applications of the principle to achieve more rights-consistent results than would have originally been conceived in traditional commentary.

The Australian High Court has engaged in more detailed discussion of the connection between the separation of powers and due process, but such a connection has been recognised in the UK House of Lords and Supreme Court. We saw above that in Australia, judges have opined that one requirement resulting from the separation of powers and the need to fulfil its objectives is the guarantee of due process. In the UK, the purposive relationship is reversed, with the House of Lords finding that '[o]ne of the purposes of Article 6 [ECHR], in requiring that disputes over civil rights should be decided by or subject to the control of a judicial body, is to uphold the rule of law and the separation of powers'.[68] These comments were made in Lord Hoffmann's judgment in *Begum v Tower Hamlets LBC*, with which the remaining Law Lords on the Bench agreed.[69] Tower Hamlets Council had determined that Begum was homeless and that it had a duty to provide accommodation for her. The accommodation that was offered was rejected by Begum and it was determined by an internal review that the accommodation offered her was suitable and it was reasonable for her to accept it. Begum, however, contended that this review ought to have been conducted by an independent and impartial tribunal. After the County Court held that the local authority's failure to refer the matter to an independent and impartial tribunal constituted a violation of Article 6 of the ECHR, the main issue before the House of Lords was whether, as the internal review officer was not an independent and impartial tribunal, the County Court's appellate jurisdiction satisfied the requirements of Article 6. Engaging a purposive interpretation of Article 6, the Law Lords held, unanimously, that the

[68] *Begum v Tower Hamlets London Borough Council* [2003] UKHL 5, [2003] 2 AC 430 (HL) [27] (Lord Hoffmann), citing *Golder v United Kingdom* (1975) 1 EHRR 524.
[69] *Begum* (ibid) [1], [73], [107], [108].

County Court's jurisdiction did satisfy ECHR requirements. This reflects a recurring theme and practice across the two applications of the separation of powers principle—a purposive approach to the principle and to rights interpretation.[70] That is, the interpretation is informed by the interpreters' assessment of the objective of the norm in question—whether the separation of powers principle or fundamental rights norms. Lord Hoffmann's purposive analysis mirrors his views on Article 6 as expressed in *Matthews v Ministry of Defence*, which also concerned the scope of Article 6, but on the very different issue of the entitlement of servicemen to institute an action for damages in tort against the Crown. Further, Hoffmann's view on the purpose of the natural justice protections in Article 6 has been endorsed in subsequent case law.[71]

The requirements derived from the separation of powers with respect to the allocation of the task of fixing criminal penalties to judges and the requirements that the judicial task be carried out with respect for due process are consistent with Masterman's views on the operation of the separation of powers in the UK. Masterman argues that the application of the separation of powers in the UK requires judicial independence and that the right to a fair hearing before an independent and impartial tribunal is as much part of the longstanding respect for independence of the judiciary as it is of natural justice rules.[72] The treatment of the relationship between these doctrines in Australia and the UK—jurisdictions which share a basis in the Westminster model constitution—shows that due process rights can be implied from the separation of powers and, vice versa, that where due process rights are recognised in rights legislation, one objective of those rights is to uphold the separation of powers.

A. Deference and Judicial Restraint

The flexibility allowed by reasoning from the separation of powers is on display in the role that the principle plays in guiding the level of deference shown by judges in constitutional and fundamental rights cases. Deference is manifested in the judicial practice ascribing varying degrees of respect to the judgement of other branches of state, on the basis of institutional

[70] FAR Bennion, *Understanding Common Law Legislation: Drafting and Interpretation* (Oxford University Press, 2009) 37–40. Bennion argues that in the common law world purposive construction of statutes is now accepted and expected, in preference to a purely literal approach. See Peter Gerangelos, *The Separation of Powers and Legislative Interference in Judicial Process: Constitutional Principles and Limitations* (Hart Publishing, 2009) 29–37.

[71] *Wilson v First County Trust Ltd (No 2)* [2004] 1 AC 816 (HL) [35] (Lord Nicholls).

[72] Roger Masterman, 'Determinative in the abstract? Article 6(1) and the separation of powers' [2005] *European Human Rights Law Review* 628, 631.

capacity or legitimacy.[73] Two strains of reasoning can be discerned in the impact of the separation of powers principle on the extent of judicial intervention in rights cases: a traditional restraint oriented understanding of the separation of powers and a more interventionist strain of reasoning. The traditional notion is that the institutional position of the judiciary demands judicial restraint in the review of tasks performed by the other branches of government. This traditional view was expressed by Lord Diplock in *Duport Steels v Sirs*, in a passage which it is useful to quote at length:

> My Lords, at a time when more and more cases involve the application of legislation which gives effect to policies that are the subject of bitter public and parliamentary controversy, it cannot be too strongly emphasised that the British constitution, though largely unwritten, is firmly based upon the separation of powers; Parliament makes the laws, the judiciary interpret them. When Parliament legislates to remedy what the majority of its members at the time perceive to be a defect or a lacuna in the existing law (whether it be the written law enacted by existing statutes or the unwritten common law as it has been expounded by the judges in decided cases), the role of the judiciary is confined to ascertaining from the words that Parliament has approved as expressing its intention what that intention was, and to giving effect to it. Where the meaning of the statutory words is plain and unambiguous it is not for the judges to invent fancied ambiguities as an excuse for failing to give effect to its plain meaning because they themselves consider that the consequences of doing so would be inexpedient, or even unjust or immoral.[74]

Similarly, it was maintained by Lord Scarman, in the same case, that:

> in the field of statute law the judge must be obedient to the will of Parliament as expressed in its enactments. In this field Parliament makes, and un-makes, the law: the judge's duty is to interpret and to apply the law, not to change it to meet the judge's idea of what justice requires… Great judges are in their different ways judicial activists. But the constitution's separation of powers, or more accurately functions, must be observed if judicial independence is not to be put at risk.[75]

These traditional sentiments were echoed by Lord Hoffmann extrajudicially in a lecture delivered in 2001, in which he argued that the judicial branch must show restraint as '[n]othing would be more destructive of its authority than a perception that it was making decisions which were properly the territory of the elected branches of government.'[76] Reasoning along these lines was also evident in the judgment of the High Court of Australia in *Al-Kateb v Godwin*, in which the court was petitioned for a ruling that

[73] See Aileen Kavanagh, *Constitutional Review under the UK Human Rights Act* (Cambridge University Press, 2009) 169; Jeffrey Jowell, 'Judicial Deference: Servility, Civility or Institutional Capacity?' [2003] *Public Law* 592.
[74] [1980] 1 All ER 529 (HL) 540.
[75] ibid 168–69.
[76] Lord Hoffmann, 'Separation of Powers' (n 31 above) 139; Carolan (n 14 above) 30.

the state's detention of a stateless person under the Migration Act 1958 (Cth, Australia) was unlawful. In concluding that the detention was lawful and that the detention of non-citizens by the Executive did not intrude upon the power allocated to the judiciary in Chapter III of the Constitution of the Commonwealth of Australia, McHugh J issued the following comment on the limits of the court's powers:

> It is not for courts, exercising federal jurisdiction, to determine whether the course taken by Parliament is unjust or contrary to basic human rights. The function of the courts in this context is simply to determine whether the law of the Parliament is within the powers conferred on it by the Constitution. The doctrine of separation of powers does more than prohibit the Parliament and the Executive from exercising the judicial power of the Commonwealth. It prohibits the Ch III courts from amending the Constitution under the guise of interpretation.[77]

That traditional view is still sometimes reflected in fundamental rights cases but in jurisdictions where a fundamental rights instrument has been enacted, which enjoins the courts to interpret acts of public authorities in accordance with the rights therein declared, or to invalidate acts that do not comply with the rights instrument, the traditional view must contend with an altered constitutional context. In this context, there remain incantations of institutional separation as a basis for judicial restraint but these arguments have in some cases been overshadowed by invocation of the argument from democratic legitimacy to support judicial restraint, in addition to—or instead of—a separation of powers argument. In other notable fundamental rights cases, where judicial restraint was encouraged by a judge on the bench, the argument was fortified by the existence of other factors affecting the court's perception of its institutional legitimacy in relation to the question at hand, including the argument from democratic legitimacy or situational arguments specific to the court in question. One such case was *Grape Bay Ltd v Bermuda (Attorney General)*. In delivering the judgment, the Privy Council explained that:

> Their Lordships would accept that Bermudians are in the best position to know what the public interest of Bermuda requires. But the Constitution lays down a separation of powers between the executive, legislature and judiciary. On a matter such as the desirability or otherwise of franchise restaurants, which is a pure question of policy, raising no issue of human rights or fundamental principle, the decision making power has been entrusted to those Bermudians who constitute the legislative branch of government and not to the judges.[78]

Local public interest was central where the Bermudian legislature, having decided that it was undesirable to give free rein to overseas franchise

[77] *Al-Kateb v Godwin* (2004) 219 CLR 562 (HC, Australia) [74] (McHugh J).
[78] [2000] 1 WLR 574 (JCPC, Bermuda) 585 (Lord Hoffmann).

restaurants, passed legislation barring the operation of such restaurants in the future, except for such restaurants that were already in operation. The appellant company, which was making arrangements to operate branches on behalf of an American company, alleged a breach of its right not to be deprived of property without compensation. On appeal to the Judicial Committee of the Privy Council, it was held, inter alia, that the facts of the case did not give rise to a deprivation of property and that a wide margin of appreciation should be afforded the legislature in this case where the legislature was making a determination as to whether the public interest would be harmed by the operation of further franchise restaurants.

Similarly, in the rights context, when institutional arguments are made, arguments from democratic legitimacy often supply the basis for the restraint impulse or support the separation of powers argument being made. Viewed in this light, it is not the separation of powers principle on its own that is said to justify restraint, but rather the democratic underpinning of the legislative act in question. This was how the argument from judicial restraint was framed in cases such as *Lichniak*.[79] In considering whether the mandatory life imprisonment required by section 1 of the Murder (Abolition of Death Penalty) Act 1965 interfered with the appellants' ECHR rights, Lord Bingham took into account that 'the fact that section 1(1) represents the settled will of a democratic assembly is not a conclusive reason for upholding it, but a degree of deference is due to the judgment of a democratic assembly on how a particular social problem is best tackled'.[80] His Lordship made this point again in *R (Countryside Alliance) v Attorney General* in determining the consistency with the ECHR of legislation proscribing fox-hunting:

> After intense debate a majority of the country's democratically elected representatives decided that there was a pressing need for the ban. It is of course true that the existence of duly enacted legislation does not conclude the issue ... The degree of respect to be shown to the considered judgments of a democratic assembly will vary according to the subject matter and the circumstances.[81]

When the institutional relationship is described in such terms, it is based on a view not merely of the imperative for divided governmental functions, but also, of the hierarchical ordering of the output of these institutions. The emphasis on democratic legitimacy in addition to separation of powers recognises that the human rights instruments have altered the calculus of the division of functions such that the law-making power of the court is strengthened,[82] the ability of the court to make general laws on sensitive

[79] *Lichniak* (n 4) [14] (Lord Bingham).

[80] ibid.

[81] *R (Countryside Alliance and others) v Attorney General* [2007] UKHL 52, [2008] 1 AC 719 (HL) [45]; Kavanagh, *Constitutional Review under the UK HRA* (n 73 above) 192.

[82] Aileen Kavanagh, 'The elusive divide between interpretation and legislation under the Human Rights Act 1998' (2004) 24 *Oxford Journal of Legal Studies* 259.

issues of policy affecting the populace being increased. In this setting, traditional appeal to the division between the branches as a demand for judicial restraint is less compelling. In a constitutional setting in which there is a Bill of Rights, the separation of powers is also often used to support a more activist use of the judicial power. This 'interventionist' impact of the separation of powers is explored in the following section on the post-HRA use of the separation of powers principle.

V. THE SEPARATION OF POWERS IN UK COURTS POST-HRA

There are two observed effects of the HRA 1998 and the CRA 2005 on the separation of powers doctrine in the UK. First the doctrine has evolved to require sharper distinctions among the legislative, executive, and judicial branches,[83] and secondly, the doctrine has featured more significantly in superior court decisions.[84]

The sharpening of personnel distinctions was chiefly focused on the separation of the judicial branch from the executive and the judicial branch from the legislature. These changes were formally facilitated by the CRA 2005, but as shown below, the rights narrative that developed after the HRA 1998 partly informed the drafting of the CRA 2005. The refinement of the distinctions between executive and judiciary were primarily apparent in the changes made to the position of the Lord Chancellor. Prior to the Act, the Lord Chancellor was not only a member of Cabinet, but also the Head of the Judiciary, a judge, and Speaker of the House of Lords.[85] In detailing the functions of the Lord Chancellor, the CRA 2005 preserves the Lord Chancellor's position as a Cabinet Minister, but not the judicial functions. Pursuant to section 18 and Schedule 6 to the CRA 2005, the Lord Chancellor is no longer permitted to sit as a judge or to preside over legislative matters in the House of Lords. Enhanced distinctions between legislature and judiciary were also achieved by section 137(3) of the CRA 2005, which prevents members of the House of Lords from sitting or voting in the House or otherwise participating in the legislative business of the House while holding judicial office.

While the CRA 2005 was the immediate facilitator of this increased separation of personnel, these changes were precipitated by the HRA 1998. The very terms of the ECHR which are scheduled to the HRA 1998 called into question the institutional arrangements of the UK government,

[83] Masterman, 'Determinative in the abstract' (n 72 above) 628–29.
[84] ibid 628.
[85] Jack Beatson, 'Reforming an Unwritten Constitution' (2010) 126 *Law Quarterly Review* 48, 54.

specifically the arrangements regarding the judiciary. Attention was drawn to Article 6(1) of the ECHR, which states, in relevant part:

> In the determination of his civil rights and obligations or of any criminal charge against him, everyone is entitled to a fair and public hearing within a reasonable time by an independent and impartial tribunal established by law.

It was questioned whether the requirements of Article 6(1) of the ECHR were flouted by the fact that the highest appellate tribunal in the state, the Judicial Committee of the House of Lords, was, as the name indicates, a committee of the Upper Chamber of Parliament, the House of Lords. The impact of the ECHR provisions on the terms of the CRA 2005 was apparent by the comments made in the lead up to the enactment of the Constitutional Reform Act. Regarding Law Lords sitting and voting in the House of Lords, the Department of Constitutional Affairs commented:

> The Human Rights Act, specifically in relation to Art 6 of the European Convention on Human Rights, now requires a stricter view to be taken not only of anything which might undermine the independence or impartiality of a judicial tribunal, but even of anything which might appear to do so. So the fact that the Law Lords are a Committee of the House of Lords can raise issues about the appearance of independence from the legislature.[86]

The Department also stated that:

> It can no longer be appropriate for a senior judge to sit in Cabinet or for a Government Minister to be our country's senior judge.[87]

Additionally, by increasing judicial power to review executive and legislative acts, and increasing their potential impact in politically sensitive cases, the HRA 1998 brought more media scrutiny to the judiciary.[88] This, in turn, heightened the importance of the structural design and personnel of the UK's highest appellate body.[89]

The impact of the HRA 1998 on the separation of powers is also reflected in judicial decisions in which Article 6 played a role. The Article has also been applied to the issue of separation of personnel. A particularly dramatic example occurs in *Davidson v Scottish Ministers (No 2)*.[90] Davidson was an inmate in Barlinnie Prison in Glasgow. He complained that the prison conditions violated his rights guaranteed under Article 3 of the ECHR, and requested a transfer. His application for judicial review was refused by

[86] Department of Constitutional Affairs, *Constitutional Reform: A New Supreme Court for the United Kingdom* (CP 11/03), July 2003, para 3.

[87] Department of Constitutional Affairs, *Constitutional Reform: Reforming the Office of Lord Chancellor* (CP 13/03) September 2003, 5.

[88] Lord Mance, 'Constitutional reforms, the Supreme Court and the Law Lords' (2006) 25 *Civil Justice Quarterly* 155, 164.

[89] ibid.

[90] [2004] UKHL 34; 2005 1 SC 7. See also *McGonnell v United Kingdom* (2000) 30 EHRR 289.

the Lord Ordinary, on the ground, inter alia, that section 21 of the Crown Proceedings Act 1947 (UK) precluded the grant of coercive orders against the Scottish Ministers. The appellate court refused to grant an interim order of specific performance against the Scottish Ministers. Davidson then sought leave to appeal to the House of Lords. The application for leave was refused by an Extra Division of the Court of Session, a Bench that included Lord Hardie. Davidson subsequently learned that in his capacity as Lord Advocate, Lord Hardie had advised the House of Lords on the effect of section 21 of the Crown Proceedings Act 1947 in the relation to the Scotland Act 1998 (UK). Davidson applied to the Inner House to set aside the decision refusing permission to appeal, on the ground that Lord Hardie's participation in the appeal breached Article 6 of the Convention. Davidson argued that there was apparent bias and lack of impartiality on the grounds of Lord Hardie's legislative involvement as Lord Advocate, his advice to his ministerial colleagues on the issue of the scope of section 21 of the Crown Proceedings Act and his resistance to an amendment to the provision which prevented the courts from making an order for specific performance against the Scottish Ministers. The Inner House granted the application and the Scottish Ministers appealed to the House of Lords. The Law Lords held, applying case law of the ECtHR on the requirements of Article 6, that there was a risk of apparent bias.

Louis Blom-Cooper penned a blistering critique of the decision, arguing that the law as applied in *Davidson* failed to distinguish between preconceptions (which Blom-Cooper maintains are natural in any human, and consequently, any judge) and bias.[91] Blom-Cooper also criticises the decision for failing to distinguish between the trial judge, who performs a fact-finding role, and the appellate judge, who reviews the law and who acts as one of (usually) three members of the appellate bench. His conclusion is that the law too easily leads to automatic disqualification. Despite the vigour of Blom-Cooper's commentary, it is respectfully submitted that his criticisms of the decision on the issue of bias can perhaps be viewed as missing a key aspect of the case. It is arguable that the decision, while framed and phrased in terms of judicial impartiality and bias, reflected a developing understanding of the demands of institutional and personnel division in the HRA era. In these terms, the decision represents a shift towards a stricter demand for separation of personnel. This conclusion is supported by Lord Woolf's comments in the case that an issue of 'structural' impartiality was raised because the remarks were made by Lord Hardie in his capacity as a government minister. The position is further reinforced by Lord Cullen's statement that:

> The fact that Lord Hardie expressed an opinion as to the effect of s 21 is not in itself decisive. What he said cannot be considered in isolation: he said it in the

[91] Louis Blom-Cooper, 'Bias on Appeal' [2005] *Public Law* 225.

> context of his role as a Government Minister in promoting the Bill, including its provision for the extension of the protection of s 21 to the Scottish Ministers. It follows that as a Government Minister, and presumably in the light of considerations of policy, he was promoting the protection of Scottish Ministers from judicial review. It was the exercising of that role, rather than simply his expression of an opinion about the effect of s 21, that persuades me that Lord Hardie was disqualified from sitting as a member of the Extra Division.[92]

As Masterman argues, Lord Woolf's and Lord Cullen's judgments lend support to the position that the courts are requiring a stricter separation as between the judiciary and the executive.[93] Two other judges (Lords Hope and Bingham) placed more emphasis not on the dual executive and judicial roles, but rather on the fact that the statements made by Lord Hardie in Parliament were on the same issue that arose in Davidson's case. Lord Bingham did state that his decision was not based on the 'theory of the separation of powers alone', but that is consistent with the ethos of this chapter, that the courts do not adopt and apply a purely *theoretical* concept of the separation of powers and that it is in the nuances of judicial application that much is revealed about the practical implications of the separation of powers as a legal principle. In fact, it is arguable that the totality of the judges' approach in this case is consistent with a purposive approach to the separation of powers principle, which considers the objectives of the doctrine and whether the functions of the relevant branch (in this instance, the court) were undermined in the case. In this case, the House of Lords decided that there was a risk of apparent bias arising from Lord Hardie's function as a judge considering the effect of legislation that he has drafted or promoted in the legislature.

A similar dynamic of Article 6 resulting in stricter separation occurred in *R (Barclay) v Lord Chancellor.*[94] Sark is a Crown dependency to which the ECHR and the First Protocol to the ECHR are applicable. The Acting Chief Judge of Sark was the Seneschal, who also served as President of Chief Pleas (which was the legislature and executive of Sark). In 2008 the Reform (Sark) Law 2008 received Royal Assent from Her Majesty in Council, on the advice of the Lord Chancellor and other officials with responsibility for advising on the matter. Under the Reform Law the Seneschal would continue to sit as a member and President of the Chief Pleas as well as chief judge for Sark, though the Law removed his right to vote and speak in Chief Pleas. The claimants challenged the defendants' decision to advise the Queen to give Royal Assent to the Law, on several grounds, citing inconsistency with the ECHR and First Protocol. The claims were dismissed at first instance

[92] *Davidson* (n 90 above) [81].
[93] Masterman, *Separation of Powers* (n 6 above) 235–36.
[94] [2008] EWCA Civ 1319, [2010] 1 AC 464 (CA).

and on appeal to the Court of Appeal, one ground of appeal was that the functions and powers conferred on the Seneschal under the Reform Law are inconsistent with Article 6 of the ECHR, in particular because under the Reform Law 2008 the Seneschal would continue to perform a dual role as President of Chief Pleas and senior judge on Sark. The Court of Appeal allowed the appeal on that ground, granting a declaration that the Seneschal's dual role violated Article 6(1), but the Court refused to quash the defendants' decision.[95] The leading judgment in the Court of Appeal was delivered by Pill LJ, who explained that he perceived 'the combination in Sark of the judicial with the other functions of the Seneschal as inconsistent with the Article 6 requirement to establish by law an independent and impartial tribunal' and that it is required that 'the principal judicial officer … is not linked with the executive and legislature in the manner and to the extent that the Seneschal is.'[96] Pill LJ did explain that '[t]his is not slavish adherence to an *abstract* notion of separation of powers but a recognition that it follows from the Seneschal's functions in his non-judicial capacity in Chief Pleas, as already described, that his independence and impartiality are capable of appearing open to doubt.'[97] Again, we see that the judges are not beholden to a theoretical concept of the separation of powers principle, but that the decisions applying Article 6 through the HRA 1998 have worked to emphasise the separation of the judicial branch.

An evolution in the jurisprudence on the separation of powers principle is also seen in 'tariff' cases. These cases emerged out of a series of challenges to the exercise of the power of the Home Secretary to fix a tariff for life sentence prisoners. In the tariff cases, we see judges ascribing greater force to the separation of powers principle, not in a way that justifies judicial restraint, but with a more defensive and in some cases, interventionist posture. In this way, the power of the Home Secretary to perform sentencing roles has been significantly limited by the courts. Most significant among these cases for the purposes of our discussion are *R v Secretary of State for the Home Department, ex parte Venables*,[98] decided prior to the entry into force of the HRA 1998, and *Anderson v SSHD*,[99] decided subsequent to the implementation of the HRA 1998. In both cases, the House of Lords deployed the separation of powers principle to articulate the position that sentencing is a judicial function. However, in *Anderson*, the principle was applied in interpreting Article 6 of the ECHR to result in a requirement of

[95] ibid [65]–[110]. The claimants appealed to the Supreme Court but the Article 6(1) claim was not in issue there so it is the Court of Appeal judgment that merits our attention in this chapter.

[96] ibid [65].

[97] ibid [67] (emphasis added).

[98] [1998] AC 407 (HL).

[99] *Anderson* (n 37 above).

not only a functional distinction but also a personnel difference predicated on that function.

Venables and Thompson were convicted of a murder committed when they were both 10, and were sentenced to detention during Her Majesty's pleasure pursuant to section 53(1) of the Children and Young Persons Act 1933 (UK). While the trial judge recommended that the minimum period of detention before consideration for release on licence (tariff) should be eight years and the Lord Chief Justice recommended ten years, the Home Secretary, in the exercise of his powers under the Criminal Justice Act 1991 (UK), set a tariff period of 15 years. The Secretary of State indicated that he took into account petitions and correspondence from the public, and opinions supplied by a national newspaper, in support of a long or whole-life tariff. On appeal to the House of Lords against the Home Secretary's decision, it was held that in fixing the tariff, the Secretary of State was performing a role analogous to that of a judge and that, in taking account of public protests, the Secretary of State had unlawfully exercised his discretion.[100]

In *Anderson*, the House of Lords went further by holding that Home Secretary's power to set tariffs for prisoners convicted of murder could not persist under the HRA 1998. Anderson was convicted of two murders and sentenced to mandatory life imprisonment pursuant to section 1 of the Murder (Abolition of Death Penalty) Act 1965 (UK). The trial judge recommended that the appellant serve a minimum period of 15 years but, similarly to the *Venables* case, but this time pursuant to section 29 of the Crime (Sentences) Act 1997 (UK), the Home Secretary prescribed a longer tariff period than that recommended by the trial judge. Anderson challenged the Secretary of State's decision and raised the issue whether the Secretary of State's power to fix the tariff was inconsistent with Article 6 of the ECHR. The Court of Appeal rejected Anderson's argument, finding that the jurisprudence of the ECtHR had recognised a distinction between mandatory and discretionary life sentences, and thus between the effects of tariffs in the context of Article 6. However, subsequent to the Court of Appeal's decision, the ECtHR recognised that, for mandatory life sentences, the punitive element was generally reflected by the tariff, and that there was no material distinction between mandatory and discretionary life prisoners with respect to the nature of tariff fixing. The House of Lords subsequently held, referring to the recent ECtHR judgments, that Article 6 demanded that fixing a tariff was a sentencing exercise which must be performed by the judicial arm of the state. Lord Steyn spoke to the demands that Article 6 places on the separation of powers in the UK, stating that, 'Article 6(1) requires effective separation of powers between the courts and the executive, and further requires that what can in shorthand be called judicial functions may only

[100] *Venables* (n 98 above) 528.

be exercised by the courts.'[101] Lord Steyn commented, quite appropriately, on 'the evolution and strengthening of the principle of separation of powers between the executive and judiciary which underlies Article 6(1)' and the influence of these changes on the development of Article 6 decisions relating to the sentencing exercise.[102]

Despite the sharpening distinctions between the branches that has resulted from the HRA 1998 and which therefore can be said to have led to observance of a stricter separation of powers doctrine, it is sometimes contended that the HRA 1998 has undermined the separation of powers by creating conditions for greater 'politicisation' of the judiciary.[103] The argument has been made that the HRA 1998 increases the politicisation of the judiciary by giving judges substantial power to effect significant social and political change. This objection is also presented as a claim that the HRA 1998 invites judges to be legislators, and in so doing, undermines the separation between judges and the legislature. This increased politicisation is primarily said to flow from the exercise of the judicial duty arising from section 3(1) of the Act, which states:

> So far as it is possible to do so, primary legislation and subordinate legislation must be read and given effect in a way which is compatible with the Convention rights.

Examples of the impact of section 3(1) can be seen in cases concerning equality such as *Ghaidan v Godin-Mendoza*,[104] in which succession rights for same-sex couples was in issue, cases concerning national security such as *A v SSHD*[105] in which the court ruled on central features of the Anti-Terrorism, Crime and Security Act 2001 (UK), and other cases concerning crime and punishment such as *Anderson v SSHD* in which, as discussed above, the power of the Secretary of State to set the tariff for life sentence prisoners was challenged.[106] There is voluminous literature on the distinction between legislating and interpreting and on the extent to which judges act consistently with this distinction in applying the HRA 1998. Instead of rehashing those arguments, I will comment briefly on the extent to which judges have been criticised for engaging in socio-political engineering under the HRA 1998. I maintain here that, while there has been some politicisation of judges, this should not be exaggerated, and secondly, that despite

[101] *Anderson* (n 37 above) [40] (Lord Steyn).
[102] ibid [40]–[41].
[103] Diana Woodhouse has stated that politicisation 'tends to lack definition': Diana Woodhouse, 'The English judges, politics and the balance of power' (2003) 22 *Modern Law Review* 920, 931.
[104] [2004] UKHL 30, [2004] AC 557 (HL).
[105] [2004] UKHL 56, [2005] 2 AC 68 (HL); Steve Foster, 'Anti-terrorism, Human Rights and the Constitutional Role of the Courts' (2005) 10 *Coventry Law Journal* 63, 67–70.
[106] *Anderson* (n 37 above).

increased politicisation, the overall impact of the HRA has been to fortify respect for the separation of powers in the UK.

On the issue of 'politicisation', Diana Woodhouse relies on evidence that there has been increased media investigation into the values and backgrounds of judges involved in contentious cases. She gives the example of the media inquiry into the background and religious and moral values of the judges deciding the case *Re A (Children)*,[107] regarding the separation of Siamese twin sisters where a decision not to separate them would condemn both to death whereas separation would allow one to live but result in the death of the other. In the course of the case, the court took into account the requirements of the right to life under the ECHR. However, Woodhouse saw the background scrutiny trend developing since the *Pinochet* case of 1999 and predicted that such scrutiny was 'likely to become a feature of high profile human rights cases.'[108] Of course, this sort of scrutiny could have developed independently of the HRA 1998 and indeed, did begin to develop before the implementation of the HRA 1998. We must not lose sight of the fact that judges were engaged in controversial fundamental rights review prior to the HRA 1998. Indeed, it has been noted that for centuries, the separation of powers 'provided the means to enforce human rights though judicial review of executive action.'[109]

Judges' capacity for creating socio-political change has been lamented for years prior to the HRA 1998 by judicial review sceptics such as JAG Griffith and Adam Tomkins.[110] Woodhouse suggests that the HRA 1998 heightens these concerns by making this judicial capacity more overt. She maintains that the judicial impact in cases involving difficult moral or political decisions is more visible first, as judges must make a clear value judgment using rights language rather than the language of ordinary statutory interpretation, and, secondly, because, in her view, judges are now enabled, through the declaration of incompatibility, to effectively introduce legislation.[111] Her first proposition is convincing to some extent, with the qualification that judges in the UK have identified and protected common law 'fundamental rights', using the language of 'fundamental rights' or 'constitutional rights', for years prior to the enactment and implementation of the HRA 1998. Her latter proposition is much less convincing. The declaration of incompatibility is limited, as the name suggests, to a declaratory order:

> 4 (2) If the court is satisfied that the provision is incompatible with a Convention right, it may make a declaration of that incompatibility.

107 [2000] EWCA Civ 254, [2000] 4 All ER 961 (CA); Diana Woodhouse, 'Law and Politics: More Power to the Judges—and to the People?' (2001) 54 *Parliamentary Affairs* 223, 228.

108 Woodhouse, 'Law and Politics' (ibid) 228

109 Lord Hoffmann, 'Separation of Powers' (n 31 above) 140.

110 JAG Griffith, 'The Political Constitution' (1979) 42 *Modern Law Review* 1.

111 Woodhouse, 'Law and Politics' (n 107 above) 234.

Further, the legal impact of the declaration is expressly limited by section 4(6):

> (6) A declaration under this section ('a declaration of incompatibility')—
>
> (a) does not affect the validity, continuing operation or enforcement of the provision in respect of which it is given; and
> (b) is not binding on the parties to the proceedings in which it is made.

Therefore, it has no coercive effect as a matter of law.[112] Perhaps as a matter of politics, the impact of the declaration may be to *prompt* legislative action on the part of *Parliament* but Woodhouse's proposition that the section 4(2) power enables judges to effectively introduce legislation goes too far.

Perhaps another explanation for the increased scrutiny of judges along value-based and political lines lies in the simple fact that the extension of the court's competence in general invites greater critical attention. This point has been made by The Hon Sir Gerard Brennan, former Chief Justice of Australia, who commented that:

> [T]oday the community looks to the courts to adjudicate disputes in areas extending far beyond the areas of jurisdiction invoked 50 years ago. Reposing that function in the judiciary, the community examines judicial performance of the function more critically than hitherto.[113]

Beyond the question of politicisation, there is also the question whether the HRA 1998 has disturbed the hierarchical relationship between the Parliament and the courts. In reflecting on the changes made by the Act to the separation of powers, we see a continuation of a recurring theme in British constitutional history: the confluence of constitutional law and political reality. As a matter of strict law, it is accurate to maintain that the hierarchical relationship between the courts and the legislature remains unchanged or barely affected. From the perspective of political reality, the legislature is significantly constrained by a declaration of a court of law that a legislative provision is incompatible with human rights. Two factors produce this result. The first is the moral power of 'rights' terminology[114] and the second is the relative institutional legitimacy of the courts and Parliament on legal questions. On the institutional domains of the two branches, Tom Campbell observes that:

> Interpretation is almost universally seen as the prerogative of the courts because it is part of adjudication, and that is taken to be their exclusive function.

[112] Timothy Macklem, 'Entrenching Bills of Rights', (2006) 26 *Oxford Journal of Legal Studies* 107, 109–11; Aileen Kavanagh, *Constitutional review under the UK HRA* (n 73 above) 277–78; compare Jonathan Morgan, 'Amateur Operatics: The Realization of Parliamentary Protection of Civil Liberties' in Tom Campbell and others (eds) *The Legal Protection of Human Rights: Sceptical Essays* (Oxford University Press, 2011) 434–38.

[113] 'Judicial Independence', The Australian Judicial Conference, Australian National University, Canberra, 2 Nov 1996.

[114] Morgan, 'Amateur Operatics' (n 112 above).

> It is therefore not only politically difficult but also constitutionally questionable for parliaments to reject a court's particular interpretations or even question a court's interpretative methods.[115]

In fact, it has been argued that this political reality may soon evolve into constitutional convention and, consequently, exists at the nexus between constitutional law and politics, probably drifting further and further into the legal realm. Masterman usefully summarises the position in the following terms:

> ... as Jeffrey Goldsworthy has written: '[t]here is clearly a difference between relinquishing or disabling one's power to make certain kinds of decisions, and declining- even routinely- to exercise it.' Yet it is undeniable that to entirely avoid the consequences of a declaration of incompatibility, then the elected branches would have to articulate carefully considered reasons for so doing, and would have to face the political consequences of rejecting a judicially declared assessment of what the law requires. On this reading, borne out by the experience of the HRA to date, the coercive powers of the courts over questions of rights are significant, with a judicial declaration of incompatibility difficult to overturn.[116]

However, until this crystallisation of a constitutional convention occurs, I would submit that Alison Young's assessment that the HRA 1998 has not subverted the supremacy of Parliament over the courts is correct.[117] Without legal entrenchment of the HRA and the power of the courts to invalidate legislation, the hierarchical position remains. Indeed, Masterman's description of the interaction between courts and Parliament subsequent to the HRA 1998 indicates that, in legal terms, Parliament's hierarchical position remains, though as a political matter, Parliament would almost certainly act consistently with the court's declaration. Accordingly, while the HRA 1998 has resulted in more pronounced institutional definition and in increased power for the courts, the hierarchical dynamic outlined at the outset as part of the operation of the separation of powers in the UK remains. So at present, the legal position remains, as Christoph Möllers put it, that '[t]he Court cannot force Parliament to take action–its decisions remain formal suggestions.'[118]

[115] Tom Campbell, 'Incorporation through interpretation' in Tom Campbell and others (eds) *The Legal Protection of Human Rights: Sceptical Essays* (Oxford University Press, 2011) 87.

[116] Masterman, *Separation of Powers* (n 6 above) 58–59.

[117] Allison Young, *Parliamentary Sovereignty and the Human Rights Act* (Hart Publishing, 2008).

[118] Möllers (n 30 above) 23. Subsequent chapters will discuss in greater detail suggestions by judges in *R (Jackson) v AG* [2005] UKHL 56, [2006] 1 AC 262 and *AXA General Insurance Ltd v The Scottish Ministers* [2011] UKSC 46, [2011] 3 WLR 871 (UKSC) that the common law may provide residual power to the courts to set aside parliamentary legislation.

VI. CONCLUSION

In the Bill of Rights era, the separation of powers principle has been a key argument in support of judicial efforts to scrutinise legislative and executive interference with fundamental rights. Moreover, as Tomkins and Masterman have noted, the separation of powers is increasingly cast in 'juridical' terms.[119] It is no longer simply descriptive, but 'is increasingly used as a tool of judicial reasoning capable of lending coercive support' to the limits on governmental action.[120] In the UK there is also a shift from a functional focused separation towards greater recognition of the need for separation of personnel, particularly as between the judiciary and the executive. This shift represents part of the impact of the HRA 1998 on the structural and institutional organisation of state bodies in the UK. In this way, the HRA 1998 has sharpened the distinctions between state organs, with cases such as *Anderson* revealing that this is part of the evolution of the understanding and application of the separation of powers in the UK.

Overall, this chapter sought to demonstrate that the interaction of the separation of powers with the enforcement of fundamental rights standards by the courts is part of a complex dynamic interaction between activism and restraint, between the view of the court as the least dangerous branch and the perception of the court as the least democratic branch. The perception of the court as the least democratic branch was shown to be particularly significant in jurisdictions where parliamentary supremacy is still accepted as a mainstay of the Constitution. In jurisdictions with codified Constitutions, the application of the separation of powers is more assertive, both with respect to the content of the doctrine and its normative force, owing to the combination of constitutional judicial empowerment and relatively clear constitutional allocation of power.

[119] Adam Tomkins, 'The Rule of Law in Blair's Britain' (2007) 27 *University of Queensland Law Journal* 255, 260–61; Masterman, *Separation of Powers* (n 6 above) 244.

[120] Masterman, *Separation of Powers* (n 6 above) 244.

Part II

Functions Played by the Implied Constitutional Principles of the Rule of Law and Separation of Powers

5

Implied Principles as Interpretative Aids

I. INTRODUCTION

IT HAS BEEN said that statutory construction represents the mechanism through which the fundamentality of constitutional norms is acknowledged.[1] The interpretative exercise provides an apparatus for revealing the constitutional principles of a state and the legal content of such principles. It is with this in mind that this chapter examines the reasons for the appeal to these principles among the judiciary and the functions played by the interpretative use of such principles. The inclination towards dismissal of the impact of constitutional principles on adjudication is pronounced where principles are invoked in judicial reasoning but do not function as distinct grounds for the court's decision. This chapter confronts this inclination by analysing the ways in which principles function as interpretative devices, explaining that implied principles are used as distancing devices in hard cases, as common grounds between conflicting positions, and as tools of institutional respect.

Part II of this chapter presents the argument that the use of implied principles is designed to function as a distancing device in hard cases. This discussion incorporates Raz's notion of the use of distancing devices in delivering reasons for public decisions and the concept of 'hard cases' as articulated by Dworkin.[2] The central argument is that even where the invocation of a constitutional principle does not form the basis for the court's decision, the principle nonetheless plays an important role in distancing the decision from the personal tastes of the judge and positioning the judge as a legitimate legal decision-maker. This positioning, aided by the use of constitutional principles as sources of legal argumentation, is particularly useful in rights cases as a rebuttal to complaints that human rights adjudication is

[1] Christopher Forsyth and Mark Elliott, 'The Legitimacy of Judicial Review' [2003] *Public Law* 286.

[2] Ronald Dworkin, *A Matter of Principle* (Clarendon Press, 1986) 74; Joseph Raz, 'On the Authority and Interpretation of Constitutions: Preliminaries' in Larry Alexander (ed), *Constitutionalism: Philosophical Foundations* (Cambridge University Press, 2001) 190.

comprised of political or moral judgements, rather than legal judgments. In Part III I argue that constitutional principles can be conceptualised at a high level of generality that allows for them to function as a common ground between conflicting normative viewpoints. Using Dworkin's characterisation of principles, as these norms do not apply in an all or nothing fashion and can be accorded varying weight depending on the particulars of a case,[3] they permit flexibility that generates broad agreement with the core of the principle. Accordingly, the flexibility of principles facilitates a common ground from which normative disputes may be settled through adjudication. In Part IV, institutional tensions between courts and other state branches are highlighted, revealing the use of implied principles as tools to define the constitutional distribution of powers among the institutions of the state and to maintain mutual institutional respect for that distribution.

As a final step in examining implied constitutional principles' function as distancing devices, debates over ouster (privative) clauses are used to reveal the operation of these principles in the intercourse between the courts and Parliament, and in the discourse over the limits of judicial intervention in fundamental rights disputes. The discourse relating to privative clauses highlights an institutional element of the use of implied principles, in delineating and preserving the province of judges to conduct judicial review and adjudicate allegations of rights violations. This discussion is also indicative of constitutional principles functioning as legal norms, with the principles being cited by judges, legal commentators, and parliamentarians as sources of specific legal effects.

II. DISTANCING DEVICES IN HARD CASES

The importance of exploring the reasons for judicial recourse to invocations of implied principles is heightened in cases in which implied principles are used as interpretative aids; in such cases the decision rests on a finding that the governmental act in question violated a provision of the relevant bill of rights or was *ultra vires* the powers conferred on the governmental authority in question by statute or some other source. Accordingly, while the decision did not rest on the inconsistency of the impugned governmental act with an implied principle, one or more of the judges measured the impugned act against the requirements of the rule of law or separation of powers.

In such cases a compelling explanation for the appeal of references to implied constitutional principles in cases where the principle does not constitute the *ratio* of the decision is that they appeal to judges in *hard cases.*

[3] Ronald Dworkin, *Taking Rights Seriously* (Harvard University Press, 1978) 35; John McGarry, 'The principle of parliamentary sovereignty' (2012) 32 *Legal Studies* 577, 578–579.

A hard case exists 'when competent lawyers are divided about which decision is required because the only pertinent statutes or precedents are ambiguous, or there is no doctrinal authority directly in point, or for some other reason the law is not ... settled.'[4] Lord Steyn suggested the 'hard case' explanation for the judicial use of constitutional principles in his judgment in *R v Secretary of State for the Home Department, ex parte Pierson*. The *Pierson* case itself highlights some of the controversies surrounding such fundamental rights cases, as the court was required to address the extent of the Secretary of State's sentencing powers in relation to mandatory life sentence prisoners, as well as challenges to the legitimacy of judicial decision-making in rights cases, which was raised in argument by the Secretary of State.

A plurality of the Law Lords held that there was an unlawful increase in the minimum sentence fixed by the Secretary of State, but Lord Steyn added further comments regarding the resolution of hard cases in public law:

> The answer to the question before the House is important. It is a difficult question. Professor Neil MacCormick observed that: 'there is often a need in hard cases to dig down to the level of constitutional theory in order to solve questions about private rights and public powers': see 'Jurisprudence and the Constitution' (1983) 36 CLP 13, 20. That is so in this case. The structure of the law matters. It is necessary to find the exact location of this case on the map of public law.[5]

He then proceeded to outline what he described as the fundamental constitutional principles of the rule of law and of non-retrospectivity in sentencing. Interestingly, what Lord Steyn suggests in this excerpt from his judgment in *Pierson* is not only that principles may be useful in resolving questions in hard cases, but that the most useful principles are those which are so fundamental that they reside at the level of constitutional theory. The Law Lord's reflections on the difficulty of solving 'questions about private rights and public powers' indicates the constitutional predicament often presented by cases concerning allegations that a governmental act has interfered with individual rights.

A similar interpretative technique has more recently been called in aid to tackle the controversial issue of the court's jurisdiction to order 'closed material procedure' in civil cases. In *Al-Rawi*, a hard case involving questions of institutional power and the balance between due process rights and security interests—where there was insufficient clarity in the rulings of the European Court of Human Rights—the UK Supreme Court cited the necessity of 'the rule of law and the administration of justice' as guides to determining the circumstances under which closed material procedure may be permitted.[6]

[4] Dworkin, A Matter of Principle (n 2 above) 74.

[5] *R v Secretary of State for the Home Department, ex p Pierson* [1997] UKHL 37, [1998] AC 539 (HL) 584.

[6] *Al Rawi v Security Service* [2011] UKSC 34, [2012] AC 531 [84] (Lord Dyson).

As Lord Dyson explained, the mere consent of the parties in a case to the use of closed material procedure is not sufficient to meet the demands of the rule of law. As the issues related to administrative justice, open justice and the rule of law, much more was at stake than mutual party consent: 'the public too has a vital interest'.[7] Similar to Lord Steyn's interpretative approach in *Pierson*, the dispute in *Al-Rawi* was cast in terms of fundamental constitutional principle, affecting both the terms of the resolution of the debate and the stakes involved in the court's reasoning and decision.

The issues confronted in fundamental rights cases such as *Al-Rawi* and *Pierson* give rise to the courts' appeal to 'distancing devices' such as constitutional principles including the rule of law. Raz has argued that where public officials, including judges, are faced with the task of choosing between incommensurable reasons, they must point to rational explanations for the decisions they make. In short, they 'should develop or adopt distancing devices—devices they can rely on to settle such issues in a way that is independent of the personal tastes of the judges'.[8] This technique is particularly relevant in fundamental rights cases in which the questions confronted, as well as the active role played by courts in resolving these questions, raise concerns regarding the legitimacy of the courts' decision-making. The legitimacy issue strikes at the heart of the interplay between political constitutionalist thought and legal constitutionalist ideas.[9] The question of legitimacy asks whether the judge is actually making a legal (as opposed to political) judgment in human rights cases. Griffith, for instance, maintained that bills of rights 'merely pass political decisions out of the hands of politicians and into the hands of judges or other persons. To require a supreme court to make certain kinds of political decisions does not make those decisions any less political.'[10] If the judgment employed in rights cases is viewed as political, rather than legal, then the judge has no more authority or legitimacy in making such judgments than does a politician. In fact, the judge may have less legitimacy than a politician, holding office without the democratic imprimatur of popular election. However, legitimacy may derive from a range of sources.[11] The legitimating source depends in part on the institution in question; for courts, legitimacy derives from the extent to which the decision-making is based on legal norms, and consistent with the constitutional role of the judiciary. Therefore, in order to establish that judgments in fundamental rights cases are like other *legal* judgments, judges utilise these

[7] ibid.

[8] Raz, 'On the Authority and Interpretation of Constitutions: Preliminaries' (n 2 above) 190.

[9] Graham Gee and Grégoire Webber, 'What is a Political Constitution' (2010) 30 *Oxford Journal of Legal Studies* 273.

[10] JAG Griffith, 'The Political Constitution' (1979) 42 *Modern Law Review* 1, 16.

[11] Jeremy Waldron, *Partly Laws Common to All Mankind* (Yale University Press, 2012) 153–55.

'distancing devices'. In addition to the authority of text and rules, principles also play this role. Thus, even where the implied constitutional principle does not form part of the *ratio* in a case, a judge's reference to the principle in the reasoning may yet reveal institutional and doctrinal factors at play in the decision-making process.

What transpires through the use of implied constitutional principles is a twin dynamic of earnest judicial attempts to arrive at a correct, well-reasoned decision and an effort on the part of the court to reinforce its legitimacy within the polity as a legal institution. The first arm of the process can be labelled a process of 'internal decisional legitimation' while the second arm speaks to the court's 'external legitimacy'. While internal decisional legitimation refers to the decision-maker's engagement in activities that seek to arrive at a decision based on sound justification, external legitimacy is more outward looking and concerns the extent to which the decision-maker's activities can be justified in terms of embedded standards and others' normative expectations.[12]

In this sense, legitimacy 'encompasses the social practice of legitimation: it needs to be claimed, sustained and recognized.'[13] The internal self-reflective process is one whereby the decision-maker—for our purposes, the judge—engages in a practice that justifies to herself and to others the decision she is taking.[14] This is the manifestation of an attempt to arrive at a justifiable and justified decision and an attempt by the judge to communicate her claims to other state institutions and to the wider community. It is in this manner that constitutional principles play a role in both enabling judges to arrive at reasoned legal decisions while communicating to the outside world the court's claims to the legitimacy of its decisional power.[15] Grounding decisions in principles that supply the very groundwork of democratic constitutionalism projects a message that, far from resting on personal inclinations or political and moral preferences, the court's decision is supported by the very fabric of the Constitution.

By that process, legitimisation efforts by the courts address the legitimacy challenge often presented by rights cases by confirming and defending the judicial authority to decide the issue.[16] An illustration of this dynamic is present in the Canadian Supreme Court's approach to questions relating to amendment of the Constitution and structure of government in Canada.[17] In

[12] David Beetham, *The Legitimation of Power* (Macmillan Publishers, 1991) 11.

[13] Dominik Zaum, 'International Organisations, Legitimacy, and Legitimation' in Dominik Zaum, *Legitimating International Organizations* (Oxford University Press, 2013) 10.

[14] ibid 11.

[15] Beetham (n 12 above) 15; Zaum (n 13 above) 9.

[16] See, in connection, Zaum (n 13 above) 11.

[17] *Reference re Secession of Quebec* [1998] 2 SCR 217 (SC, Canada); *Reference re Senate Reform* [2014] 1SCR 704 (SC, Canada).

submissions in the *Secession Reference* on the substantive issue of whether there was a right to unilateral secession on the part of Quebec, there was robust opposition to the justiciability of this question.[18] Though questions of justiciability are routinely raised when a court is asked to deliver a judgment on a reference or in its advisory jurisdiction, the challenge to the Court's jurisdiction in this case was particularly pointed in suggesting that a judicial pronouncement might usurp the democratic will of Quebecers (Québécois). In crafting its opinion on this *Reference*, the court's invocation of constitutional principles of federalism, the rule of law, constitutionalism, and the protection of minorities contributed to the delineation of the 'legal framework' within which the political decision regarding secession must be resolved. The constitutional principles were advanced as norms that must be respected by the Court, the provinces, and the federal government. Having defended the Court's decision to give an answer to the reference question as being 'within its area of expertise: the interpretation of law', the constitutional principles cited were said to 'assist in the interpretation of the text and the delineation of spheres of jurisdiction, the scope of rights and obligations, and the role of our political institutions'.[19] The assistance provided by the principles was on display in the Court's reasoning that '[t]he rule of law principle requires that all government action must comply with the law, including the Constitution.'[20] Taking account of constitutional development in Canada, obedience to the rule of law and the Constitution in this case meant that there must be recognition that the political representatives of a province have bound the province 'into the future', that the Constitution is entrenched and cannot be changed by a simple majority vote in the province. This reasoning contributed to the Court's conclusion that secession of a province was, in legal terms, 'an amendment to the Constitution, which perforce requires negotiation.'[21]

A challenge presented by sceptics of the normative significance of rule of law and separation of powers is the claim that invocation of such principles is merely rhetorical. Yet, case law in which these principles are invoked actually demonstrates a derivative process that coheres with common law adjudicative practices. The derivative process of extracting specific rules from constitutional principles has been observed in the *Secession Reference* judgment's identification of the 'organising principles' of the Constitution, including the rule of law, and 'then proceeded to fashion a set of rules to govern the secession of a province of Canada, including the need for

[18] *Secession Reference* (ibid) [27].
[19] ibid.
[20] ibid [72].
[21] ibid [84].

negotiation'.[22] Similarly, in *Polyukhovich v The Commonwealth of Australia* the general separation of powers principle was seen to underpin more specific norms that proscribe bills of attainder and laws which undermine judicial decisional independence by requiring a court to give effect to the decision of an executive authority as if it were a judicial decision.[23] It is through this derivative process that constitutional principles serve as grounds of argument on which courts can and do base their application of particular norms to the facts of the case.

The spatial dynamic of distancing is particularly pronounced where the institutional or personal interests of the judiciary are at stake, in which context the principles function as techniques to situate decision-making in the normative demands of the constitution, rather than the personal and institutional interests of the judiciary. The dynamic is evident in the interpretation of separation of powers and judicial independence by the Australian High Court and the Canadian Supreme Court.[24] Constitutional principles have been enlisted by these courts to explain the need for extension of judicial independence protections to provincial courts. The separation of powers performed this function in the *Remuneration Reference*, where the Canadian Supreme Court accepted arguments that pay reductions for provincial judges constituted a violation of the right to trial by an independent and impartial tribunal under section 11(d) of the Canadian Charter of Rights and Freedoms 1982. Lamer CJ cast the case as one concerning judicial independence, which he described as a concept that was 'inextricably bound up with the separation of powers'.[25] For the Chief Justice, 'the institutional independence of the judiciary reflects a deeper commitment to the separation of powers between and amongst the legislative, executive and judicial organs of government'.[26] The distancing function was central to the decisional legitimation exercise as the decision—that only a body independent from the branches of government can order a reduction in judges' salaries[27]—resulted in the protection of the financial interests of the judiciary itself. The personal and institutional judicial interests served by the decision were such that there was (or seemed to be) an added impetus to justify the

[22] Robin Elliot, 'References, Structural Argumentation and the Organizing Principles of Canada's Constitution' (2001) 80 *Canadian Bar Review* 67, 94; See also *Reference re Senate Reform* (n 17 above) [30]–[48].

[23] *Polyukhovich v The Commonwealth* (1991) 172 CLR 501 (HC, Australia).

[24] *New South Wales v Commonwealth of Australia* (the *Wheat case*) (1915) 20 CLR 54 (HC, Australia); *Hinds v R* [1977] AC 195 (JCPC, Jamaica); *Kable v DPP (NSW)* (1996) 189 CLR 51 (HC, Australia); *Reference Re Remuneration of Judges of the Provincial Court of Prince Edward Island* [1997] 3 SCR 3 (SC, Canada).

[25] *Remuneration Reference* (ibid) [138].

[26] ibid [125].

[27] ibid [147].

decision in terms that were constitutionally embedded. In looking to the separation of powers and judicial independence as bases for the court's reasoning, the principles played an integral dual role in the court's legitimisation efforts by contributing to the reasoned decision and by communicating claims justifying the court's exercise of its authority.

In such cases regarding judicial independence, the legitimacy of the court's decision-making would be particularly vulnerable to criticism[28] on the ground that the result of the case protects personal interests and the need for a distancing device to justify the court's decision would become even more compelling. Such criticism is at its height in a case protective of the financial interests of judges, as in the *Remuneration Reference*. By relying on the constitutional text as well as constitutional principles, which the Court's jurisprudence has repeatedly embraced as part of 'the constitution',[29] the Court indicates that its judgment is guided by the appropriate legal approach to constitutional interpretation. Moreover, the connection to foundational constitutional principle seeks to clarify that protection of the independence of the judiciary serves not only judicial institutional interests, but also the constitutional balance of the state and the constitutional protections afforded to individuals within the state.

Ultimately, the attempt at distancing is an objective, an end that is not always achieved. As with other distancing techniques—such as text or framers' intent—principles are not unequivocally successful in displacing doubts about the court's role and impact in resolving difficult rights issues. The subjectivity and complexity of constitutional rights questions will often permit room for doubts about the decision-making process and conclusions of the court. Moreover, as interpretative aids, principles work alongside other interpretive techniques in serving a distancing function as well as related interpretive and institutional ends.

III. COMMON GROUND

The challenge to the legitimacy of judicial decision-making in fundamental rights cases, which the concept of distancing devices seeks to meet, is also an institutional question that requires attention to institutional theory. Viewed in the light of institutional roles, public adjudication is a means by which the court, as an institution of the state, simultaneously maintains public faith in the central values of the constitution while persuading the public of

[28] See, eg, Jean Leclair, 'Canada's Unfathomable Unwritten Constitutional Principles' (2002) 27 *Queen's Law Journal* 389.

[29] *Re: Resolution to amend the Constitution* (*Patriation Reference*) [1981] 1 SCR 753; *Wheat case* (n 24 above); *R v Kirby, ex p Boilermakers' Society of Australia* (1956) 94 CLR 254 (HC, Australia).

the constitution's continued relevance as a response to changes in society. Thus, through the process of public adjudication, the court 'allows the state to position any emerging social views within the parameters of the existing understanding of the constitution.'[30] This understanding also reflects the interaction between the use of implied principles and the common law tradition. It is allied with the view that common law adjudication plays a similar role of ensuring the responsiveness of the law to changing social mores while affirming tradition and custom. As Selznick puts it:

> By inviting argument and making the law forever fluid and debatable, the common law tradition ensures that the law that is merges with the law that ought to be ... Common law reason cannot escape social and political tradition: 'Custom must stand the test of reflection; reflection must yield to the verdict of experience.'[31]

This interplay of the future and the past, and of constancy and change, is evoked in Dworkin's concept of 'interpretative integrity'. The idea of law as integrity 'insists that legal claims are interpretive judgments and therefore combine backward- and forward-looking elements; they interpret contemporary legal practice seen as an unfolding political narrative.'[32] This concept is particularly useful in unpacking the role of public adjudication in responding to emerging social views and judges' response to hard cases in the field of fundamental rights. Accordingly, the court invokes principles that have become authoritative by public repetition in order to explain and justify changes in the understanding of the law. In so doing, the court is 'investing these new social understandings with the authoritative reputation cultivated by the public use and repetition of the "old"'.[33] This use of principles in common law courts evinces a perception of the common law as a vision of the law as both 'given' and 'adaptable'. This is the 'paradox of the common law': that it is 'centred on a vision of law as *given*—if not by divine authority, then by history and practice—and yet as *adaptable* to changing needs and circumstances.'[34]

This conceptualisation of the process of the common law assists in explaining references to the traditional principles of the rule of law and separation of powers in two contexts. The first is the development of the requirements of the law in hard cases that arise from controversial human rights issues. In this context, references to the separation of powers and rule of law may perform the function of connecting tradition with changes in society. The

[30] Eoin Carolan, *The New Separation of Powers: A Theory for the Modern State* (Oxford University Press, 2009) 14.

[31] Philip Selznick, *The Moral Commonwealth: Social Theory and the Promise of Community* (University of California Press, 1992) 450; ibid.

[32] Ronald Dworkin, *Law's Empire* (Harvard University Press, 1986) 225.

[33] Carolan (n 30 above).

[34] Selznick (n 31 above) 449.

second context occurs where there are competing views on a divisive social or political issue. In this context, references to the separation of powers or the rule of law allow the court to identify and present a notional common ground between conflicting normative positions on the issue in question.

In the first context, references to implied constitutional principles enable judges to tie traditional values with changes in society, thereby allowing judges to anchor evolution of the law and social mores to traditionally accepted principles. Accordingly, in *Ghaidan,* the House of Lords cited changing societal perceptions regarding the appropriate treatment of gay couples as one element in favour of including gay couples within the scheme for succession to secure tenancies.[35] The Law Lords held that the exclusion of gay partners from secure tenancies violated the right to privacy, in conjunction with the right to non-discrimination. In delivering the judgment of the majority, Lord Nicholls invoked the rule of law in admonition of discriminatory law.[36] Linking such evolution in social mores and the evolution in the law that would result from the court's decision to the need to respect the rule of law provided an air of tradition to an otherwise progressive development in the law and society, particularly as the decision showed a strong use of the interpretative power of the court under section 3 of the HRA 1998.

In the second context, as the rule of law and separation of powers are widely accepted by judges as foundational constitutional principles, references to them provide a foothold of mutual understanding between conflicting normative positions on the issue in question. An issue as morally and politically divisive as the legality of assisted suicide has been presented partly in rule of law terms in the UK Supreme Court decision in *R (Nicklinson) v Ministry of Justice*, where the terms of the ECHR and the judgments of the Strasbourg Court provided insufficient guidance. While the House of Lords had previously indicated that the rule of law required guidance on the policy to be used by the Director of Public Prosecutions in determining whether to prosecute for assisted suicide,[37] the rule of law was also invoked by Lord Sumption in *Nicklinson* to clarify that the DPP could not be required to pre-emptively exempt certain persons from prosecution.[38] The iterative use of the rule of law in *Purdy* and *Nicklinson* on the issue of the extent of policy guidance required to be published on assisted suicide is indicative of both the enduring relevance of the unifying common ground role of constitutional principles and the use of principles as norms applied to specific issues to achieve legal conclusions.

[35] *Ghaidan v Godin-Mendoza* [2004] UKHL 30, [2004] 2 AC 557 (HL) [55] (Lord Millett).
[36] ibid [9] (Lord Nicholls).
[37] *R (Purdy) v Director of Public Prosecutions* [2009] UKHL 45, [2009] 3 WLR 403 (HL).
[38] *Nicklinson v Ministry of Justice* [2014] UKSC 38, [2014] 3 WLR 200 [238] (UKSC).

Of course, beyond the common ground of respect for the 'rule of law' or 'separation of powers' lie profound debates about the true content of such principles. However, there is a level of indeterminacy in many constitutional and rights norms—whether written or unwritten, rules or principles—which results in inevitable substantive disagreements on the part of interpreters. So for instance, there is spirited debate about which conception of the rule of law is desirable, often manifesting in tensions between more formalistic views on the rule of law and the more substantive conceptions of the rule of law.[39] These tensions were reflected in the decision of the Judicial Committee of the Privy Council in *Lewis v Attorney General for Jamaica* that the 'protection of the law' invokes the rule of law and that the rule of law required the completion of the appellants' international human rights petitions and consideration of the reports of the human rights bodies in the appellants' petitions for mercy before the Jamaican Privy Council.[40] The latter holding on the procedure for the applications for mercy departed from previous decisions of the Judicial Committee of the Privy Council which had held that the exercise of the prerogative of mercy fell outside the realm of constitutional rights protections.[41] This departure from previous authority led to a rather different application of the rule of law by the dissenting judge in *Lewis*, Lord Hoffmann. For Lord Hoffmann, 'If the Board feels able to depart from a previous decision simply because its members on a given occasion have a "doctrinal disposition to come out differently", the rule of law itself will be damaged and there will be no stability in the administration of justice in the Caribbean.'[42] Accordingly, while Lord Hoffmann applied the rule of law as a need for certainty in the law, the majority adopted an application that resulted in greater procedural protection for persons sentenced to death.

Similar conflicts in the configuration of the rule of law arose in contested decisions in *Regina (Corner House Research) v Director of the Serious Fraud Office*. Both the Divisional Court's ruling that the Director of the Serious Fraud Office erred in discontinuing an investigation in the wake of threats from Saudi Arabia and the House of Lords' contrary judgment that the Director's decision was lawful, made use of rule of law arguments. The cleavage between the decisions resonates in divergent conceptions of the rule of law whereby the Divisional Court articulated an application of the rule of law that privileged adherence to the law above threats while Lord Bingham's approach, in the House of Lords, was to uphold the Director's

[39] NW Barber, 'Must Legalistic Conceptions of the Rule of Law Have a Social Dimension?' (2004) 17 *Ratio Juris* 474; Alison L Young, 'The Rule of Law in the United Kingdom: Formal or Substantive?' (2012) 6 *Vienna Journal on International Constitutional Law* 259; Graham Gee and Grégoire Webber, 'Rationalism in Public Law' (2013) 76 *Modern Law Review* 708.

[40] *Lewis v Att Gen of Jamaica* [2001] 2 AC 50 (JCPC, Jamaica) 82–85.

[41] *Reckley (No 2)* [1996] AC 527 (JCPC, Bahamas) 539–542.

[42] Lewis (n 40 above) 90.

decision by funnelling rule of law requirements through the ordinary rules of judicial review. Thus, while the course chosen by House of Lords has been assailed as unduly deferential and unsupportive of the rule of law,[43] the more accurate assessment is that the decisions reflected varying views of the rule of law's implications.

Notwithstanding these stark representations of the distinction between general acceptance of the implied principle and the specific application of that principle, the likelihood of conflicting interpretations is certainly not unique to implied constitutional principles; textual norms are similarly susceptible to differing interpretations. Contested interpretations are part and parcel of judicial construction of constitutions and bills of rights, which leaves requires judges to act as 'mediators between the high generalities' of the constitution and 'the messy detail of their application to concrete problems'.[44] Thus, the meaning of the terms 'equality' and 'discrimination' lead to fiercely differing interpretations and the concept of human dignity which has appeared in multiple constitutions and human rights texts since the 1940s continues to perplex courts and commentators.[45] The task of interpretation in constitutional and rights cases is one that is subject to substantive evaluation on the part of the interpreter and, as explained by Lord Hoffmann, 'the concepts used in a constitution ... may expressly state moral and political principles to which judges are required to give effect in accordance with their own conscientiously held views of what such principles entail.'[46] The constitutional interpretive process is therefore one that inexorably involves a level of indeterminacy and interpretive contestation. What constitutional principles—alongside constitutional text—accomplish is measured consensus on the terms of the debate and on the doctrinal mechanisms for resolution of constitutional and rights issues.[47] They provide processes and tools for 'managing disagreement'[48] about the public good and individual rights.

[43] Jeffrey Jowell, 'Caving In: Threats and the Rule of Law' (2008) 13 *Judicial Review* 273, 275–276.

[44] *Boyce v R* [2004] UPKC 32, [2005] 1 AC 400 (JCPC, Barbados) [28] (Lord Hoffmann).

[45] Hugh Collins, 'Equality, Discrimination and Social Inclusion' (2003) 66 *Modern Law Review* 16; Christopher McCrudden 'Equality and Discrimination' in David Feldman (ed) *English Public Law* (Oxford University Press, 2009); Christopher McCrudden, 'Human Dignity and Judicial Interpretation of Human Rights' (2008) 19 *European Journal of International Law* 655.

[46] *Matadeen v Pointu* [1998] 3 WLR 18 (JCPC, Mauritius) 25.

[47] Constitutional principles play a similar role in constitutional design, as in the negotiation and drafting of the Interim and Final Constitution of South Africa. See Heinz Klug, 'South Africa's Experience in Constitution-Building' available at http://papers.ssrn.com/sol3/papers.cfm?abstract_id=1808168 (accessed 9 September 2016) 3–5, 19, 31–38.

[48] David Feldman, 'Which in Your Case You Have Not Got: Constitutionalism at Home and Abroad' (2011) 64 *Current Legal Problems* 117, 123.

IV. INSTITUTIONAL RESPECT

At the core of every Constitution is an exercise in the allocation of state power and the creation and maintenance of a constitutional balance of power. Exactly where this balance lies is, of course, dependent on the particulars of constitutional design of respective states, but the operation of the rule of law and separation of powers underpinning the constitution function as tools to maintain the institutional divisions and interactions required by the constitution and thereby facilitate continuing constitutional stability. The separation of powers and those facets of the rule of law that speak to institutional design and respect—specifically the independence of the judiciary and the requirement of access to courts—are invoked in rights cases as indicators of the institutional distribution required of the constitution.

In the United Kingdom, judicial opinions address concerns for institutional respect in adjudicating rights issues by seeking a balance between respect for parliamentary supremacy and responsiveness to the oft-repeated constitutional staple that 'society depends on the courts to act as guardians of the rule of law.'[49] The UK Supreme Court's approach to the compatibility of the ban on assisted suicide with Convention rights in *Nicklinson* was significantly impacted by such considerations. As Lord Mance phrased it, in weighing rights against public interests and convictions, the court 'will attach great significance to the judgment of the democratically informed legislature' while being mindful that 'the function of independent judges charged to interpret and apply the law is ... a cornerstone of the rule of law'.[50] It is in line with this division of power that the Court decided to defer to Parliament to deliberate and legislate further on the legality of assisted suicide while reaffirming its jurisdiction to order a declaration of incompatibility upon convincing evidence of the inconsistency of the law with rights under the ECHR.

A. Ouster Clauses and Access to Court

The struggle over ouster clauses provides useful case studies that reveal the role of implied constitutional principles in attempts to settle and maintain the constitutional allocation of powers. There has been a lengthy dialogue between the courts and parliament on the acceptable scope of ouster clauses, with the rule of law and separation of powers emerging as powerful bases

[49] *A v British Broadcasting Corporation* [2014] UKSC 25, [2015] 1 AC 588 (UKSC) [23] (Lord Reed). See also SA De Smith et al in Lord Woolf and others (eds), *De Smith's Judicial Review*, 6th edn (Sweet & Maxwell, 2007), para 5-016.

[50] *Nicklinson* (n 38 above) [190] (Lord Mance).

of argumentation within that conversation. In this section of the chapter, I highlight three case studies that demonstrate this point well. While the focus of this discussion is on case law emerging out of these case studies, I will also note discussions outside the courtroom by legal and political actors that contributed to the course of these debates. In these cases as well as the arguments advanced by legal commentators, practitioners and parliamentarians, implied principles are employed as a source of other norms relating to access to courts and supervisory jurisdiction by courts over tribunals and other bodies. The principles thereby assist not only in the demarcation of institutional roles, but also the inter-institutional relationship of state organs. This dynamic is evident in three case studies. The first centres on the Foreign Compensation Act 1950 (UK) and the *Anisminic* case, the second concerns the Asylum and Immigration Appeals Tribunal Bill, and the third concerns the Tribunals, Courts and Enforcement Act 2007 (UK) and the *Cart v Upper Tribunal* case.

The *Anisminic* case arose as a challenge to the decision of the Foreign Compensation Commission (FCC), established under the Foreign Compensation Act 1950. Under the Act, the FCC had the responsibility of distributing funds received from foreign governments to compensate for losses suffered by British nationals in overseas territories. The appellants Anisminic Co. Ltd made an application to the FCC claiming that they were entitled to participate in the Egyptian Compensation Fund. The FCC made a determination that Anisminic had sold its property to another company, that that company was the appellants' successor in title, and that, as the successor was not a 'British national' as required under the Foreign Compensation Act, Anisminic had not established its claim that it was entitled to receive compensation from the Fund.

Anisminic brought an action against the FCC for declarations that the Commission's determination was a nullity and that the appellants were entitled to participate in the Fund. On appeal, the House of Lords held that the FCC had made an error of law. The House of Lords had to overcome the hurdle of an ouster clause in section 4(4) of the Act, which read: 'The determination by the Commission of any application made to them under this Act shall not be called in question in any court of law.' A majority of the House of Lords surmounted this hurdle by holding that the FCC made an error of law as to the very breadth of its powers, so since the FCC's error was a jurisdictional error, their 'determination' was a nullity and, in truth, no determination at all. Accordingly, the ouster clause was inapplicable. While *Anisminic* was not a 'fundamental rights case' properly so called, the decision and its aftermath reveal applications of implied constitutional principles that have implications for the use of these principles in fundamental rights adjudication. The House of Lords' response to the ouster clause contributed to discussions on ouster clauses in cases where rights were engaged, as well as to the development of discourse on access to courts as a fundamental right.

The bold judgment in *Anisminic* elicited a strong and swift reaction of the Government to shield decisions of the FCC from judicial scrutiny but the breadth of the privative clause proposed by the Government led to powerful rule of law arguments being made within the legal fraternity and even by judges themselves in their capacity as members of the House of Lords. The Government quickly introduced an amendment to a Foreign Compensation Bill which happened to be before the House of Commons, the purpose of the amendment being retrospective nullification of the *Anisminic* decision. The Bill passed the House of Commons but then met with fierce opposition.

The legal profession reacted strongly, with a joint letter to *The Times* from Desmond Ackner, Chairman and General Council of the Bar, and H Edmund Sargant, President of the Law Society, protesting the proposed provision. The letter, entitled 'Foreign Compensation Bill: Threat to the Rule of Law', argued that the provision's attempt to remove judicial scrutiny of the FCC's decisions 'is a serious encroachment on the Rule of Law and in our view should not be made part of the law of this country save after full and thorough debate and then only for compelling reasons.'[51] These eminent lawyers ended their letter by stating that they 'consider that it is an undesirable development of the law to make the Commission sole and final judges of the limits of their own jurisdiction and to take away from the Courts the power, which they have always possessed and which is a vital facet of the Rule of Law, of ensuring that an inferior tribunal keeps within the four walls of whatever limited jurisdiction the legislature has entrusted to it.'[52] The letter was published on the morning of 3 February and that very afternoon, when the Bill was debated in the House of Lords, the privative clause was met with withering attacks from Peers. A strong amendment was introduced and passed by the House of Lords, an amendment which was supported by the Law Lords sitting in the Upper Chamber.

In the Upper Chamber, Lord Denning levelled a scathing attack against the amendment, protesting that 'It was one of the cardinal features of the rule of law in this country that tribunals and other bodies should in the last resort be controlled by the judges of the High Court or of the Court of Appeal'.[53] The remarks of Lord Denning and the Law Society and Bar Council letter identify the extraction from the rule of law of a specific norm that courts should have supervisory jurisdiction over tribunals and executive bodies. Ultimately, the Government capitulated; the eventual provision in the Foreign Compensation Act provided for appeal to the Court of Appeal on points of law. Otherwise, except in cases of breach of natural

[51] Desmond Ackner QC and Edmund Sargant, 'Foreign Compensation Bill: Threat to the Rule of Law' *The Times* (London, 4 February 1969).

[52] ibid.

[53] HL Debate 4 February 1969, vol 299, col 55; See also Hugh Noyes, 'Lords Attack Foreign Compensation Bill', *The Times* (5 February 1969).

justice, all determinations (including purported determinations) were shielded from judicial review.

A similar dynamic occurred in the second case study: the dispute over the Asylum and Immigration Appeals Tribunal. Analysing the saga that developed over this issue, Richard Rawlings aptly described the conflict as one that raised 'a series of linked themes', including 'the practical interplay of rule of law arguments with developments in common law constitutionalism; and an expanded role for legal elements in the political process.'[54] The Asylum and Immigration (Treatment of Claimants, etc) Bill was introduced in response to government concern about the extent of, and delays engendered by judicial supervision of the immigration and asylum process through appeals and judicial review. The Bill sought to address the government's concerns through three prongs: restriction of the availability of funding for legal services in such cases; reduction of the formal right of appeal by abolition of the Immigration Appeal Tribunal; and ouster of the supervisory jurisdiction of the court regarding status determination decisions in immigration and asylum cases.

It is the third prong that is most relevant to this discussion the ouster clause which appeared in clause 14 of the Bill:[55]

(1) No court shall have any supervisory or other jurisdiction (whether statutory or inherent) in relation to the Tribunal.
(2) No court may entertain proceedings for questioning (whether by way of appeal or otherwise):
  (a) any determination, decision or other action of the Tribunal (including a decision about jurisdiction) ...

Subsection 3 of the clause then proceeded to plug any potential loopholes that might permit the courts to intervene:

(1) Subsections (1) and (2):
  (a) prevent a court, in particular, from entertaining proceedings to determine whether a purported determination, decision, or action of the Tribunal was a nullity by reason of:
    (i) lack of jurisdiction;
    (ii) irregularity;
    (iii) error of law;
    (iv) breach of natural justice; or
    (v) any other matter [save for a Tribunal member acting in bad faith].

Notably, in light of *Anisminic*, the clause would have prevented the court from inquiring into a 'purported determination'. This fact was noted by

[54] Richard Rawlings, 'Review, Revenge and Retreat' (2005) 68 *Modern Law Review* 378, 378.

[55] Formerly clause 11, when the Bill was before the House of Commons.

Lord Mackay of Clashfern (a former Lord Chancellor) in debate in the Upper Chamber:

> Those who are familiar with that branch of the law will recognise those words as coming from a speech of the late Lord Reid in the case of Anisminic. Those were the grounds on which he held that the decision of the Foreign Compensation Commission in that case was not protected by the statutory ouster ... However broad that protection is, if there is no true determination of the commission, there is nothing to protect. Alert to that problem, those who have put the Bill together sought to avoid it.[56]

The proposed ouster clause was subjected to pointed critique by members of the legal profession, including members of the senior judiciary. The rule of law and separation of powers occupied a central place in those critiques. Within Parliament, the clause was assailed by the Joint Committee on Human Rights on the ground that '[o]usting the review jurisdiction of the High Court over the executive is a direct challenge to a central element of the rule of law, which includes a principle that people should have access to the ordinary courts to test the legality of decisions of inferior tribunals.'[57] In referring to the clause as 'a serious affront to the rule of law', Lord Mackay of Clashfern specified that removing access to the courts even in the face of a breach of natural justice 'strikes at the very heart of the rule of law'.[58] In thoughtful extra-judicial comments on the Bill, the Lord Chief Justice, Lord Woolf, revealed that:

> This clause is undoubtedly unique in the lengths to which it goes in order to prevent the courts from adjudicating on whether the new appeal tribunal has acted in accordance with the law. As the House of Commons Constitutional Affairs Committee stated in its report of 26 February: '... As a matter of constitutional principle some form of higher judicial oversight of lower Tribunals and executive decisions should be retained. This is particularly true when life and liberty may be at stake.' Extensive consultation took place with myself and other members of the judiciary before the Bill was introduced. ... our advice was that a clause of the nature now included in the Bill was fundamentally in conflict with the rule of law and should not be contemplated by any government if it had respect for the rule of law.[59]

These critiques indicate a continuing dialogue between the judiciary and the government that preceded even the introduction of the Bill.[60] Further, the pointedness and specificity of the comments reveal that the references

[56] HL Deb 15 March 2004, vol 659, col 67 (Lord Mackay of Clashfern).
[57] Fifth Report of Session 2003–04, HL Paper 35, HC 304, 10 February 2004, para 57.
[58] ibid.
[59] Lord Woolf, 'The Rule of Law and a Change in the Constitution' (2004) 63 *Cambridge Law Journal* 317, 328.
[60] The wisdom and constitutional propriety of this form of informal dialogue is open to doubt. See Rawlings, 'Review, Revenge and Retreat' (n 54 above) 400, 410.

to the rule of law were not mere rhetorical grandiloquence; the comments reveal that in the view of these judges and other legal professionals, access to courts and judicial supervision of the executive are essential to the maintenance of the rule of law.[61] Incidentally, these are elements of the rule of law that have been recently identified by a plurality of the UK Supreme Court in *Evans* as constitutional principles that must guide the court's statutory interpretation.[62] The critiques therefore reveal a clear attempt to marshal a legal principle in the context of a political debate in order to achieve a legal consequence. The manner in which the rule of law was invoked in the debate in these case studies therefore supports Jowell's position that the rule of law is a legal principle from which courts can derive specific, applicable norms. This derivation of more specific norms from the implied principle is a process that has also been observed in the Canadian Supreme Court's use of constitutional principles in cases such as the *Secession Reference*.[63] Therefore, the evidence indicates that the principles do serve as grounds of argument on which lawyers and courts can and do base their application of particular norms to the legal issues.

The rule of law arguments were reinforced by the claim that the ouster clause would also offend the separation of powers by interfering with the court's constitutional sphere. Some commentators placed this separation of powers argument within the framework of the notion of dual sovereignty or bipolar sovereignty, whereby parliamentary supremacy is respected but courts remain supreme within their province. Thus, Michael Fordham in an Opinion which was presented to the Constitutional Affairs Committee, argued that:

> The modern view of the constitution is not that Parliament has sole supreme power, but that it and the Courts each have constitutional sovereignty, based on a separation of powers involving mutual respect each for the other. A statutory ouster of judicial review would trespass on the duality, separation and mutual respect. ... in reviewing and disapplying a statutory ouster of judicial review, ... the Court would be doing no more than restoring the proper division of labour reflected in the separation of powers on which 'the British constitution, though largely unwritten, is firmly based' (*Duport Steels Ltd v Sirs* (Lord Diplock)).[64]

[61] This is reflected in an opinion piece penned by Jeffrey Jowell: Jeffrey Jowell, 'Immigration Wars', *The Guardian* (London, 2 March 2004) http://www.guardian.co.uk/world/2004/mar/02/law.immigration (accessed 9 September 2016).

[62] See ch 3, Judicial Conceptions of the Rule of Law.

[63] Robin Elliot, 'References, Structural Argumentation and the Organizing Principles of Canada's Constitution' (2001) 80 *Canadian Bar Review* 67, 94.

[64] Michael Fordham, 'Common Law Illegality of Ousting Judicial Review' (2004) 9 *Judicial Review* 86, 92 (citations omitted). These arguments were echoed by the Joint Committee on Human Rights: Fifth Report of Session 2003-04, HL Paper 35, HC 304, 10 February 2004, paras 58–60. For more on dual sovereignty, see Sir Stephen Sedley, 'The Common Law and the Constitution' in Michael Patrick Nolan and others (eds), *The Making and Remaking of the British Constitution* (Blackstone Press, 1997); Paul Craig, 'Public Law, Political Theory and Legal Theory' [2000] *Public Law* 211.

According to this reasoning, if the courts were to 'disapply' the ouster clause, they would be justified on the ground that they were acting within the judicial province, in which judges are supreme. Further, they would be taking the necessary measures to protect constitutional fundamentals—the rule of law and separation of powers—and to maintain mutual respect between the courts and Parliament. The marshalling of the dual sovereignty approach in addition to rule of law arguments in this context is that the dual sovereignty approach seeks to resolve the tension between the rule of law as protected by the courts, and parliamentary supremacy, by framing the issue in the language of the separation of powers. Within a separation of powers framework, the courts would be entitled—in fact, duty-bound—to protect the rule of law against any encroachments, even encroachments by Parliament.

The furore over the provision and the warnings issued by members of the senior judiciary were heeded by the government, which agreed to withdraw clause 14 from the Bill. The significance of the warnings by the judiciary was noted by Lord Donaldson in a debate on the Bill in the Upper Chamber:

> My Lords, many people, both within and outside this House, have condemned the ouster provisions ... as a constitutional outrage and an affront to the rule of law. Suffice it to say that I wholeheartedly agree. Fortunately, it appears that the Government have now had second thoughts. We need not, therefore, stop to consider, as otherwise we would have done, what would and should have been the response of the judiciary had the clause been law, interesting and important though that would have been.[65]

The government settled on a provision that allowed some (albeit limited) access to the courts for appeal for error of law and appeals on a point of law.[66] Though the expansive ouster clause was removed from the Asylum and Immigration Bill before it was enacted, the conversation regarding the extent to which tribunals could be placed outside the reach of the courts persisted. That conversation led to the Tribunals, Courts and Enforcement Act 2007 (UK) (Tribunals Act) and became part of the context of *Cart v Upper Tribunal* in which the issue was the scope for judicial review of unappealable decisions of the Upper Tribunal established by the Tribunals Act 2007.[67] The Act sought to unify the tribunals system, in response to the recommendations of the Report of the Legatt Committee. It created a unified structure, with a First-tier tribunal and an Upper Tribunal organised into chambers, each of which had its own president. Section 3(5) of the Act provides that 'The Upper Tribunal is to be a superior court of record'. An important contextual note here is that when the government was developing its proposals for reform of the asylum and immigration decision-making

[65] HL Deb 15 March 2004, vol 659, col 72.
[66] Asylum and Immigration (Treatment of Claimants etc) Act 2004 (UK), s 26(6).
[67] [2011] UKSC 28, [2012] 1 AC 663.

process, one of the suggestions was that the Immigration Appeal Tribunal should be reframed as a superior court of record. This suggestion and its purpose were advanced in the government's White Paper of February 2002, in which it was explained that 'As a Superior Court of Record there should be no scope for judicial review of its decisions, particularly of refusals to grant leave to appeal that are made in an attempt to frustrate removal.'[68] The proposal was shelved following what a minister from the Lord Chancellor's department referred to as 'helpful discussions' with senior members of the judiciary. That the Upper Tribunal that emerged from the Tribunals Act of 2007 was legislatively termed a 'superior court' serves as a further reminder of the continuing nature of discussions regarding the supervisory jurisdiction of the ordinary courts over administrative tribunals.

The Upper Tribunal has three roles, operating first as a tribunal of first instance for some matters, secondly, as a tribunal exercising judicial review jurisdiction which is equivalent to that of the High Court in England and Wales or Northern Ireland, and thirdly, as an appellate body hearing appeals on a point of law arising from a decision of the First-tier tribunal. There is no express provision in the Act limiting the supervisory jurisdiction of the High Court but the question arose whether the system established by the Tribunals Act 2007 had the effect of limiting the exercise of that jurisdiction. The theme of mutual respect emerged again as the Supreme Court held unanimously that in order to provide the independent scrutiny required by the rule of law, while respecting the tribunal structure established under the Act, judicial review by the High Court of Upper Tribunal decisions was not excluded and should be exercisable upon the same criteria for which permission to make an appeal to the Court of Appeal was granted.[69] Most significantly, the rule of law was not merely raised as dicta but formed part of the *ratio decidendi* in the Supreme Court judgment. The judgment was built solidly and explicitly on the ground that the rule of law is the basis of judicial review and, accordingly, the ultimate factor in interpreting the relevant terms of the Tribunals Act 2007 was the scope of supervisory jurisdiction over the tribunals system demanded by the rule of law. Hence, Lady Hale's judgment, with which all the other justices concurred, stated that '*[t]he real question*, as all agree, is what level of independent scrutiny outside the tribunal structure is required by the rule of law.'[70]

Deployment of the language of the rule of law serves as a meaningful part of the dialogic interchange between the judiciary and Parliament and supports the argument that the rule of law is used as an anchor for common

[68] Home Office, *Secure Borders, Safe Haven: Integration with Diversity in Modern Britain* (Cm 5387, 2002), para 466.

[69] *Cart* (n 67 above) [37], [56]–[57].

[70] *Cart* (n 67 above) [51] (emphasis added).

values that transcend issues, political positions, and even institutions. This is not to suggest that multiple institutions and normative contingents mean the same thing when they speak or hear the language of the rule of law, and it is not to propose that there is no difference between the rule of law as legal principle, as political principle, and the rule of law in any of its other permutations. What is evident is that there is substantial power in this language, and this power sounds across institutions and across political factions. Accordingly, lawyers and judges are able to deploy rule of law language convincingly in a dialogue with the Executive and Parliament.

The application of the rule of law and separation of powers by courts in the United Kingdom is affected and limited by the dominant constitutional principle operative in the UK Constitution: parliamentary supremacy. Indeed, parliamentary supremacy affects the constitutional balance that the courts seek to maintain, with courts acknowledging that their interpretative exercise must ultimately bow to, and avoid trampling, parliamentary supremacy. The division of power shifts under written constitutions under which courts are empowered to invalidate unconstitutional legislation. Courts in such jurisdictions have been insistent that within a separation of powers construct, the courts would be entitled—in fact, duty-bound—to protect the rule of law against encroachments, even encroachments by Parliament. That line of argument is seen in full force in *Plaintiff S/157* in which the Australian High Court imposed a limited construction of a clause in the Migration Act 1958 (Cth) which—similarly to the draft Asylum and Immigration Bill (UK)—sought to exclude decisions (including 'purported decisions') from the scope of judicial review. In Australia, where the Commonwealth of Australia Constitution Act 1900 provided doctrinal impetus to separation of powers arguments, Gleeson CJ remarked that in addition to the rule of law:

> In a federal nation, whose basic law is a Constitution that embodies a separation of legislative, executive, and judicial powers, there is a further issue that may be raised by a privative clause. It is beyond the capacity of the Parliament to confer upon an administrative tribunal the power to make an authoritative and conclusive decision as to the limits of its own jurisdiction, because that would involve an exercise of judicial power.[71]

The court's supervisory jurisdiction over the Refugee Review Tribunal was secured through the interpretive influence of the rule of law as a requirement for executive obedience to the law and the separation of powers as protection of the exclusivity of judicial power.

[71] *Plaintiff S157/2002 v Commonwealth* of Australia [2003] 211 CLR 476 (HC, Australia) [9] Gleeson CJ. For an alternative account of UK and Australian courts' treatment of privative clauses, see David Dyzenhaus, *The Constitution of Law: Legality in a Time of Emergency* (Cambridge University Press, 2006) 102–17.

Similarly, the Privy Council has employed the separation of powers to interpret statutory provisions interfering with access to courts, though in a case implicating a tension between parliamentary privilege and access to courts. In a claim against the Government of St Vincent and the Grenadines for constitutional relief, the appellant in *Toussaint (Randolph) v Attorney-General of St Vincent and Grenadines* sought to rely upon a statement allegedly made by the Prime Minister during a budget debate.[72] The Attorney-General applied to strike out the claim, arguing, inter alia, that the statement which the appellant sought to adduce in evidence was privileged pursuant to section 16 of the House of Assembly (Privileges, Immunities and Powers) Act 1966 (St Vincent and the Grenadines). Section 16 of the Privileges Act 1966 did, on its face, prevent the appellant from adducing that evidence by preventing the admissibility of evidence relating to proceedings in the House except with the permission of the Speaker of the House. In finding that there had been a violation of the appellant's right of access to court under sections 8(8) and 16 of the Constitution, the Privy Council ordered that section 16 of the Privileges Act 1966 must be read with the modifications necessary to enable evidence of the Prime Minister's statement to be admissible in the appellant's claim. In interpreting the requirements of the constitutional right of access to courts, the Board was influenced by the impact of section 16 of the Privileges Act 1966 on the separation of powers, thereby viewing the issue through the lens not only of respect for fundamental rights, but also respect for the role of the courts as a scrutineer of executive activity. Thus, in delivering the opinion of the Board, Lord Mance protested that:

> the exclusion relied upon by the Attorney General ... involves a potentially very significant inroad into the doctrine of separation of powers. Nothing in the nature of, or need to protect, parliamentary activity requires an officer of the legislature to have so unconstrained a power over the use before the courts, to explain and review executive action, of statements made in Parliament.[73]

Both *Plaintiff S/157* and *Toussaint* demonstrate the interpretive impact generated by implied principles in attempts to respect the legislative and administrative roles of other branches of government while (re)asserting the constitutionally instrumental role of the courts in interpreting the law and protecting individual rights.

The marshalling of rule of law and separation of powers arguments in construing ouster clauses and determining the contours of other restrictions on access to courts in fundamental rights cases furnish a framework for settling disputes over the jurisdiction of state organs. In particular, as legislatures and governments strive for efficiency and finality in decisions in

[72] [2007] UKPC 48, (2007) 70 WIR 167 (JCPC, St Vincent and the Grenadines).
[73] ibid [31] (Lord Mance).

sensitive areas such as immigration and asylum, these constitutional principles remain a base from which to ensure that attempts at efficiency operate within the bounds of the constitutional allocation of, and restraints on, power.

Implied constitutional principles provide a framework for resolving disputes; reliance on these principles as an interpretive technique does not lead to identical results, and in particular, does not automatically produce wider access to court in each individual case. For instance, reflecting on the *Cart* case, while the Divisional Court, the Court of Appeal, and the Supreme Court in *Cart* employed the same category of application of the rule of law—that is, the rule of law as a requirement of supervisory jurisdiction by an independent judicial source—the resulting interpretation of the Tribunals Act 2007 by the two appellate bodies diverged.[74] The Court of Appeal sanctioned review of the Upper Tribunal where there was outright excess of jurisdiction or fundamental denial of justice but not where the tribunal made an error of law within jurisdiction. The Supreme Court, on the other hand, preferred an alternative formulation which allowed judicial review of the Upper Tribunal using the same criteria upon which applications for permission to make a second-tier appeal to the Court of Appeal were determined. The Supreme Court thus 'made it clear that it envisaged judicial review in circumstances broader than those for which the lower courts' decisions in *Cart* would have allowed.'[75] Nonetheless, what the reasoning in the cases does indicate are first, an emerging similarity of interpretive technique and methodology and, secondly, a framework for resolving issues of access to courts, regardless of the result in the particular case.

V. CONCLUSION

Rather than dismissing as inconsequential judges' invocations of implied constitutional principles, these references are better understood as tools to determine the spheres of decision-making authority of respective institutions, and decide the normative terms on which decisions should be made. The continued function of implied constitutional principles as an interpretive technique is the product of a mixture of historical, institutional, and rhetorical factors. This chapter advanced some reasons for the methodological choice to refer to constitutional principles, central among those being that the principles function as distancing devices in hard cases, that they furnish a common basis from which to argue and resolve normative disputes and that

[74] See discussion in Mark Elliott and Robert Thomas, 'Tribunal justice and proportionate dispute resolution' [2012] *Cambridge Law Journal* 297.
[75] ibid 307–08.

they serve as tools to assist in the delineation and maintenance of respect for institutional boundaries. Judicial decisions thereby make use of the implications of the separation of powers and the rule of law for the organisation and relationship of state institutions and for the relationship between the individual and state organs. The constitutional allocation of power in the state in turn influences the incidence and manner of 'principled reasoning'; therefore, we can discern the interpretative use of implied principles taking on special significance in the United Kingdom. As we see in the following chapter, constitutionally conferred powers lead to implied principles serving a more significant role as invalidating grounds in those countries that have adopted codified constitutions and judicial review of legislation.

6

Implied Principles as Grounds for Invalidating Legislation

I. INTRODUCTION

THE PHENOMENON WHEREBY judges either use the implied constitutional principles of the rule of law and the separation of powers to invalidate legislative provisions, or assert that these principles may be used as grounds for invalidation of legislation, have constitutional and institutional implications beyond the use of implied constitutional principles as interpretative aids. When used as an interpretative aid, the interpreted text itself remains the ground on which legislation is invalidated, however when an implied principle becomes the ground of invalidation, the court's decision is based not on the text, but on a principle that is not expressed in substantive provisions of the constitutional or rights instrument. Part II of this chapter proposes that there are three circumstances that give rise to the use of implied constitutional principles as a ground for invalidating legislation or an assertion of the power to do so. The first occurs where there is a gap in the Bill of Rights with respect to the fundamental right or interest that appears to be engaged in the case before the court. That is, where the case before the court arguably engages a particular individual right but the Bill of Rights does not expressly guarantee this right. The second circumstance occurs where there is a gap in the constitutional text relating to the court's power to invalidate legislation. Finally, in the third scenario the legislation at issue challenges or removes the court's power of review of governmental action that affects individual rights. This third category differs from the second in that the challenge to the court's power comes not from the Bill of Rights itself but from subsequent legislation.

Dissecting and analysing the case law in those three categories exposes common threads, which leads to the argument in Part III of the chapter that two trends are evident in the case law that arises in this area. First, where courts have invalidated legislation on the basis of an implied constitutional principle or otherwise asserted the power to do so, they have relied on an application of the principle that protects jurisdictional boundaries. Jurisdictional boundaries transcend both principles as they may reflect the separation of powers principle or an application of the rule of law as a requirement of the separation of state organs. Secondly, courts are most protective of the borders of the judicial sphere; accordingly an implied principle is sometimes used as a proxy or synonym for separation and protection of the judicial branch from other branches. Against this background, Part III will also discuss the idea that invalidation on a jurisdictional basis allows for judicial review on structural grounds—such as an argument that a decision should be made by the judicial branch—rather than substantive grounds—such as an argument that a decision has violated a right not to be subjected to inhuman and degrading punishment. In that sense, structural bases allow the court to purport to review and potentially strike down legislation on grounds that do not involve evaluation of policy or values. Accordingly, invalidation on jurisdictional grounds may appear less interventionist and reinforce the utility of constitutional principles as devices that distance the court from value judgments. However, I also intend to demonstrate that this technique is more presentational than actual and that the attempt to present structural grounds as devoid of value judgments is ultimately unconvincing.

II. THE PRACTICE OF INVOKING IMPLIED PRINCIPLES AS GROUNDS FOR INVALIDATING LEGISLATION

A. A Gap in the Bill of Rights or Constitutional Text with Respect to the Individual Interest that is Engaged in the Case before the Court

This first category of cases is a product of jurisdictions in which there is a bill of rights or constitution that confers on the court jurisdiction to review legislation but where the rights protections lack comprehensiveness. The decision of the Privy Council in *Hinds v R* is one of the key cases that arise within this category.[1] The Privy Council invalidated sections 8 and 10 of the Gun Court Act 1974, Jamaica, on the ground that they violated the constitutional principle of the separation of powers by vesting sentencing powers in the Governor General of Jamaica and a Review Board comprised mainly of non-judicial appointees. It appears that one reason for the Privy Council's reliance on the separation of powers as the ground for striking down parts of the Gun Court Act 1974 was the judges' assumption that no provision in the Bill of Rights text clearly applied to the sentencing power at issue, that is, that there was a gap in the Bill of Rights in the Jamaican Constitution. It was not firmly established at the time of *Hinds*, in 1977, that either the right not to be deprived of liberty except in execution of the order of a court of law in section 15 of the Jamaican Constitution, or the right to trial by an impartial and independent tribunal in section 20 of the Constitution, was applicable to the facts of the case.

[1] *Hinds v R* [1977] AC 195 (JCPC, Jamaica).

At the time of *Hinds*, section 15 provided that no person should be deprived of liberty except in the execution of the order of a court of law but, again, the Privy Council in *Hinds* did not identify this right as being applicable to the facts of the case. The right was not even cited in *Hinds*. Correspondingly, section 20 included a right to trial by an independent and impartial tribunal but there are indications in the law report (Appeals Cases) that the Board did not regard this section as dispositive of the case. The Privy Council described the section in terms which seemed to limit its application to the determination of whether the defendant ought to be convicted of a crime;[2] there was no mention of the application of that provision to the sentencing stage of a trial.

This omission was, perhaps, unsurprising given the approach that was taken to the scope of section 20 in legal commentary at that time. Lloyd Barnett did not refer to sentencing as an aspect of the right to fair trial in his discussion of the rights to fair trial in his text *The Constitutional Law of Jamaica*, which, like the *Hinds* decision, was published in 1977.[3] Margaret Demerieux also made no mention of sentencing in her study of 'Constitutional Protections for the Criminally Accused', which discusses the right to trial by independent and impartial tribunal.[4] Demerieux's text, *Fundamental Rights in Commonwealth Caribbean Constitutions*, published in 1992, was one of the few leading authorities on Commonwealth Caribbean constitutional law and her treatment of the subject, together with that by Lloyd Barnett, suggests that during the time of *Hinds* (and for a significant period of time following), case law and academic thinking on Caribbean constitutional law had not yet confirmed that the vesting of sentencing powers in an officer of the executive violated the right to trial by an independent and impartial tribunal.

Further, in the Appeal Cases report, counsel for the appellants failed to invoke section 20 of the Constitution to support the argument that the conferral of sentencing powers on members of the executive was unconstitutional.[5] Instead, counsel cited structural provisions, such as section 97 of the Constitution, which provided, in subsection (1) that '[t]here shall be a Supreme Court for Jamaica which shall have such jurisdiction and powers as may be conferred upon it by the Constitution or any other law', and in subsection (4), that the 'Supreme Court shall be a superior court of record

[2] ibid 223, 225–26.

[3] Lloyd G Barnett, *The Constitutional Law of Jamaica* (Oxford University Press, 1977) ch 14.

[4] Margaret Demerieux, *Fundamental Rights in Commonwealth Caribbean Constitutions* (Faculty of Law Library, University of the West Indies, 1992).

[5] Section 20 was only invoked to argue that sections of the Gun Court Act 1974 providing for in camera proceedings were unconstitutional. This argument, which was unsuccessful, was that the 'in camera' provisions of the Gun Court Act 1974 contravened the provision in s 20(3) that court proceedings be held in public. See *Hinds* (n 1 above) 223–24.

and, save as otherwise provided by Parliament, shall have all the powers of such a court.' On this foundation, the attorneys argued that Parliament could by ordinary legislation increase the powers of the Supreme Court, but could not use ordinary legislation to erode the jurisdiction of the Supreme Court. It was also asserted in the course of argument that '[t]he structure of the Constitution shows that it was based on the principle of the separation of powers and that it was intended to preserve basic institutions and principles in existence before the Constitution came into force.'[6]

The relevance of the right to trial by an independent and impartial tribunal to the sentencing stage has now been more conclusively established. In particular, case law on Article 6 of the ECHR has established that the right includes an entitlement to have one's sentence determined by an independent and impartial tribunal, an interpretation that is assertively represented in the judgment of the House of Lords in *Anderson v Secretary of State for the Home Department*, in which the Law Lords stated that:

> as the imposition of sentence was part of a trial for the purposes of ensuring a fair hearing by an independent and impartial tribunal guaranteed by Article 6 [ECHR] and the fixing of the tariff was required to be set by such a tribunal, and the Secretary of State was neither independent of the executive nor a tribunal, he should play no part in fixing the appellant's tariff, and to that extent the appeal succeeded.[7]

The *Anderson* judgment enhances our understanding of the right to fair trial in Jamaican constitutional law for two reasons. First, the Bill of Rights in the Jamaican Constitution was modelled on the ECHR catalogue of rights. Secondly, the judges of the House of Lords (now the Supreme Court of the UK) also sit on panels of the Privy Council that decide cases on appeal from the Court of Appeal of Jamaica. Indeed, in subsequent case law from Jamaica and the wider Commonwealth Caribbean, the approach in *Anderson* has been adopted and it has become clear that the right to fair trial as outlined in section 20 includes the right to have both conviction and sentence determined by an independent and impartial tribunal,[8] but these developments post-date *Hinds*.

B. A Gap in the Power Conferred on the Court by the Bill of Rights or other Constitutional Text

The second circumstance occurs when the Bill of Rights or constitutional text does not expressly confer on the court a power to invalidate legislation,

[6] *Hinds* (n 1 above) 200.

[7] *R (Anderson) v SSHD* [2002] UKHL 46, [2003] 1 AC 837 (HL) 838.

[8] *DPP of Jamaica v Mollison* [2003] UKPC 6, [2003] 2 AC 411 (JCPC, Jamaica) [11]; *Reyes v The Queen* [2002] 2 AC 235 (JCPC, Belize) [44].

or confers a general power to invalidate legislation but omits express extension of that power to the legislation in question. This gap in judicial power is a feature of several Commonwealth Caribbean Constitutions, including the Constitution of Jamaica 1962. Section 2 of the Jamaican Constitution provides that, subject to the terms of the Constitution, 'if any other law is inconsistent with this Constitution, this Constitution shall prevail and the other law shall, to the extent of the inconsistency, be void.' Section 25 of the Bill of Rights in Chapter III of the Jamaican Constitution entitles individuals to apply to the Supreme Court of Jamaica for redress for contravention of their rights and empowers the Supreme Court of Jamaica to make such orders as it considers appropriate for the purpose of enforcing the guarantees listed in the Chapter.

The Jamaican Constitution was amended in 2011 by the Charter of Fundamental Rights and Freedoms (Constitutional Amendment) Act 2011, which replaced Chapter III with a new catalogue of rights. Prior to the 2011 amendment, the Bill of Rights provisions sat alongside a clause—referred to as the general savings law clause—that limited the power of the courts to enforce the rights provisions in Chapter III by purporting to prevent the court from invalidating legislation that pre-dated the Constitution itself. Section 26(8) of the Constitution provided that:

> Nothing contained in any law in force immediately before the appointed day shall be held to be inconsistent with any of the provisions of this Chapter; and nothing done under the authority of any such law shall be held to be done in contravention of any of these provisions.[9]

Chapter III as amended retains the power of the court to make orders for the enforcement of the rights provisions contained in the Chapter,[10] but it modifies the general savings law clause. Henceforth, the court may hold legislation pre-dating the 2011 Charter of Rights to be inconsistent with the provisions of the Bill of Rights, with the exception of legislation regarding sexual offences, obscene publications, and offences relating to the life of the unborn.[11]

The Privy Council used the implied principle technique to obviate the original general savings clause restrictions on the power of the court in *DPP v Mollison*,[12] which was decided nine years before the constitutional amendment. The respondent was a prisoner who had been convicted of a murder which was committed when he was 16 years old and was sentenced to detention during the Governor General's pleasure, in accordance with

[9] The 'appointed day' is the day when the Constitution entered into force.
[10] Constitution of Jamaica 1962, s 13(19).
[11] Constitution of Jamaica 1962, s 13(12).
[12] *Mollison* (n 8 above).

section 29 of the Juveniles Act 1951 (Jamaica). He appealed against his sentence, arguing: (i) that the sentence infringed his right, guaranteed by section 15(1)(b) of the Constitution of Jamaica, 1962, not to be deprived of liberty except in accordance with the sentence of a court; (ii) that the sentence violated his right to a fair hearing within a reasonable time by an independent and impartial tribunal, as guaranteed by section 20(1) of the Constitution; and (iii) that the sentence infringed the fundamental constitutional principle of the separation of powers because the length of the sentence was to be determined by a member of the executive rather than a member of the judiciary. It was conceded that the sentence did infringe the rights expressed in sections 15(1)(b) and 20(1) of the Constitution. However, because the Juveniles Act 1951 was a pre-1962 statute, the general savings law clause prevented the court from holding that the Act was inconsistent with the Constitution. Accordingly, the only argument that could permit the court to invalidate the sentence was the submission that the sentence infringed the implied constitutional principle of the separation of powers. Lord Bingham, delivering the judgment of the Privy Council, held that the statutory provision violated the separation of powers by vesting a sentencing power in the hands of the executive. In his words:

> Whatever overlap there may be under constitutions on the Westminster model between the exercise of executive and legislative powers, the separation between the exercise of judicial powers on the one hand and legislative and executive powers on the other is total or effectively so. Such separation, based on the rule of law, was recently described by Lord Steyn as 'a characteristic feature of democracies': *R (Anderson) v Secretary of State for the Home Department* [2003] 1 AC 837, 890–891, para 50. In the opinion of the Board, [the respondent] has made good his challenge to section 29 based on its incompatibility with the constitutional principle that judicial functions (such as sentencing) must be exercised by the judiciary and not by the executive.

In arriving at this holding, Lord Bingham said, in relation to *Hinds*, that:

> the sentencing provisions under challenge in the *Hinds* case were held to be unconstitutional not because of their repugnancy to any of the rights guaranteed by sections in Chapter III of the Constitution but because of their incompatibility with a principle on which the Constitution itself was held to be founded.[13]

What the Privy Council developed in *Mollison* was a clever technique for circumventing a textual gap in the court's power to invalidate legislation that infringes fundamental rights. With the court being barred from striking down the law for violation of fair trial rights, the implied principle of the separation of powers provided a means by which the court could fill the gap in its powers. A lacuna in the jurisdiction of the court to invalidate

[13] ibid [13].

inconsistent legislation has led the recently constituted Caribbean Court of Justice (CCJ) to follow in the steps of the Judicial Committee by finding creative grounds for protecting the fundamental rights guaranteed in the constitutions subject to the court's jurisdiction. The CCJ flexed its muscles—in a somewhat similar fashion to the Judicial Committee—in *Attorney General for Barbados v Joseph and Boyce*,[14] though the implied principle relied on by the CCJ was the rule of law, rather than the separation of powers.

Joseph and Boyce had been sentenced to death upon conviction for murder. After their appeals against sentence to the Court of Appeal and to the Judicial Committee were dismissed, they petitioned the Inter-American Commission on Human Rights (IACHR) for declarations that Barbados had violated their rights to, inter alia, life, humane treatment, and fair trial, under the American Convention on Human Rights. On the application of the IACHR, the Inter-American Court of Human Rights issued provisional measures requiring Barbados to preserve the respondents' lives pending the outcome of the IACHR proceedings. In a further application to the Court of Appeal, the respondents were successful, the Court holding that the respondents were entitled to have their executions suspended pending the outcome of the IACHR proceedings and to have the outcome of the IACHR proceedings considered in clemency proceedings in Barbados. The Attorney General appealed to the CCJ, which had by the time of the appeal replaced the Judicial Committee as the final appellate court for Barbados. The CCJ dismissed the Attorney General's appeal, holding that the respondents had a legitimate expectation that the State would not execute them without permitting a reasonable time within which their proceedings before the IACHR could be completed.

It is, however, the Court's holding that it had jurisdiction to provide redress to uphold the 'protection of the law' that is most pertinent to this discussion. The Court held that it had jurisdiction to determine whether the respondents' right to protection of the law was infringed and to provide redress if such a violation was found, though in this case it was held that the right to protection of the law was not violated. The issue arose as a result of section 11 of the Constitution of Barbados 1966, which the CCJ characterised as the preamble to the Bill of Rights Chapter in the Constitution.[15] Section 11 expresses the right to protection of the law in the following terms:

> 11. Whereas every person in Barbados is entitled to the fundamental rights and freedoms of the individual, that is to say, the right, whatever his race, place of origin, political opinions, colour, creed or sex, but subject to respect for the rights and freedoms of others and for the public interest, to each and all of the following, namely.

[14] *AG v Joseph and Boyce* (2006) 69 WIR 104 (Caribbean Court of Justice (CCJ), Barbados).
[15] ibid [58] (de la Bastide P and Saunders J).

> ...
>
> (*c*) *the protection of the law;*
>
> ...
>
> the following provisions of this chapter shall have effect for the purpose of affording protection to those rights and freedoms subject to such limitations of that protection as are contained in those provisions ...[16]

Sections 12–23 then detail the specific rights which correspond to the rights referred to in section 11, with section 24 then conferring on the court jurisdiction to provide redress for violation of sections 12–23. There is no section, however, that unambiguously corresponds with 'the protection of the law' in section 11, but section 18 most appears to correspond with the protection of law. This is indicated by its marginal note which reads 'Protection of the law', and its subject matter, which seeks to ensure that both the process of establishing guilt or innocence in criminal cases is determined as well as the determination of the existence or scope of a civil right or obligation is established, are conducted fairly.[17]

In the view of the CCJ, the terms of section 18 could not, however, be intended to capture the *full* extent of the 'protection of the law'. In support of this position, the Court referred to *Thomas v Baptiste*, in which Lord Millett stated that due process of the law, which has the same meaning as the protection of the law, invokes universal standards of justice that inhere in the rule of law.[18] Accordingly, it was argued that the court's power to provide redress for violations of the protection of the law could not be limited to section 18. De la Bastide and Saunders JJ of the CCJ summed up the Court's conclusion in this way:

> We are of the view that Lord Millett's observations on the meaning of the word 'law' in the context of the phrase 'due process of law' are equally applicable to the phrase 'protection of the law'. Procedural fairness is an elementary principle permeating both concepts and therefore, pursuant to s 11, a condemned man has a constitutional right to procedural fairness as part of his right to protection of the law. Correspondingly, *the courts have an inherent jurisdiction, and a duty, to grant an appropriate remedy for any breach of that right.*[19]

Since section 24 of the Barbadian Constitution did not grant the Court jurisdiction to provide redress for breaches of section 11, the Court asserted an 'inherent jurisdiction' to grant relief for breaches of this right, but did not elucidate the basis for this jurisdiction.

[16] Emphasis added.
[17] *Joseph and Boyce* (n 14 above) [60].
[18] *Thomas v Baptiste* [2000] 2 AC 1 (JCPC, Trinidad and Tobago) 22 (emphasis added).
[19] *Joseph and Boyce* (n 14 above) [64] (emphasis added).

Inferring from the references to the rule of law in explaining the right to due process, the root of the court's jurisdiction was the 'rule of law'.[20] This conclusion is supported by Justice Wit's more explicit judgment, which, after referring to the affirmation that 'that men and institutions remain free only when freedom is founded upon respect for moral and spiritual values and the rule of law' in the preamble to the Barbadian Constitution, continued:

> It is clear that this concept of the rule of law is closely linked to, and broadly embraces, concepts like the principles of natural justice, procedural and substantive 'due process of law' and its corollary, the protection of the law. It is obvious that the law cannot rule if it cannot protect. The right to protection of the law requires therefore not only law of sufficient quality, affording adequate safeguards against irrationality, unreasonableness, fundamental unfairness or arbitrary exercise of power; but it also requires the availability of effective remedies. These requirements are inherent in the Barbados Constitution. Section 24 which expressly guarantees the right to an effective remedy is, therefore, merely a reflection of that fundamental right to the protection of the law. Hence, the existence of that section, cannot, without more, be construed in a manner so as to limit that right or to frustrate the granting of an effective remedy for a breach of the Constitution.[21]

The positioning of the rule of law as a source of the court's jurisdiction to review legislation is also consistent with statements by members of the House of Lords in the *Jackson* case[22] that the court has a duty to safeguard the rule of law. *Jackson* is discussed in more detail in the following section of this chapter. However, for the moment, it suffices to point to Lord Steyn's dictum expressing the possibility of judicial rejection of legislation:

> In exceptional circumstances involving an attempt to abolish judicial review or the ordinary role of the courts, the Appellate Committee of the House of Lords or a new Supreme Court may have to consider whether this is constitutional fundamental which even a sovereign Parliament acting at the behest of a complaisant House of Commons cannot abolish.[23]

What is particularly momentous about this argument is that it expands upon the idea that the rule of law simply legitimises judicial review of *executive* organs, and raises the prospect of judicial review of legislation. The rule of law justification for judicial review of administrative action is championed by supporters of common law constitutionalism as a substitute for the

[20] See commentary on the Court's lack of conceptual clarity in Tracy Robinson, 'Our Inherent Constitution' in David S Berry and Tracy Robinson (eds) *Law-Making, Constitutionalism and the Convergence of National and International Law* (Ian Randle Publishers, 2013) 256–60.

[21] *Joseph and Boyce* (n 14 above) [20].

[22] *R (Jackson) v AG* [2005] UKHL 56, [2006] 1 AC 262.

[23] ibid [102].

traditional argument that the *ultra vires* doctrine justifies judicial review.[24] In an article published in 2002 Lord Steyn framed the argument in the following terms:

> As a department of state the judiciary is charged with the constitutional duty to control abuse of power by the state, its officials and emanations. In a democracy the rule of law itself legitimises judicial review. I now accept that the traditional justification in England of judicial review is no longer supportable. By overwhelming weight of reasoned argument the *ultra vires* theory has been shown to be a dispensable fiction.[25]

This is significant, because, as Lord Steyn noted in that piece, '[t]he theoretical underpinning of the principles of judicial review ... may affect their reach.'[26] This seems to be borne out by his dictum in *Jackson* and mirrors the comments made by Justice Wit in *Joseph and Boyce*, which show that perhaps the rule of law justification may be expanded so that it not only justifies review of executive action, but also justifies review of legislation in some circumstances.

Despite this significant common thread that runs through *Joseph and Boyce* and *Jackson*, an important distinction affects the lines of reasoning in the two cases. The distinction arises as a result of the doctrine of parliamentary supremacy which persists in the United Kingdom, but not in the Commonwealth Caribbean. The judges in *Joseph and Boyce*—quite correctly—did not acknowledge any need to justify their assertion that the protection of the law or the rule of law could be a basis for invalidating legislation, beyond identifying this principle within the 'unstated assumptions' of the Constitution. On the other hand, Lord Steyn in *Jackson* was at pains to restrict the normative power of the rule of law as against legislation by limiting its application to 'exceptional circumstances' and to account for its conflict with parliamentary supremacy by suggesting that in such circumstances the court would 'qualify' parliamentary supremacy by establishing a different hypothesis of constitutionalism.[27] In this respect therefore, while both *Jackson* and *Joseph and Boyce* suggest that the rule of law argument used in common law constitutionalism could be applicable to judicial review of legislation, *Joseph and Boyce* is bolder in asserting a broader, more robust role for the rule of law. In fact, it indicates that the common law constitutionalist argument coupled with a constitution that explicitly empowers the court to invalidate legislation (even if the scope of this power

[24] Justin Leslie, 'Vindicating Common Law Constitutionalism' (2010) 30 *Legal Studies* 301, 307; Lord Steyn, 'Democracy through law' (2002) 6 *European Human Rights Law Review* 723, 723, 725; TRS Allan, 'The Constitutional Foundations of Judicial Review' (2002) 61 *Cambridge Law Journal* 87, 88. See discussion of common law constitutionalism in ch 2 above.

[25] Lord Steyn (ibid).

[26] ibid.

[27] *Jackson* (n 22 above) [102].

is limited) helps to produce a more robust normative role for the rule of law, leading the court to expand the scope of legislative review.

Lord Steyn's dictum in *Jackson* was criticised by Trevor Allan who expressed dissatisfaction with the theoretical reasoning outlined in this dictum. For Allan, Lord Steyn's position in *Jackson* was based on the existence of a conflict between a commitment to parliamentary supremacy and a commitment to constitutional legal principle, including the principle of the rule of law.[28] Allan contends that this conflict could be resolved if judges would accept that the rule of law imposes limits on parliamentary supremacy. Allan therefore argues that Lord Steyn's suggestion that in 'exceptional circumstances' judges might have to 'qualify' a doctrine of parliamentary supremacy 'established on a different hypothesis of constitutionalism', is unnecessary as all such limitations on legislative supremacy as may be necessary to comply with the rule of law are already implicit in Britain's unwritten constitution.[29] Allan also protests that Lord Steyn's dictum amounts to a threat of judicial revolt in exceptional circumstances, which runs the risk of 'portraying the courts, implausibly, as free political agents in a political process disguised as constitutional adjudication.'[30] For Allan, this quandary would be solved by accepting the force of an already existing normative rule of law against Acts of Parliament. Whether one subscribes to Steyn's or Allan's position, it does demonstrate that the enduring presence of parliamentary supremacy in the UK adds a further element to discourse on the normative force of the rule of law that accounts for some of the subtle differences in approach between courts in the UK and courts of the Commonwealth Caribbean.

The continued role of parliamentary supremacy also accounts for some of the features of the use of the doctrine of separation of powers in the High Court of Australia.[31] As noted in chapter two, while the Commonwealth Constitution of Australia imposes some limits on the legislative powers of the Federal Parliament of Australia,[32] judicial review of legislation under the Commonwealth Constitution is only possible due to implication of that power by judges. More specifically, as the text of the Constitution does not give the judiciary the power to review the Acts of Parliament for rights-consistency, the principle of parliamentary supremacy remains operative in Australia. In this jurisdiction, which has not (unlike the UK) introduced a Bill of Rights according courts some power to scrutinise legislation

[28] TRS Allan, 'Questions of Legality and Legitimacy: Form and Substance in British Constitutionalism' (2011) 9 *International Journal of Constitutional Law* 155, 155–56.

[29] ibid 156.

[30] ibid 160.

[31] See, eg, Julie Taylor, 'Human Rights Protection in Australia: Interpretation Provisions and Parliamentary Supremacy' (2004) 32 *Federal Law Review* 57.

[32] ibid 60.

for rights-consistency, the courts have found creative ways to strike down rights-infringing statutes.

One method through which this has been accomplished is by way of the implied doctrine of the separation of powers. As stated in chapter four, the enshrinement of the separation of powers in the Constitution of the Commonwealth of Australia 1900 was established in a series of landmark cases in Australian constitutional law, including *New South Wales v Commonwealth of Australia* (the *Wheat case*),[33] *R v Kirby, ex p Boilermakers' Society of Australia*,[34] and, more recently, *Polyukhovich v Commonwealth of Australia*,[35] *and Kable v DPP (NSW)*.[36] In a number of these cases, it was stated that the separation of powers can be used not only as an interpretative guide, but also as an independent ground of normative limitations on legislation. The *Polyukhovich* Court held that the separation of powers would invalidate a law that punished specified persons without trial, on the ground that such a law was a usurpation of judicial power.[37] It has been noted that it is difficult to identify a clear ratio from the *Kable* case,[38] but it has been observed that the case expanded the impact of the separation of judicial power in the Federal Constitution by using it as a source of limitations on state parliaments in their interaction with state courts vested with federal jurisdiction.[39] From that basic principle the statute in *Kable* was invalidated, a plurality of the judges holding that the division of functions envisioned by the Act was incompatible with the independence, impartiality, and integrity of the Supreme Court of New South Wales as a court endowed with federal jurisdiction.[40]

The idea in *Kable* has been further developed and was recently affirmed in *South Australia v Totani*[41] in which the court invalidated a statutory provision on the ground that it undermined the institutional independence and impartiality of the courts of South Australia. The statute under challenge was the Serious and Organised Crime (Control) Act 2008 (South Australia), section 14(1) of which provided that '[t]he Court must, on application by the Commissioner, make a control order against a person (the "defendant") if the Court is satisfied that the defendant is a member of a declared organisation.' If, on application by the Commissioner of Police under section 8 of

33 (1915) 20 CLR 54 (HC, Australia) 88–93 (Isaacs J).
34 (1956) 94 CLR 254 (HC, Australia) 267–88.
35 (1991) 172 CLR 501 (HC, Australia) 502, 532–40 (Mason CJ).
36 (1996) 189 CLR 51 (HC, Australia).
37 *Polyukhovich* (n 35 above) 502.
38 Mirko Bagaric, 'Editorial: The revived Kable doctrine as a constitutional protector of rights?' (2011) 35 *Criminal Law Journal* 197, 197.
39 ibid.
40 *Kable* (n 36 above).
41 *South Australia v Totani* (2010) 242 CLR 1 (HC, Australia).

that Act, the Attorney-General is satisfied that members of an organisation associate to commit serious crime that threatens public safety, he may make a declaration in respect of that organisation. Section 3 defined 'organisation' and 'member' very broadly. Breach of a control order was a criminal offence punishable by a maximum of five years' imprisonment.

The majority of the High Court held that section 14(1) was invalid as it sought to enlist a court in the implementation of executive policy by an adjudicative process in which the court was acting at the behest of the Attorney General to an unacceptable degree.[42] Part of the ratio for this important decision was that the state cannot deprive state courts of the characteristics of institutional independence and impartiality—the minimum characteristics of courts—because Chapter III of the Constitution assumes the rule of law, an assumption predicated in part on state courts' retention of the defining characteristics of courts.[43] The High Court's decision, therefore, directly relied on that area of the rule of law that overlaps with the separation of powers—the requirement of an independent and impartial judiciary.[44]

C. Non-Bill of Rights Legislation Challenges or Threatens to Reduce the Power of the Court

The phenomenon of invoking unwritten principles as a ground for invalidating legislation has also manifested itself in the United Kingdom, in a legal context dominated by parliamentary supremacy (although as noted above, this is under challenge). A central feature of the doctrine of parliamentary supremacy in the UK is that no law passed by Parliament may be set aside by the courts. There have been statutes that have caused debate about the definition of the parliamentary supremacy, such as the European Communities Act 1972 (UK) (ECA) and the Human Rights Act 1998 (UK) (HRA). However, neither of these statutes explicitly empowered the courts to invalidate parliamentary legislation. Yet, in obiter dicta in *Jackson*, it was accepted by two judges in the House of Lords that there is a residual power at common law for judges to 'reject' legislation.[45]

The two judges—Lord Steyn and Lady Hale—argued that this residual power could be utilised where there is an attempt to remove the power of the courts to review governmental actions that affect individual rights. The judgments suggest two potential approaches to such legislative attempts. The first of these seeks to justify review on the principle of legality and

[42] ibid 82, 149, 236, 428, 436, 481.
[43] ibid 58–66 (French CJ), 232–33 (Hayne J).
[44] See ch 4 above.
[45] *Jackson* (n 22 above) [102] (Lord Steyn), [159] (Lady Hale).

the second is 'exceptional circumstances review' as outlined by Lord Steyn. Indeed, Lady Hale envisioned the use of these two approaches to legislation that threatens to remove the power of the courts to review challenges to individual liberty in her judgment in *Jackson*. She warned that '[t]he courts will treat with particular suspicion (and might even reject) any attempt to subvert the rule of law by removing governmental action affecting the rights of the individual from all judicial scrutiny.'[46]

As an interpretative tool, which inhibits Parliament's ability to override fundamental rights or the rule of law by general or ambiguous words,[47] the principle of legality arguably extends only to interpretative choices and not to invalidation of parliamentary legislation. In *AXA General Insurance Ltd v The Scottish Ministers*, Lord Reed articulated this presumption of legality as a potential ground for invalidating legislation of a subordinate legislature (the Scottish Parliament), but not the Westminster Parliament. However, Lord Reed's reasoning in *AXA* opens the door for further development in the utilisation of this principle and it remains to be seen whether the courts would assert a power to invalidate legislation of a sovereign legislature on this basis. The power of invalidation may also be based explicitly on the rule of law, without an interpretative restriction; this is the basis of 'exceptional circumstances review' as articulated by Lord Steyn. These 'exceptional circumstances' include occasions where a statute seeks to remove the power of the court to adjudicate issues related to individual liberties. As stated above, in *Jackson*, Lord Steyn argued that in 'exceptional circumstances' involving an attempt by the legislature 'to abolish judicial review of flagrant abuse of power by a government or even the role of the ordinary courts in standing between the executive and citizens', the courts may have to reject those legislative attempts.

The legislature's usage, or proposed usage, of privative clauses (also known as ouster clauses) has been a driving force behind the court's assertiveness in professing the power to reject legislation which is wholly inconsistent with constitutional principle. 2004 to 2005 saw repeated and vociferous denunciations of privative clauses from within the legislature and from various branches of the legal profession. These denunciations were largely in response to the Asylum and Immigration (Treatment of Claimants, etc.) Bill 2004 (UK). As discussed in chapter five, the draft Bill that was introduced in Parliament contained a clause purporting to oust completely the jurisdiction of the court over decisions of the Asylum and Immigration Tribunal,

[46] *Jackson* (n 22 above) [159] (Lady Hale).

[47] *AXA General Insurance Ltd v The Scottish Ministers* [2011] UKSC 46, [2011] 3 WLR 871 (UKSC) [152] (Lord Reed); *R v Secretary of State for the Home Department, ex parte Pierson* [1997] UKHL 37, [1998] AC 539, 591 (Lord Steyn); *R v Secretary of State for the Home Department, ex p Simms* [2000] 2 AC 115, 131 (Lord Hoffmann).

even in the face of allegations of breach of natural justice.[48] Along with denunciations from the Chief Justice and a former Lord Chancellor, Roger Smith, solicitor and Director of JUSTICE, likened a tribunal created under such rules to the Star Chamber and described the ouster clause as not only 'offensive to all who value good governance', but also, 'objectionable under the principles both of common law and human rights'.[49] So, as Mark Elliott notes, when Lord Steyn referred in the *Jackson* case to the possibility of Parliament abolishing judicial review of 'flagrant abuse of power', he 'delicately omitted to say' that the Government of the day had sought to do just that in the Asylum and Immigration Bill.[50] Accordingly, these previous government threats to the jurisdiction of the court where fundamental rights or interests were engaged are a crucial part of the context of the judicial claim to jurisdiction to invalidate legislation for breach of implied constitutional principles in the United Kingdom.

Jackson—which addresses instances in which non-Bill of Rights legislation may threaten the power of the court—is quite relevant to any discussion of the impact of implied constitutional principles on fundamental rights adjudication, despite not being a case in which there was an allegation of violation of a fundamental right. The relevance of *Jackson* lies in the framing of the jurisdiction of the court in fundamental rights cases by Lady Hale and Lord Steyn. Lady Hale, as stated above, spoke to the supervisory jurisdiction of the court in cases concerning 'governmental action affecting the rights of the individual' and Lord Steyn's robust defence of judicial review and the 'ordinary role of the courts' must be thought to include judicial review in cases in which there are allegations of state interference with fundamental rights.

Parts of the dicta in *Jackson* were recently reasserted by the UK Supreme Court in *AXA General Insurance v Lord Advocate*.[51] *AXA* was a fundamental rights arising out of the enactment of the Damages (Asbestos-related Conditions) (Scotland) Act 2009. Sections 1 and 2 of the Act provided that asymptomatic pleural plaques constitute an injury capable of giving rise to harm under the law of tort, despite the fact that these plaques do not increase an individual's susceptibility to other asbestos-related diseases or shorten life expectancy. Section 4 of the Act provided that sections 1 and 2 were to have retrospective effect. The appellants were insurers who alleged, inter alia, that their right to peaceful enjoyment of their possessions under Article 1 of the First Protocol to the ECHR, were violated by the Act. Under

[48] Asylum and Immigration (Treatment of Claimants, etc.) Bill 2004 (UK).

[49] Roger Smith, 'Rights and Wrongs: Asylum Star Chamber' (2004) *Law Society Gazette*, 15 January, 16, 17.

[50] Mark Elliott, 'The Sovereignty of Parliament, the Hunting Ban, and the Parliament Acts' (2006) 65 *Cambridge Law Journal* 1, 3.

[51] *AXA General Insurance v Lord Advocate* (n 47 above).

section 29(2)(d) of the Scotland Act 1998 legislation incompatible with any right protected by the ECHR was outside the legislative competence of the Scottish Parliament, and under section 33(1) the court was empowered to determine whether Acts of the Scottish Parliament were within its legislative competence. One issue that arose in the course of the case was whether in addition to the limits on legislative competence specified in the Scotland Act 1998, the Scottish Parliament was also subject to the supervisory jurisdiction of courts on common law grounds.

In a judgment delivered by Lord Hope, with which the remaining judges concurred, the justices identified two scenarios that are central to the discussion in this chapter. First, Lord Hope referred to Lord Steyn's dictum on exceptional circumstances review. Lord Hope correctly framed this as a question of the relationship between the rule of law and parliamentary sovereignty and regarded it as an open question how a conflict between those two principles ought to be reconciled.[52] This, although *obiter*, endorses the potential for the courts to enforce the rule of law by 'rejecting' legislation passed by the Westminster Parliament. The second scenario envisioned by Lord Hope was part of the court's holding in the *AXA* case that Acts of the Scottish Parliament would be subject to judicial review and subject to refusal of recognition by the courts if legislation of the Scottish Parliament was passed seeking to 'abolish judicial review or to diminish the role of the courts in protecting the interests of the individual.'[53] Lord Hope justified this power of rejection by invoking the rule of law as the ground on which this purported jurisdiction of the court rests. In his words: 'The rule of law requires that judges must retain the power to insist that legislation of that extreme kind is not law which the courts would recognise.'[54]

The first scenario explored by Lord Hope was already foreshadowed in *Jackson* and certainly has implications for the use of unwritten constitutional principles in judicial review in UK courts. It is arguable that the second scenario discussed by Lord Hope may also have implications for such review in jurisdictions where there is constitutional, rather than legislative, supremacy. It is important to note that one reason the Supreme Court held conclusively that superior courts would be entitled to review the legislation of the Scottish Parliament on grounds that it rejected fundamental rule of law principles, was that the Scottish Parliament is not a sovereign Parliament. So a factor in the court's willingness to clearly assert this power to invalidate legislation on rule of law grounds is the question whether the legislature is sovereign. This suggests that in jurisdictions where there is constitutional rather than legislative supremacy, there could be a corresponding

[52] ibid [51].
[53] ibid.
[54] ibid.

willingness and justification for asserting a power to invalidate legislation on grounds of violation of rule of law principles.

Yet, the implications of the *AXA* judgment for jurisdictions with constitutional supremacy are not entirely clear. There is a relevant similarity between devolved legislatures and legislatures in jurisdictions with constitutional supremacy, such as the Commonwealth Caribbean states, in that their legislatures are not sovereign. However, an equally relevant *distinction* is that the Scottish Parliament has delegated powers[55] while parliaments in the latter jurisdictions, while not sovereign, are in no sense delegated bodies. Accordingly, while the judgment on this point in *AXA* provides useful lessons on the court's view of its powers of review under common law, some elements of the reasoning might not be directly applicable to legislatures in jurisdictions such as those of the Commonwealth Caribbean.

With this caveat in mind, the *AXA* judgment may yet be instructive in jurisdictions without parliamentary supremacy because of the Supreme Court's holding that the constitutional principle of the rule of law can found the basis of the court's rejection of 'extreme' legislation that seeks to abolish judicial review or diminish the role of the courts as protector of the citizen. Particularly illuminating for other states is that the court came to this conclusion despite the presence of statutory grounds, embodied in the Scotland Act 1998, which has been described as a constitutional statute,[56] which empower the court to invalidate legislation of the Scottish Parliament. This suggests a potentially significant role for constitutional principles such as the rule of law as complementary grounds for striking down legislation if the terms of the constitution do not suffice.

As two Law Lords in *Jackson* and the Court in *AXA* have stated, this is only likely to occur in 'exceptional circumstances'. In countries with written bills of rights which confer jurisdiction on the courts to invalidate legislation, the circumstances in which the terms of the bill of rights would not suffice may be exceptional, yet they are not impossible. Indeed, most bills of rights in Commonwealth Caribbean Constitutions are based on the ECHR and therefore bear a close resemblance to Schedule 1 of HRA. Moreover, Caribbean Constitutions allow for the amendment of the Constitution, including the Bill of Rights, with the Constitution of Trinidad and Tobago even permitting the enactment of 'Special Acts' that derogate from the Constitution.[57] This may open the door for privative clauses that amend

[55] ibid [46].

[56] ibid.

[57] Derogation by Special Acts is permitted if passed in accordance with special majority requirements prescribed in the Constitution. See, eg, section 13, Constitution of Trinidad and Tobago 1976. Section 50 of the Constitution of Jamaica 1962 also allowed for Special Acts but has now been repealed by the Charter of Fundamental Rights and Freedoms (Constitutional Amendment) Act 2011 (Jamaica).

the Constitution and severely restrict the court's power of review for violations of fundamental rights. Accordingly, while the circumstances would be exceptional, it is not inconceivable that if those circumstances were to occur, a court in a jurisdiction with constitutional supremacy might be without a constitutional textual ground on which to base its review of or refusal to recognise such a statute, and would be forced to resort to unwritten constitutional principles.

III. TRENDS AND FAULT LINES

There are two trends evident in cases where judges lay claim to the power to invalidate legislation on the ground of an implied principle. First, the cases in which the judges hold or state in obiter dicta that implied principles are grounds on which legislation may be invalidated involve applications of constitutional principle in defence of jurisdictional spheres. Thus, the separation of powers is often used, and, when the rule of law is called upon, it is that area of the rule of law which intersects with the separation of powers doctrine.[58] Secondly, there are more instances of the courts using principles in this way to delineate and protect the sphere of the judiciary than those of the other two branches of government.

A. Invalidation to Protect Jurisdictional Boundaries

An examination of the cases discussed above reveals that judges more readily lay claim to a power to invalidate legislation through the application of an implied principle in defence of the boundaries between the institutions of state. Invalidation was either based on the separation of powers, or an application of the rule of law as a requirement of judicial independence, access to courts, or a combination thereof. Therefore, if the rule of law is suggested as a ground on which courts can invalidate legislation, it is that category of the rule of law which overlaps with the separation of powers principle. This claim does not mean that judges *generally* appeal to the separation of powers principle in more cases than they do to the rule of law principle, but rather, that when judges assert a power to invalidate legislation based on an implied constitutional principle of the separation of powers or rule of law, there are more instances in which the application of the principle is one that protects jurisdictional spheres. For ease of reference, in the remainder of this section, these grounds will be referred to collectively as jurisdictional grounds.

[58] See ch 4 above.

This trend is arguably based on the following factors. First, while there is significant dispute about the true content of both the separation of powers and the rule of law, there appears to be significantly more debate regarding the content of the rule of law as well as greater scepticism about its usefulness as a legal principle. This accounts for part of the trend, but more is needed to explain the higher incidence of use of jurisdictional grounds (whether expressed as aspects of separation of powers or the rule of law) as bases for invalidation, especially since these jurisdictional grounds are sometimes expressed as part of the rule of law principle.

This leads to the second factor, that is, the appeal of jurisdictional applications of the principles as direct grounds for invalidating legislation is partly attributable to such grounds allowing for judicial review to be presented as proceeding along structural rather than substantive or rights-based reasoning. Rights-based grounds recognise and protect individual interests or community values which the state is not permitted to infringe, while structural review relies on rules regarding the operation of the institutions of the state and the apportionment of powers among them. Jurisdictional grounds in general and the separation of powers in particular, are therefore structural in this sense. The rule of law in general has been included within the category of structural grounds by Adrienne Stone,[59] but this is mistaken. Only those meanings of the rule of law that are limited to the functioning of governmental institutions should be classified as structural, excluding from this category the aspects of the rule of law that explicitly invoke substantive values.[60] This would accord with the definition of structural review as review that is based on the rules regarding the operation of the institutions of government. Thus, the separation of powers would qualify as structural and some (but by no means all) applications of the rule of law would be considered structural.

Structural review generally attracts less stringent criticism than rights-based review.[61] For instance, in Canada and Australia, political and academic debate contests the desirability of judicial engagement in rights-based review but this sort of objection is not raised to structural judicial review.[62] While structural review is sometimes the subject of debate, the disagreement usually involves the manner of exercise of this review but does not tend to involve arguments that the courts be denied this power of structural

[59] Adrienne Stone, 'Judicial Review Without Rights: Some Problems for the Democratic Legitimacy of Structural Judicial Review' (2008) 28 *Oxford Journal of Legal Studies* 1, 3–4, 12–13.

[60] See alternate definitions of 'structural judicial review' in ibid; James Allan, 'Not In for a Pound—In for a Penny? Must a Majoritarian Democrat Treat All Constitutional Judicial Review as Equally Egregious?' (2010) 21 *King's Law Journal* 233, 242–43.

[61] Stone (n 59 above) 3; Allan, 'Not In for a Pound' (ibid) 243.

[62] ibid 5–6.

review *in toto*. It may be proposed that structural review is less susceptible to strident criticism as it is not open to arguments that it reflects elite judicial values on contentious moral or political questions. Accordingly, if a judge can base her decision regarding the constitutionality of the death penalty on the division of powers between the judiciary and the executive, she may avoid the charge that her ruling is a mask for her own moral views of the death penalty. Of course, it is doubtful whether structural judgments can truly be said to avoid value judgments. For instance, in the context of separation of powers, decisions regarding which branch of government should be accorded particular functions may involve evaluative judgements regarding the function in question, the potential difference of results depending on which body exercises the function and the relative attributes of each body. Structural review in the context of the separation of powers may also reflect the judge's evaluative judgement regarding competing conceptions of the separation of powers.[63] In writing on the democratic legitimacy of structural judicial review, Adrienne Stone put the argument this way:

> courts must make choices when interpreting the structural elements of a constitution and those choices are driven, at least in part, by judges' own assessments of the merits of competing conceptions of those structures.[64]

Therefore, while structural review, like rights-based review, may *actually* involve evaluative judgement, there is a perception that it does not.

Accordingly, there is some dissonance between perception and reality, but it is the perception that is relevant for the purposes of this chapter. For our purposes, it is necessary to consider that this perception of the merits of structural as opposed to rights-based review partly accounts for the higher incidence of judges relying on jurisdictional grounds as bases for invalidating legislation. What perhaps supplements the impact of this perception is that when courts rely on jurisdictional grounds, they tend to rely on traditionally established propositions about the relative functions and powers of the relevant branches of government. This idea is explored in the next section on the divisions protected by courts.

B. Divisions Protected

Within the trend whereby judges identify jurisdictional applications of implied principles as grounds on which legislation may be invalidated, a further trend is identifiable. This is the trend whereby judges protect the

[63] For instance a judge may adopt a material, as opposed to formal, conception of the separation of powers. For the distinction between material and formal conceptions of the separation of powers, see ch 4 above.

[64] Stone (n 59 above) 17.

judicial sphere to a greater extent than they protect the spheres of the legislature or of the executive.[65] This is evident in the majority of the cases in this study, from *Hinds* in the Commonwealth Caribbean to *Jackson* in the UK.

An exception to this general rule is the case of *Astaphan v Comptroller of Customs of Dominica*.[66] The question before the court was the constitutionality of section 27(4) of the Dominican Customs (Control and Management) Act 1985. Section 27 of the Act provided that if an importer signs a declaration that, due to lack of documentation or information, he is unable to make a correct and complete entry of goods, he will be allowed to take delivery of the goods on payment of a specified sum. Under section 27(4) the specified sum was comprised of the customs duty in addition to a further sum determined by the customs officer, provided that the further sum is at least half of the customs duty. The appellants, who were required to pay the specified sum, challenged the constitutionality of the section, arguing before the Court of Appeal of the Eastern Caribbean States that the 'further sum' referred to in section 27(4) was either a tax or duty [which were regarded as the same], or a penalty, and that in either case, it was unconstitutional. The appellants contended that if the further sum was regarded as a tax or duty, it was inconsistent with the basic constitutional principle of the separation of powers and that if it was regarded as a penalty, it also violated the principle of the separation of powers and/or violated section 6 of the Constitution of the Commonwealth of Dominica 1978, which prohibits compulsory acquisition of property except under the conditions permitted in the Constitution.

These arguments were accepted by the Court of Appeal which held, first, that if the 'further sum' is a tax it violates the separation of powers as between the legislature and the executive. The Court reasoned that the power to impose taxes and duties is inherently legislative and that if the further sum was a tax or duty, the legislature had delegated its legislative power to the executive without prescribing a maximum sum or otherwise circumscribing the power and without prescribing guidelines or a policy for the imposition of the further sum.[67] The Court further held that the compulsory acquisition of the further sum constituted a violation of the right not to be deprived of property and fell outside the constitutional exception of acquisition of property by way of penalty for breach of the law because the Customs Act did not provide that the inability to make perfect entry of goods due to want of documentation or information constituted an offence. Yet, the court sought to further bolster the judgment by holding that, even

[65] This trend is unsurprising when considered in light of a model of public choice theory or institutional theory. See William Mitchell and Randy Simmons, 'Public Choice and the Judiciary: Introductory Notes' [1990] *Brigham Young University Law Review* 729; Jack Knight and Lee Epstein, 'On the Struggle for Judicial Supremacy' (1996) 30 *Law & Society Review* 87.

[66] (1996) 54 WIR 153 (Eastern Caribbean CA, Dominica).

[67] ibid 158–59.

assuming that the further sum was a penalty, it violated the separation of powers by purporting to vest the discretion to fix the appropriate penalty in the hands of the executive, rather than the judiciary.

It was thought prior to this decision that the separation of powers only had partial normative application in the Caribbean context, in that the courts would only enforce the separation of the judiciary from the legislative and executive branches, but would not demarcate or enforce divisions between the executive and the legislature.[68] Indeed, *Astaphan* is the only the case that is located in any of the jurisdictions in this study in which legislation has been struck down on the ground of violation of the separation of powers by purporting to transfer legislative powers to the executive. How then do we account for the decision in *Astaphan*? First, this finding on the ground of separation of powers was shielded by other grounds. In fact, the entire reasoning and decision in the case could be characterised as an attempt to construct a 'bullet-proof judgment' in that the judgment was constructed upon so many foundations that it could be defended even if the separation of powers finding is assailed. A further explanation for the exception of the *Astaphan* decision is that the Court of Appeal was emboldened by the Privy Council decision in *Hinds*. Finally, the court was arguably also emboldened by the powers of review accorded under the Constitution, specifically, the fact that the Constitutions of the Commonwealth Caribbean, including that of Dominica, prescribe judicially enforced limits on the legislature. *Astaphan* suggests that in Commonwealth *Caribbean* jurisdictions, courts may be prepared to invalidate legislation on the ground of violation of the separation of powers as between the legislature and executive, at least where fundamental rights are engaged.

Why is there a higher incidence of judges using jurisdictional bases as grounds on which to invalidate legislation where the legislation affects judicial independence but not where it affects the division between the legislature and the executive? Most apparent is that judges may be more comfortable policing the boundaries of their own province of power as they can justifiably claim to be the appropriate guardians of their own sphere of activity. This relative sense of comfort may be enhanced by the notion that the judiciary is the 'least dangerous' branch of government;[69] in this sense, an attempt by the courts to protect the powers of the judiciary may be deemed to pose less risk than attempts to protect the power of the other branches. Indeed,

[68] Stephen Fraser, 'Constitutional Protection of Fundamental Rights in Guyana' (25 November 2000), http://datametric.net/clients/guyanalaw/present00-2.html (accessed 8 October 2016).

[69] See Alexander Hamilton, (Michael A Genovese ed), *The Federalist Papers* (Palgrave Macmillan Publishing, 2009) 236.

attempts to guard against reduction of the judiciary's power seem all the more justifiable if the judiciary is viewed as weaker than the other branches and more vulnerable to the force of the more dominant branches.

Further, in terms of constitutional design, in the Westminster system of the UK and modified Westminster system of the Commonwealth Caribbean, Canada, and Australia, the line between the executive and the legislature is less defined, whereas the division between the judiciary on the one hand, and the executive and legislature on the other, is much more concrete. This was the prevailing view in twentieth century commentary on the separation of powers in the Westminster system.[70] This view was also evident in early twentieth century constitutional case law, such as the Australian High Court decision in *Victorian Stevedoring & General Contracting Co Pty Ltd v Dignan*[71] in which the Court rejected the argument that legislation delegating power to the Governor General to make regulations which could override Acts of Parliament violated the separation of powers between the legislature and the executive. In his judgment, Evatt J emphasised the close relationship between the executive and legislature which exists in the Westminster system. This understanding continues to dominate today; while there have long existed disputes in the academic literature regarding the existence of separation of powers as a feature of the British Constitution, there has been much greater acceptance of the notion of an independent judiciary.[72] This notion has become so firmly established that it may perhaps be seen as not only an accepted facet of the separation of powers and the rule of law, but also a characteristic that is fundamental to the very understanding of the separation of powers, the rule of law, and the Westminster Constitution. As Masterman indicates, this idea has been based on and supported by statute, common law and convention, which reinforced judicial independence as a fundamental feature of the Constitution, including the Act of Settlement 1701, the House of Commons Disqualification Act 1975 (UK), the HRA 1998, the CRA 2005, the rule against bias, and fair hearing requirements.[73]

Finally, the judicial protection trend is encouraged by the presence in those cases of two central elements: individual interests are affected, and the

[70] Gordon Hewart, *The New Despotism* (Ernest Benn, 1929) 37–45; Trevor C Hartley and JAG Griffith, *Government and Law: An Introduction to the Working of the Constitution in Britain*, 2nd edn (Weidenfeld and Nicolson Publishers, 1981) 175.

[71] *Victorian Stevedoring & General Contracting Co Pty Ltd v Dignan* (1931) 46 CLR 73 (HC, Australia); Leslie Zines, *The High Court and the constitution*, 5th edn (The Federation Press, 2008) 198–207.

[72] Roger Masterman, *The Separation of Powers in the Contemporary Constitution: Judicial Competence and Independence in the United Kingdom* (Cambridge University Press, 2011) 4, 26–30.

[73] *Ridge v Baldwin* [1964] AC 40; *R v Bow Street Magistrates ex p Pinochet (No. 2)* [1999] 1 All ER 577; noted Timothy H Jones, 'Case Comment: Judicial Bias and Disqualification in the Pinochet case' [1999] *Public Law* 391.

court's power of review in relation to government action that affects those interests is limited to some extent by a statutory text. In these circumstances, the court may view itself as the last bastion of fundamental rights protection and therefore resist efforts to remove this final layer of protection for individuals. Where the issue only arises as a question of the division between legislative and executive power, there are other layers of protection that may yet be explored so judicial intervention would not be urgent.

IV. CONCLUSION

The development of judicial acceptance that implied constitutional principles are grounds for invalidating legislation is emblematic of the tension between the elected and judicial branches of government. This tension is pronounced whenever legislatures seek to limit the jurisdiction of the courts to restrain governmental interference with fundamental rights. What is particularly poignant about this struggle is that because the legislature defines and redefines the *textual* bases of judicial enforcement of fundamental rights, whenever the legislature exercises its control over the text in order to narrow the judiciary's sphere of influence in rights protection, judges may resort to looking outside the text in order to ground their protective actions. The judicial resolve to peer outside the text and to restrain legislative will by recourse to non-textual principles is more pronounced in jurisdictions with a written Constitution that confers the power of legislative review, and most pronounced where a constitutional bill of rights has effectively erased parliamentary supremacy. Institutional relationships are central to the use of principles as invalidating grounds, and most importantly, courts are especially assertive in the face of a threat to the judicial role of protecting individual rights from state infringement.

7

Implied Principles as Gateways to Comparative Law

I. INTRODUCTION

OUR DISCUSSION NOW takes us to the intersection of the institutional and the methodological. This chapter taps into an important thread that runs through the practice of reasoning by implied constitutional principles. Such reasoning often situates the institutions of state, the substance of the law, and the reasoning of the judges within a transnational[1] or even global context. Implied constitutional principles are used in a manner that expressly connects the court's reasoning to foreign institutions and jurisdictions, by creating a form of connection to foreign judicial decisions. There is a significant degree of commonality of language and discourse that feeds and is fed by the comparative methodology employed by judges, a commonality around the language of constitutionalism, the rule of law, separation of powers, and fundamental rights. The relationship between reasoning by implied constitutional principles and reasoning by comparative analysis can flow in two directions: implied constitutional principles can fuel and justify comparativism in adjudication, while the use of foreign judgments by courts can also result in references to such principles.

The chapter proceeds by briefly noting the trend of judicial comparativism in constitutional law and human rights. Specifically, I will propose reasons why judges cite foreign judgments and show that the appeal of comparative law intersects with the appeal of implied constitutional principles, specifically in fundamental rights adjudication. This analysis highlights the importance of legitimation of institutions, of institutional processes, and of the state *qua* state. Part III of the chapter then discusses two ways in which implied principles function as gateways to foreign judgments. First, the court may state that the principle is a feature of the local legal system by virtue of inheritance from another jurisdiction. Accordingly, in Canada and the Commonwealth Caribbean, the legitimacy of invoking the rule of law and separation of powers is traced to the inheritance of the British legal

[1] The term 'transnational' is used to denote an extension beyond national jurisdictions.

tradition.[2] Courts also refer to foreign law in identifying and justifying the content given to these principles.[3] From these mechanisms of connecting the principles to foreign law, specific themes emerge. First, the use of implied constitutional principles in conjunction with comparative legal analysis is evocative of a connection between transition and continuity. Secondly, there is evident judicial effort to preserve and reinforce institutional legitimacy. Part IV then engages with the colonial legacy that is reflected in reliance on unwritten principles while Parts V and VI of the chapter discuss the extent to which the case law shows courts developing common approaches to common problems and the impact of the cross-jurisdictional exchanges considered in this study.

In the countries examined, which were once part of the colonial structure of Great Britain, invocation of implied principles as a pathway to adopting the reasoning of judges in the United Kingdom is also, in some respects, an acknowledgment of—and a beckoning towards—a historical framework. This historical gaze challenges the situation of the institution within the new state and the degree of autochthony and intellectual independence manifested by judicial and other legal institutions. Alongside the tensions generated by a historical outlook, the chapter also addresses the extent to which reference to domestic instruments contribute to the development of 'nationalised' conceptions of implied principles, and considers how this interacts with references to foreign law. This analysis will expose a tension between transnationalism and nationalisation which is a key feature of both comparativism and the constitutional principles of the rule of law and the separation of powers.

II. COMPARATIVISM IN CONSTITUTIONAL LAW AND HUMAN RIGHTS

The trend of judicial comparativism in constitutional and human rights cases has been influenced by concurrent events in constitutional states.[4]

[2] *Reference re Language Rights Under s 23 of Manitoba Act, 1870 and s 133 of Constitution Act, 1867* [1985] 1 SCR 721 [63].

[3] *Thomas v Baptiste* [2000] 2 AC 1 (JCPC, Trinidad and Tobago) 21–22.

[4] On comparativism in Australian constitutional law, see Adrienne Stone, 'Comparativism in Constitutional Interpretation' [2009] *University of Melbourne Law Research Series* 15. On comparativism in Canadian constitutional law, see Gianluca Gentili, 'Canada: protecting rights in a "worldwide rights culture", an empirical study of the use of foreign precedents by the Supreme Court of Canada (1982–2010)' in Tania Groppi and Marie-Claire Ponthoreau (eds), *Use of foreign precedents by constitutional judges* (Hart Publishing, 2013). On comparativism in UK constitutional law, see Esin Örücü, 'Comparative Law in British Courts', in Ulrich Drobnig and Sjef van Erp (eds), *The Use of Comparative Law by Courts* (Kluwer Law International, 1999); Tom Bingham, *Widening Horizons: The Influence Of Comparative Law And International Law On Domestic Law* (Cambridge University Press, 2010) 5. On comparativism in Commonwealth Caribbean constitutional law, see Albert Fiadjoe, 'Judicial Attitudes to Commonwealth Caribbean Constitutions' (1991) 20 *Anglo-American Law Review* 121.

The first significant occurrence is the existence—and growth—of constitutions, whether written or unwritten, which feature a number of modern elements. Secondly, there is the impact of the recognition of fundamental rights and freedoms and emerging rights discourse across constitutional jurisdictions, often alongside rights instruments. Thirdly, these jurisdictions have developed institutional mechanisms, often including courts, to settle disputes regarding the scope of fundamental rights and to contribute to the realisation of such rights.[5] These developments foster, and in some cases spring from, a transnational dialogue on constitutionalism and rights protection. They encourage and enhance comparative work among scholars, legislators, advocates, and judicial actors.[6]

The level of generality of principles makes them particularly attractive in comparative judicial exchanges. The universalistic nature of constitutional principles such as the rule of law and separation of powers at a high level of abstraction means that their invocation does not, *ipso facto*, threaten commitment to the local values and conditions of the state in question. If one then digs deeper into the content of such principles there is revealed a range of applications ascribed to them in foreign jurisdictions, depending on the perspectives of the judges in the case, the textual arrangements of the constitution, and the social and political circumstances of the society. This range of applications may include a decision by the court to reject an understanding of the principle that has been adopted or championed in another jurisdiction.

There is a significant point of overlap between the appeal of reasoning by principles and the appeal of comparative methodology. This is the perceived reputational impact of these two analytical tools, which operates on two levels. First, both techniques are indicative of the legitimacy of the state. They send a signal to internal and external forces that the state has embraced the tradition of democratic constitutionalism. This can either be, as in the case of South Africa, a message that the state has rejected an undemocratic past,[7] or, as in the case of many Commonwealth Caribbean states, a message that the new state will retain the democratic traditions of the former ruling state. Interestingly, the reputational impact on the perception of the legitimacy of the state can be used to reinforce either an image of transformation, an

[5] Wen-Chen Chang and Jiunn-Rong Yeh, 'Internationalization of Constitutional Law' in Michel Rosenfeld and András Sajó (eds), *The Oxford Handbook of Comparative Constitutional Law* (Oxford University Press, 2012) 1168–69.

[6] Vicki C Jackson, 'Comparative Constitutional Law: Methodologies' in Michel Rosenfeld and András Sajó (eds), *The Oxford Handbook of Comparative Constitutional Law* (Oxford University Press, 2012).

[7] Heinz Klug, 'South Africa's Experience in Constitution-Building' University of Wisconsin Law School, Legal Studies Research Paper Series Paper No 1157, http://papers.ssrn.com/sol3/papers.cfm?abstract_id=1808168 (accessed 22 January 2013).

image of continuity, or some combination of both.[8] On the intra-state level, reputational impact is meant to accrue to the institutional legitimacy of the court. Referring to the 'legitimacy generating' effects of comparative judicial reasoning, it has been remarked that 'judicial borrowing helps courts to deliver decisions that appear objective and impartial, which is particularly valuable to newly establish [sic] constitution courts. Engagement with foreign peers can also boost the external prestige of courts even when it leads to the rejection of foreign approaches.'[9] The case has also been made that courts employ citation of foreign judgments as a 'distancing device' to enable the courts' audience to view human rights judgments as legal, as opposed to policy or political judgments.[10]

III. INHERITANCE FROM FORMER COLONIAL POWER

Implied constitutional principles provide a base from which the substantive and structural borrowing that occurred during constitution-making processes in new nation-states can be maintained. Indeed, Allan contends that Western liberal democracies are founded on the rule of law, and consequently, share unwritten constitutional principles and 'should ... be understood to share a common law constitution'.[11] There is a similar sentiment of commitment to common constitutional principles, including the rule of law and the separation of powers, which may be used as a gateway to transnational judicial reasoning. The implied constitutional principles of the rule of law and separation of powers are sometimes expressly linked to the legal system and legal tradition inherited from Britain. In this way, the colonial history and the legal tradition of a foreign jurisdiction are used to justify the invocation of an implied constitutional principle. This also has the effect that foreign law—including foreign judgments—is referred to in judicial analysis.

In Canada the recognition of the rule of law as an 'unwritten postulate' of the Constitution has been based in part on its status within the English constitution, interpretive support for that position being drawn from the

[8] See further examples and discussion in Part III of this chapter.

[9] Vlad Perju, 'Constitutional Transplants, Borrowing, and Migrations' in Michel Rosenfeld and András Sajó (eds), *The Oxford Handbook of Comparative Constitutional Law* (Oxford University Press, 2012) 1318.

[10] Christopher McCrudden, 'Human Rights and Judicial Use of Comparative Law', in Esin Örücü (ed) *Judicial Comparativism in Human Rights* (Martinus Nijhoff Publishers, 2004) 1.

[11] TRS Allan, *Constitutional Justice: A Liberal Theory of the Rule of Law* (Oxford University Press, 2001) 4–5.

preamble to the Canadian Constitution Act 1867. Accordingly, in *Reference re Manitoba Language Rights*, it was explained that:

> The rule of law has always been understood as the very basis of the English Constitution characterising the political institutions of England from the time of the Norman Conquest (AV Dicey, *The Law of the Constitution* (10th ed 1959), at p 183). It becomes a postulate of our own constitutional order by way of the preamble to the *Constitution Act, 1982*, and its implicit inclusion in the preamble to the *Constitution Act, 1867* by virtue of the words 'with a Constitution similar in principle to that of the United Kingdom'.[12]

This reasoning did not directly refer to British case law, but, of course, it opens the door for references to case law from the UK in expounding on the principles of the Canadian Constitution. The blend of historical and textual interpretive bases that link constitutional principles to former colonial powers generates prominent contested pursuits that reveal the complexity of constitutional inheritance.

A. Transition and Continuity

The use of implied constitutional principles as a conduit between Britain and the new state evokes a connection between transition and continuity. For instance, in the *Secession Reference*, the rule of law, along with other constitutional principles, was invoked in a discussion of the historical context of the Constitution and the influence of that history on the principles that form part of the current Constitution:

> Despite its federal structure, the new Dominion was to have 'a Constitution similar in Principle to that of the United Kingdom' (*Constitution Act, 1867*, preamble). Allowing for the obvious differences between the governance of Canada and the United Kingdom, it was nevertheless thought important to thus emphasize the continuity of constitutional principles, including democratic institutions and the rule of law; and the continuity of the exercise of sovereign power transferred from Westminster to the federal and provincial capitals of Canada.[13]

The passage claims for Canada the adoption of a tradition of constitutionalism and the rule of law at the founding of the new state. There is a sense that this continuity of democratic traditions adds legitimacy to the institutions of the newly independent state. Thus there are at least two elements of the appeal to continuity. The first is the assertion of the continuity of the substance of the law in the sense of the adoption of constitutional principles. The second is the continuity of state institutions.

[12] *Reference re Manitoba Language Rights* (n 2 above) [63].
[13] [1998] 2 SCR 217 (SC, Canada) [44].

The continuity of positive laws was at the heart of the decision of the Supreme Court of Canada in *Reference re Manitoba Language Rights*, as reflected in the Court's assertion of the survival of the constitutional principle of the rule of law. The *Reference* sought reaffirmation of the bilingual publication requirement—English and French—of all statutes, records and journals of the Houses of the Parliament of Canada and of the Legislatures of Quebec and Manitoba, as prescribed under section 133 of the Constitution Act 1867 and section 23 of the Manitoba Act 1870.[14] In 1890, An Act to Provide that the English Language shall be the Official Language of the Province of Manitoba 1890 (Man) (Official Language Act) was enacted by the Manitoba Legislature, which led to Manitoba ceasing publication of French versions of its records, journals and legislation. Having determined that the constitutional bilingual requirements were mandatory, the Canadian Supreme Court found that Manitoba legislation that was not printed and published in both English and French were invalid by reason of section 23 of the Manitoba Act 1870. Yet, despite the constitutional breach, the Court took the dramatic position that the rule of law required that the invalid legislation 'be deemed temporarily valid for the minimum period necessary for their translation, re-enactment, printing and publication.'[15]

The continuing presence of the rule of law as a 'fundamental postulate' of the Constitution provided a basis for the temporary validity of the Manitoba legislation. As the court put it, 'the rule of law requires the creation and maintenance of an actual order of positive laws to govern society.'[16] The maintenance of the positive legal order was perceived by the court as essential to 'avoiding a legal vacuum in Manitoba and ensuring the continuity of the rule of law.'[17] The nature of the continuity which was discussed in this aspect of the judgment was quite elemental, speaking to the need for humans in any society to be governed by norms that guide behaviour and contribute to a system of social control. This idea was made explicit in the Court's statement that the rule of law recognises that 'law and order are indispensable elements of civilised life'.[18] Hence, the court held that a 'declaration that the laws of Manitoba are invalid and of no legal force or effect would deprive Manitoba of its legal order and cause a transgression of the rule of law.'[19] The elemental nature of the concern of securing normative order through the rule of law ensures that this issue is viewed as having a global reach and not restricted to national or provincial matters. The globalised perspective engendered by the necessity of legal order for

[14] The Manitoba Act 1870 is entrenched as part of the Constitution of Canada by virtue of s 52(2)(b) of the Constitution Act 1982.

[15] *Reference re Manitoba Language Rights* (n 2 above) [157].

[16] *Reference re Manitoba Language Rights* (n 2 above) [60].

[17] ibid [67].

[18] ibid [64].

[19] ibid [68].

the survival of the state helps to justify the incorporation of foreign judicial decisions into the court's reasoning. In this way, what might initially present as an esoteric Canadian concern to preserve minority language rights, becomes both basal and global.

Thus, the *Manitoba* judgment also presented the rule of law as a connection to a global network of constitutional states in general, going beyond the connection to the former colonial ruler. Belief in the existence of this network is reflected in the court's characterisation of the rule of law as an 'unwritten but inherent principle' which 'must provide the foundation of any constitution.'[20] This argument is consistent with the Supreme Court's reference to judgments from Cyprus and Pakistan—both former British colonies—which each faced a crisis regarding the enactment of unconstitutional statutes. In both jurisdictions, the doctrine of state necessity was used to sanction acts that would otherwise have been held to be unconstitutional and invalid. In Cyprus, in *Attorney General of the Republic v Mustafa Ibrahim*,[21] the Court of Appeal of Cyprus relied on the doctrine of state necessity to hold valid a law passed in contravention of the express provisions of the Constitution of the Republic of Cyprus 1960. Similarly, the Federal Court of Pakistan in *Special Reference No 1 of 1955* upheld an action taken by the Governor General of Pakistan to fill a legal vacuum created by the Federal Court's earlier invalidation of many statutes and regulations. In an earlier case, the Federal Court had held that 44 amendments to the Indian Independence Act 1947 (which functioned as the original Constitution for India and Pakistan) were void, having been passed without royal assent. As a result of this decision, many pieces of legislation passed pursuant to the amendments were also nullities. The Governor General subsequently issued a proclamation retrospectively empowering himself to validate and enforce all laws necessary to preserve the State and the government until a new Constituent Convention could decide upon the validity of those laws. The Governor General was found to have acted out of necessity 'in order to avert an impending disaster and to prevent the State and society from dissolution.'[22] This mirrors the concerns that confronted the court in the *Manitoba Language Rights* case. For the Canadian Supreme Court, the doctrine of necessity employed by courts in Cyprus and Pakistan had its foundation in the rule of law, arguing that '[t]he cases on the necessity doctrine ... point to the same conclusion: the courts will recognise unconstitutional enactments as valid where a failure to do so would lead to legal chaos and thus violate the constitutional requirement of the rule of law.'[23] In sum, the rule of law

[20] ibid [105].

[21] [1964] Cyprus Law Reports 195.

[22] *Special Reference No 1 of 1955*, PLR 1956 WP 598 (Fed Ct, Pakistan), cited in *Reference re Manitoba Language Rights* (n 2 above) [101].

[23] *Reference re Manitoba Language Rights* (n 2 above) [104].

basis and elemental concern for the maintenance of legal order in society are features that support an appeal to foreign law and, conversely, the references to foreign law allow the court to incorporate unwritten principles and doctrines into its judgment.

In the *Secession Reference* the Supreme Court of Canada constructed a case for continuity by laying claim to the gradual evolution of the Constitution. Support for the Court's characterisation of the Constitution was based in part on the process through which independence was achieved in Canada. The Court laid a claim to gradual evolution on the basis of the process of independence. Accordingly, it was noted that 'Canada's evolution from colony to fully independent state was gradual … Canada's independence from Britain was achieved through legal and political evolution with an adherence to the rule of law and stability.'[24] After tracing Canada's journey to independence, the Court stated its conclusion that:

> We think it apparent from even this brief historical review that the evolution of our constitutional arrangements has been characterized by adherence to the rule of law, respect for democratic institutions, the accommodation of minorities, insistence that governments adhere to constitutional conduct and a desire for continuity and stability.[25]

As in the *Manitoba Language Rights Reference*, preoccupation with the rule of law as an engine of continuity and stability within the state was instrumental to the court's reasoning. It was concluded that Quebec did not have a right to unilaterally secede from Canada, and further, that all parties (including Quebec) should negotiate 'in a manner consistent with constitutional principles and values'.[26] In recognising the complex issues to which secession would give rise, the Court stated that these issues 'would have to be resolved within the overall framework of the rule of law, thereby assuring Canadians … a measure of stability in what would likely be a period of considerable upheaval and uncertainty'.[27] In this way, the continuity and stability that characterised the independence process, and which is reflected in the adoption of the rule of law as a principle of the Canadian Constitution, requires that stability must also be maintained by the negotiation of a potential secession process for Quebec.

B. Continuing Institutional Legitimacy

Another significant theme emerging from cases in which there is a confluence of reasoning by implied constitutional principle and reasoning by

[24] *Secession Reference* (n 13 above) [46].
[25] ibid [48].
[26] ibid [95].
[27] ibid [96].

comparative legal analysis is the idea of continuing institutional legitimacy. Finding that the election of the First Minister and Deputy First Minister of Northern Ireland—which fell outside of the time period envisioned by the Northern Ireland Act 1998—was valid, Lord Bingham recognised that 'it is in general desirable that the government should be carried on, that there be no governmental vacuum.'[28] Faced with the potential of even more profound consequences, the *Manitoba Language Rights* case emphasised a similar need for preserving institutional legitimacy. In holding that the rule of law demanded the declaration of temporary validity, the Court summarised the likely impact on the institutions of government in the province of Manitoba if the Acts of the province were invalidated with immediate effect:

> The situation of the various institutions of provincial government would be as follows: the courts, administrative tribunals, public officials, municipal corporations, school boards, professional governing bodies, and all other bodies created by law, to the extent that they derive their existence from or purport to exercise powers conferred by Manitoba laws enacted since 1890 in English only, would be acting without legal authority.[29]

For this institutional reason, along with the potential impact on substantive law, the Court concluded that 'declaring the Acts of the Legislature of Manitoba invalid and of no force or effect would, without more, undermine the principle of the rule of law'.[30] In this construct, the rule of law operates to secure the legal authority of the institutions of the state and the maintenance of institutional authority. The rule of law is perceived as a conduit operating within dimensions of both space and time. It connects current institutions to the past and, hence, to their past legitimacy and authority, and it connects the institutions within Canada, to the English (and subsequently British) institutions.

The *Hinds* case, the first in which a statute from an independent Commonwealth Caribbean jurisdiction was invalidated for inconsistency with the Constitution,[31] also explicitly laid claim to continuity and characterised the Constitution as 'evolutionary'. The idea of transition through continuity was present in Lord Diplock's judgment in which he expressed that one result of this continuity was survival of the separation of powers and the preservation of the institutional apparatus that existed prior to independence. In his words:

> The new constitutions, particularly in the case of unitary states, were evolutionary not revolutionary. They provided for continuity of government through successor

[28] *Robinson v Secretary of State for Northern Ireland* [2002] UKHL 32 [11].
[29] *Reference re Manitoba Language Rights* (n 2 above) [56].
[30] ibid [59].
[31] AR Carnegie, '*Floreat* the Westminster Model?' A Commonwealth Caribbean Perspective' (1996) 6 *Caribbean Law Review* 1, 1.

> institutions, legislative, executive and judicial, of which the members were to be selected in a different way, but each institution was to exercise powers which, although enlarged, remained of a similar character to those that had been exercised by the corresponding institution that it had replaced.[32]

This view has taken hold, and continues to inform constitutional interpretive approaches in the region, notably being cited in *Suratt v Attorney General* to explain that the constitutions' objective of securing continuity of government explains why 'they leave much to implication.'[33] As in *Hinds*, the Privy Council in *Suratt* was tasked with resolving whether a new tribunal—in that case the Equal Opportunities Tribunal—was inconsistent with the separation of powers. The tribunal was created under the Equal Opportunity Act 2000 (Trinidad and Tobago) to hear complaints alleging discrimination in breach of the Act, and was accorded significant powers of discovery, examination, and enforcement. While concluding that the creation of the tribunal posed no threat to judicial independence and separation of powers, the Privy Council was again concerned to protect the institutional integrity of the superior courts by preventing the transfer of part of their core jurisdiction.[34]

Institutional legitimacy was brought to the fore in the *Provincial Judges Reference*, in striking down the reduction of judicial salaries in provinces of Prince Edward Island, Manitoba, and Alberta. In the Opinion, the preambular 'reference to "a Constitution similar in Principle to that of the United Kingdom"' was acknowledged as recognition of the constitutional principle at issue, in that case the principle of judicial independence.[35] Moreover, the institutional similarity and continuity between England and Canada was asserted, the argument being made that 'the preamble indicates that the legal and institutional structure of constitutional democracy in Canada should be similar to that of the legal regime out of which the Canadian Constitution emerged.'[36] In the Court's view, this necessitated recognition of constitutional democracy and protection of mechanisms that supply definition, order, and legitimacy to those institutions.[37] By that reasoning, the implied principle of judicial independence required limitations on the use of legislative power to undermine the independence of the courts. The Court's assessment of the Constitution as evolutionary was invoked to justify an expansion of the protection of

[32] *Hinds v R* [1977] AC 195 (JCPC, Jamaica) 212.

[33] *Suratt v Attorney General of Trinidad and Tobago* [2008] UKPC 38, (2008) 73 WIR 437 (JCPC, Trinidad and Tobago) [18] (Lord Bingham), [38] (Lady Hale).

[34] ibid [47]–[51].

[35] *Reference Re Remuneration of Judges of the Provincial Court of Prince Edward Island* [1997] 3 SCR 3 (SC, Canada) [105].

[36] ibid [96].

[37] ibid [103], in reference to the protection of political institutions through the protection of free speech.

judicial independence from superior court judges to all judges in the state. The argument of Lamer CJ, delivering the opinion of the majority, proceeded as follows:

> The historical origins of the protection of judicial independence in the United Kingdom, and thus in the Canadian Constitution, can be traced to the *Act of Settlement* of 1701. As we said in *Valente*, *supra*, at p. 693, that Act was the 'historical inspiration' for the judicature provisions of the *Constitution Act, 1867*. Admittedly, the Act only extends protection to judges of the English superior courts. However, our Constitution has evolved over time. In the same way that our understanding of rights and freedoms has grown, such that they have now been expressly entrenched through the enactment of the *Constitution Act, 1982*, so too has judicial independence grown into a principle that now extends to all courts, not just the superior courts of this country.

The Court then concluded that the judicial branch constituted an institution that is part of the 'basic structure of [the] Constitution', with the result that there is an 'implied limitation [on legislative power] that the independence of those courts cannot be undermined'.[38]

The continuity of the English model of constitutionalism in new states and the impact of this continuity on the institutional apparatus of these states poses challenging questions for the distribution of powers among state organs. In *Hinds* Lord Diplock was confident that once the constitution in question is 'a Constitution on the Westminster model', that 'the absence of express words to that effect does not prevent the legislative, the executive and the judicial powers of the new State being exercisable exclusively by the legislature, by the executive and by the judicature respectively.'[39] Yet, the *Hinds* assessment of the separation of powers in the Westminster constitutional system ought to be compared with the characterisation of that constitutional model by the High Court of Australia in *R v Kirby, ex p Boilermakers' Society of Australia*.[40] Both courts referred to the adoption of 'British' ideas on the division or separation of powers, the Court in *Kirby* stating that the division in the Australian Constitution 'is a division of powers whose character is determined according to traditional British conceptions'.[41] *Kirby*—decided in 1956—described that presumably British conception of separation of powers as a 'broad division of power', with the dual consequences that 'difficulties as between executive and legislative power are not to be expected' and that 'it is in connection with judicial power that questions are apt to occur.'[42] When

[38] ibid [108].
[39] *Hinds* (n 32 above) 212.
[40] (1956) 94 CLR 254 (HC, Australia) 276–77.
[41] ibid 276.
[42] ibid.

we fast-forward 19 years to the *Hinds* decision, we see a bolder and more expansive statement of the contours of the separation of powers, which described more concrete functional and personnel divisions across all three branches.[43]

Despite reliance on English tradition in both judgments to establish and justify the court's understanding of the separation of powers, the characterisations of the implications of the separation of powers principle are inconsistent. What are the explanations for this? First, it is possible that one of the two assessments was incorrect. On this point, it is relevant that *Hinds* has been criticised by a sector of British and Caribbean commentators, the argument being made that the separation of powers was not truly a feature of the English constitution.[44] The second is that neither assessment was incorrect, as each represented an accurate application of the traditional English constitution to the constitution of the respective state. Again, the criticism of *Hinds* is relevant. Caribbean academic Carnegie argued that the statement in *Hinds* that the Westminster model had been transplanted to the Commonwealth Caribbean was dubious.[45] Carnegie challenged the transplantation argument, noting the differences in separation of powers and the organisation of institutions under Caribbean constitutions as compared with these features in the English constitution, particularly the difference engendered by the constitutions' grant of power to the courts to review and invalidate legislation. The third possible explanation is that neither assessment was incorrect as each represented the understanding of the separation of powers in the English constitution at the time of the respective judicial decision. If the third explanation holds sway, that would entail that the separation of powers principle in the English constitution underwent transformation between *Kirby* in 1956 and *Hinds* in 1975. The difference between these two cases and the variety of possible explanations for that difference are engaged here to demonstrate that references to foreign law do not necessarily add clarity to the court's decision-making. In fact, such comparative references may raise more questions than they answer.

This leads to a larger point that the adjudicative borrowing that occurs in relation to constitutional principles highlights areas of convergence as well as divergence in comparative constitutionalism. Those co-existing spheres of convergence and divergence are largely revealed by the cleavage between citation of the connection between principles and foreign law and articulation of the content of those principles in the borrowing state.

[43] *Hinds* (n 32 above) 212.

[44] O Hood Phillips, 'A Constitutional Myth: Separation of Powers' 93 *Law Quarterly Review* 11 (1977); Carnegie (n 31 above).

[45] Carnegie (n 31 above).

C. Comparison at Different Stages of Constitutional Development

A compelling facet of the transnational borrowing and the use of principles (and the connection of the two techniques) which occur in the adjudication of constitutional law and fundamental rights is that these practices are not limited to, or exclusively initiated by, judicial action. Political actors and as well as non-judicial legal actors also engage in this exercise, and their comparative engagement may influence the court to follow suit. The process of constitutional design and drafting itself often involves substantial and impactful comparative work.[46] In the Commonwealth Caribbean, for instance, there were two branches of borrowing that influenced the design of the constitutions that were enacted. On one level, the states adopted much of the structure of Westminster government. This fact was reflected in *Hinds,* where Lord Diplock discerned in independent Commonwealth constitutions 'a common pattern and style of draftsmanship which may conveniently be described as "the Westminster model."'[47] Secondly, there was a distinct belief in the influence of comparative law and constitutional principle adopted from a foreign jurisdiction as expressed by Lord Diplock in the following terms:

> All of [the Westminster constitutions] were negotiated and drafted by persons nurtured in the tradition of that branch of the branch of the common law of England that is concerned with public law and familiar in particular with the basic concept of separation of legislative, executive, and judicial power as it had been developed in the unwritten constitution of the United Kingdom.[48]

In this sense, there was an adoption of what has been referred to as the 'catholicity' of the common law, reflecting a receptivity to external sources.[49]

Constitutional principles and comparative analysis share the characteristic of bringing an external outlook and influence into the constitutional debates of a jurisdiction and this external influence on the state's constitutional debates may occur at the constitutional design stage as well as the constitutional adjudication stage. An intriguing question which arises is how the use of comparative law in conjunction with implied constitutional principles during the construction of constitutions translates into the comparative analysis that occurs in judicial interpretation of constitutions. At the interpretative stage, there are three scenarios that may emerge. First, there may be an abandonment of comparative analysis. This has not occurred in any of the jurisdictions considered in this study. Secondly,

[46] Bruce Ackerman, 'The Rise of World Constitutionalism' (1997) 83 *Virginia Law Review* 771; Klug (n 7 above); Anne Smith, 'Internationalisation and Constitutional Borrowing in Drafting Bills of Rights' (2011) 60 *International and Comparative Law Quarterly* 867.

[47] *Hinds* (n 32 above) 212.

[48] ibid.

[49] John Laws, *The Common Law Constitution* (Cambridge University Press, 2014) 58–64.

comparative judicial analysis may involve the same or similar jurisdictions to those used in the drafting stage. The cases discussed above show evidence of this, as in newly states there are repeated references to UK law. Similarly, in Trinidad and Tobago and Australia, English and British references are supplemented by references to North American laws. References to North American sources are consistent with the influence of the Constitution of Canada on the drafting of the Constitution of Trinidad and Tobago and the Constitution of the United States of America on the drafting of thc Commonwealth Constitution of Australia.[50] Thirdly, comparative discussion may occur but involving significantly different jurisdictions and issues from those used during the drafting stage. The occurrence of the third scenario may suggest that the judicial reasoning used comparison for different purposes than those which influenced the drafting process. With respect to this third circumstance, in some jurisdictions, there has been a narrowing of the jurisdictions considered between the design stage and the adjudicative stage. For instance, in Australia, the design of the Constitution and organisation of the institutions of state were largely influenced by the English constitution, as well as the constitutional framework of Canada, the USA, Germany and Switzerland.[51] Yet, in its adjudication—specifically its reasoning by constitutional principles—Germany and Switzerland are not referenced. This may reflect the influence of the 'similar cases model' of comparative methodology, which in this circumstance, narrows the comparator jurisdictions to those which possess the same legal system as the jurisdiction in question. The same patterns may occur in the use of principles in the constitutional construction stage as compared with the interpretive stage.

Beyond the legislative use of comparative law in constitutional drafting, the courts' reference to comparative law are sometimes encouraged by the attorneys in the case. Thus, Lord Diplock was able to note in *Hinds* that the Board had been 'quite properly referred to a number of previous authorities', which included cases from foreign jurisdictions, with a focus on cases from former British colonies.[52] Counsel in *Hinds* and *Zuniga v Attorney General* relied in their submissions on judicial decisions emanating from Australia, Canada, the Republic of Ireland and Ceylon [now Sri Lanka] on the relative powers of the legislature and the jurisdiction of the courts. Subsequently, some of the cases invoked by counsel were then incorporated into the judgment delivered by the Judicial Committee. This sequence makes it clear that one reason for the use of comparative reasoning in judicial

[50] Margaret Demerieux, *Fundamental Rights in Commonwealth Caribbean Constitutions* (Faculty of Law Library, University of the West Indies, 1992); Andrew Inglis Clark, *Studies in Australian Constitutional Law* (Charles F Maxwell (G Partridge & Co, 1901)) 1; Cheryl Saunders, *The Constitution of Australia: Contextual Analysis* (Hart Publishing, 2011) 15.

[51] Saunders (ibid).

[52] *Hinds* (n 32 above) 200–01, 204–08.

decisions is that lawyers rely on these judgments in their submissions. The reliance on foreign judgments and comparative analysis is prevalent among lawyers and (human rights activists) in common law jurisdictions. Accordingly, there is a network of legal professionals, wider than the judicial class, that incorporate comparative analysis into their arguments.[53] This, predictably, has an impact on the analysis of the judges to whom these arguments are made; thus it may be seen to encourage the judiciary to engage in comparative analysis.

IV. PRINCIPLED BORROWING AND A COLONIAL LEGACY

The recognition of implied constitutional principles in the former British colonies of the Commonwealth Caribbean, Canada, and Australia provide particularly fertile ground for the observance of the trends of transnational legal analysis and judicial globalisation.[54] While inheritance of some legal traditions from England may justify and perhaps almost make it inevitable that judges in the new states would refer to British judgments, it was not automatic that the new states should cross-reference each other. Perhaps it was largely the institutional and adjudicative link of the Privy Council that provided (and in some states, continues to provide) the medium through which this borrowing takes place. As Örücü has noted, an intra-familial comparativism has emerged in human rights cases in the common law world, with the Privy Council working as its anchor.[55] The comparative methodology and intra-Commonwealth judicial borrowing has been justified by the Privy Council from the early days of adjudication of Commonwealth Caribbean written constitutions.[56]

The appeal of foreign judgments in new democracies has been characterised as arising in part from a 'strong pedagogical impulse'.[57] Most importantly, there is an attempt to tie the institutions in the new democracy with older democratic states, an effort described by Slaughter in these terms: 'The court of a fledgling democracy, for instance, might look to the opinions of courts in older and more established democracies as a way of binding its

[53] McCrudden, 'Human Rights and Judicial Use of Comparative Law' (n 10 above) 19–20. See also Aharon Barak, 'Response to The Judge as Comparatist: Comparison in Public Law' (2005–2006) 80 *Tulane Law Review* 196.

[54] On transnational human rights reasoning, see Christopher McCrudden, 'A Common Law of Human Rights: Transnational Judicial Conversations on Constitutional Rights' (2000) 20 *Oxford Journal of Legal Studies* 499. On judicial globalisation, see Anne-Marie Slaughter, 'Judicial Globalization' (1999–2000) 40 *Virginia Journal of International Law* 1103.

[55] Esin Örücü, 'Whither Comparativism in Human Rights Cases' in Esin Örücü (ed) *Judicial Comparativism in Human Rights* (Martinus Nijhoff Publishers, 2004) 232.

[56] *Hinds* (n 32 above) 211; *Vasquez v R* [1994] 1 WLR 1304 (JCPC, Belize) 1314.

[57] McCrudden 'Human Rights and Judicial Use of Comparative Law' (n 10 above) 10.

country to this existing community of states.'[58] In former colonies, there are internal and external elements to this 'pedagogical impulse'. Internally, it has been argued that there is a psychologically soothing effect of adopting or maintaining links with the structure, language, and law of the former ruling state. Carnegie has argued in the Caribbean context that the manifestation of a desire to maintain such links lies in part:

> in the continuing influence of the historical attitudes even in the era of political independence. Poyers' view of the patterning of early nineteenth century Barbados government on the English system perhaps reflected a desire for self-assurance by colonial settlers which produced the fiction that the colonial systems was Westminster adapted only in relative detail. That psychological comfort still has a part to play in constitutional design is no doubt too obvious for any warning to be needed against denying its value ...[59]

Understanding the dynamics at play in the invocation of principles as a conduit to foreign legal material requires some reflection on power disparity in the migration of constitutional and fundamental rights law judgments. Chang and Yeh in their study of the 'Internationalization of Constitutional Law' point to such a power disparity in judicial comparativism in constitutional law, citing examples of the US Supreme Court and the German Federal Constitutional Court, which are often cited by foreign courts within their respective geographical regions and legal families, but which seldom refer to foreign cases in their own judgments.[60] Examination of comparative case law, including case law discussed in Part III above, reveals a greater incidence of borrowing by the former colonies than by the former imperial power. This suggests that there is a remnant of colonial power at play here, as well as a legal historical basis that encourages the investigation of historical English precedents as explanatory aids. Further dissection reveals that among the courts in the Commonwealth, there is more judicial discursive power possessed by the larger, more developed and majority white states than accrues to the smaller, less developed, majority black states.[61] The reasons for the power disparity among Commonwealth states may include the locus (both physical and intellectual) of legal training for judges, the fact that the new states have developed on the ideas of

[58] Anne-Marie Slaughter, 'A Typology of Transjudicial Communication' (1994) 29 *University of Richmond Law Review* 99, 134.

[59] Carnegie (n 31 above) 11.

[60] Chang and Yeh (n 5 above) 1176.

[61] Cheryl Saunders and Adrienne Stone, 'Reference to Foreign Precedents by the Australian High Court: A Matter of Method' in Tania Groppi & Marie-Claire Ponthoreau (eds), *The Use of Foreign Precedents by Constitutional Judges* (Hart Publishing, 2013) 33–34; Chang and Yeh (n 5 above) 1176. In Trinidad and Tobago as well as Guyana the majority ethnic group is of Indian descent, with the population of Afro-descendants the second largest group: http://www.indexmundi.com/trinidad_and_tobago/demographics_profile.html (accessed 19 October 2013), http://www.indexmundi.com/guyana/ethnic_groups.html (accessed 19 October 2013).

British constitutionalism so there may be more pedagogical value in referring to British judgments, institutional affiliation with educational facilities in the more developed states,[62] the perception that some jurisdictions are more 'developed' and therefore have greater reputational currency, functional resource-based considerations that encourage states to consult the judicial record of jurisdictions that have already addressed difficult issues in hard cases, and the increased availability of judicial decisions from more developed states.

The implications of this power disparity in the legal and cultural life of the state are significant. The first set of implications is functional. If the migration of constitutional ideas and case law travels mostly in one direction, this casts doubt on the metaphor and existence of true transnational judicial *dialogue*. If one assumes that comparativism and the internationalisation of constitutional law is useful, unbalanced migration also adversely affects the benefits of judicial comparativism as it diminishes the perspectives that inform judicial decision-making. This discussion of the implications of an imbalance in borrowing does not seek to discount the divergence that occurs in the process of comparative analyses undertaken in borrowing states; references to the use of implied principles in foreign law do not inevitably result in adoption of the particular applications of the principle in that foreign law. Foreign law has been distinguished on the basis of textual differences in the constitutional framework and local circumstances, including social, religious, and political culture. Further, while the historical roots of constitutional principles are identified as English, there is judicial acknowledgement that they continue to evolve in the constitutional context of the new jurisdiction.[63] More broadly, there are cultural implications to the imbalance of borrowing power. It reinforces a narrative—steeped in a colonial legacy—that the newly independent states, particularly those of the Caribbean, are still grasping for legitimacy, to be 'made into men'.[64] This cultural impact—while not automatically resulting in fealty to British, Canadian or Australian doctrine—affects both the legal and political culture by colouring institutional behaviour.

V. DEVELOPING COMMON APPROACHES TO COMMON PROBLEMS

It has been convincingly argued in defence of comparative judicial analysis that it may be useful for countries to harmonise their approaches to similar problems. A particular method of approaching a legal problem may prove

[62] See references to the influence of intellectual tradition in *Hinds* (n 32 above) 212.

[63] *Remuneration Reference* (n 35 above) 106.

[64] Tracy Robinson, 'Gender, Nation and the Common Law Constitution' (2008) 28 *Oxford Journal of Legal Studies* 735, 746.

so fruitful that it is sensible to regard it as a permanent resource.[65] There are features discernible in the development of the content of principles by foreign law which show some evidence that the countries under examination are developing common methodological approaches to common problems. Of course, the dominant methodological approach in our analysis is the combination of citing implied principles and foreign law.

One example of an area in which there are common problems to which common approaches have been developing is the prevalent citation of foreign law applying implied constitutional principles as guides to the organisation of state institutions. In *New South Wales v Commonwealth* (*Wheat* case) the High Court of Australia held that although section 101 of the Constitution provided for an Inter-State Commission and permitted the Commonwealth Parliament to confer powers upon the Commission to administer inter-state trade, the Constitution does not permit Parliament to confer the powers of a court on the Inter-State Commission.[66] The 'fundamental principle of the separation of powers' was employed to assist in resolving the debate regarding the correct interpretation of section 101.[67] The Court cited English and US law in clarifying the distinction between the executive and the judiciary and in establishing the circumstances in which adjudicative functions were judicial as opposed to administrative.[68] A similar dynamic was also evident in cases such as *Victorian Stevedoring*,[69] regarding the constitutional validity of section 3 of the Transport Workers Act 1928–1929 (Cth) which conferred on the Governor General the power to make regulations governing the employment of transport workers and the licensing of persons engaged as transport workers. Under the section, the Governor General was empowered to make regulations prohibiting the employment of unlicensed persons. Having been convicted of an offence against the regulations, the appellants challenged their convictions, arguing inter alia, that it was 'inconsistent with the distribution made by the Constitution of legislative, executive and judicial powers' for the legislature to delegate its powers to a member of the executive.[70] The High Court examined whether the separation of powers principle prohibited the delegation of the legislative power under consideration, ultimately finding that legislative power may be delegated to the

[65] Jeremy Waldron, *'Partly Laws Common to All Mankind': Foreign Law in American Courts* (Yale University Press, 2012) 61.

[66] The case was decided after the enactment of the Constitution of the Commonwealth of Australia 1900 but before the Statute of Westminster 1931, which may be regarded as the point at which Australian independence begins.

[67] *New South Wales v Commonwealth of Australia* (1915) 20 CLR 54 (HC, Australia) 88 (Isaacs J).

[68] ibid 89–92.

[69] *Victorian Stevedoring and General Contracting Co Pty Ltd v Dignan* (1931) 46 CLR 73 (HC, Australia).

[70] ibid 90.

executive and that there was a valid delegation in this case. In this discussion the complexities of arriving at the practical application of a constitutional principle was illustrated through references not only to the English division of power but also to federal common law systems in the USA and Canada.[71]

Foreign law is also heavily cited in reference to applications of constitutional principles in support of due process requirements, including the requirement of access to courts.[72] *Church of Scientology v Woodward*[73] provides an illustration of the way in which the procedural applications of the rule of law might be used to beckon to judicial discourse in other jurisdictions. The Church of Scientology and one of its members sought a declaration that they were not security risks under the Australian Security Intelligence Organization Act 1979 (Cth) and that the Director-General of the Australian Security Intelligence Organization (ASIO) acted outwith its powers under the 1979 Act in obtaining and distributing information about them and characterising them as security risks. One issue in the case was whether the Act had implicitly excluded judicial review for ultra vires (though allowing for review for corruption or mala fides). The majority of the Court rejected the Solicitor General's submission that judicial review of the ASIO was excluded by the Act.[74] Referring to the rule of law as a requirement of access to courts led the court to cite English authorities on the importance of allowing citizens access to courts to make complaints against the executive.[75] Notably, there is a recurrence throughout this study of access to courts as a common application of implied constitutional principles throughout the jurisdictions examined. Consequently, this application of the principles unsurprisingly provides fertile ground for comparative judicial reasoning.

There was a similar connection of due process requirements to the rule of law and the use of the rule of law principle to invoke foreign law in the Privy Council's decision in *Thomas v Baptiste*[76] holding that the right not to be deprived of life without due process under section 4(a) of the Constitution of Trinidad and Tobago 1976 prevented the state from executing the applicants before the resolution of their petitions in the Inter-American rights system.[77] In delivering the judgment, Lord Millett described the concept of due process of law as inclusive of respect for the rule of law and connected this principle to global tradition, saying that due process 'invokes the concept of the rule of law itself and the universally accepted standards of justice

[71] ibid 89–98.
[72] This application would form part of the legalistic conception of the rule of law as discussed in ch 3 above.
[73] (1980–1982) 154 CLR 25 (HC, Australia).
[74] ibid 55.
[75] ibid 70–71.
[76] *Thomas v Baptiste* (n 3 above).
[77] ibid 22.

observed by civilised nations which observe the rule of law'.[78] The judges also traced the history of the due process clause to the Magna Carta and to the Fifth Amendment to the Constitution of the USA. For the majority in *Thomas*, the due process clause embodied both the separation of powers principle by 'exclud[ing] legislative as well as executive interference with the judicial process' and the rule of law principle, 'thus giv[ing] constitutional protection to the concept of procedural fairness.'[79] Finally, the majority's statement that the right not to have the outcome of the legal proceedings superseded by executive action is a right 'accorded by the common law' and affirmed in the due process clause, also provides an avenue to a legal network beyond Trinidad and Tobago.

These points in the judgment are revealing; there is a clear, explicit, and repeated attempt to connect the constitutional principles invoked by the court in protection of due process to global standards (at least, those observed by 'civilised nations'), notably global standards that may not be limited to a particular text. This was important in light of the fact that the case concerned the extent to which domestic courts and the executive in Trinidad and Tobago were required to observe the American Convention on Human Rights and the processes of the Inter-American system. By invoking principles recognised globally, there is an incorporation of foreign and international doctrine, ostensibly without adopting a particular foreign or international text. In addition, the reference to the common law right to procedural fairness situates the case—and the state—within the common law tradition. Consequently, the majority's holding was not only a matter of respecting global standards, but a somewhat more specific matter of respecting common law standards, and one which the legal profession in a fellow common law country would find especially persuasive.

Yet, the Privy Council's references to standards observed by 'civilised nations' bear a distinctively negative cultural cast in the colonial and post-colonial context. There is influential literature on colonial and post-colonial discourse which posits that the term 'civilised' expresses adoption of—and assimilation into—European culture as well as an the superiority of European culture.[80] As Césaire put it, the colonial construct of civilisation was one in which 'the civilized world was Europe'.[81] Speaking as a Judicial Committee that stretches from the colonial to post-colonial period, and which has its geographical locus in England, the Privy Council's language in this respect is unfortunately reminiscent of a hierarchical relationship between the (former) imperial power and the (former) colonial state. This representation of hierarchy arguably influences the borrowing between the

78 ibid.
79 ibid.
80 See, eg, Ania Loomba, *Colonialism/Postcolonialism* (Routledge, 2005) 255.
81 Aimé Césaire, *Discourse on Colonialism* (Monthly Review Press, 1978) 28.

respective judicial institutions in the states concerned, and perhaps contributes to the borrowing imbalance discussed above.

VI. CYCLICAL BORROWING

As noted above, there is a greater tendency for judges in the former colonies (particularly the Commonwealth Caribbean) to cite UK judgments than vice versa, and the cases discussed in this chapter reflect the high incidence of references to the UK law in the courts of the former colonies. Despite this general imbalance, there is evidence of a feedback loop that sees judgments of the newer states which invoke implied constitutional principles being referenced in UK case law. This is evident, for instance, in UK judgments on the separation of powers. There are three main reasons for this cyclical pattern. First, there are perceptions of similarities in the structure of state as all these jurisdictions have (to varying extents)[82] a parliamentary style of government. Secondly, they are cases in which the Privy Council remains the final appellate tribunal so a Privy Council judgment would impact the UK House of Lords (now the UK Supreme Court) as they are decided by (largely) the same pool of judges. Thirdly, in light of the discussion in the previous section of this chapter, there are areas in which common techniques and solutions are being developed across jurisdictions to address common problems.

The cyclical pattern can have an impact on the accuracy of the analysis of the content principles in adjudication. There may be an opportunity for reflection and correction of errors, in a sense allowing for the correction of the court's analysis. However, there is also the possibility that the pattern simply results in the repetition and dissemination of errors. What is interesting and may be worthy of further research is the extent to which the adoption and repetition of a flawed understanding of the application of a principle may then change the reality to fit the flawed model. These ideas can be explained by way of example from the impact of the *Hinds* case. As we have seen, Lord Diplock's statements on the separation of powers in the Westminster system have been subject to criticism. Yet, segments of his comments have been repeated and adopted in important cases in the Caribbean by the Privy Council, and in the UK by the House of Lord. Whatever the accuracy of Lord Diplock's comments at the time they were made, they have arguably had a substantial impact on subsequent judicial understanding and exposition of the separation of powers doctrine. Could the argument be made that Lord Diplock's assessment of the strength of the separation of powers principle in Westminster style constitutionalism has

[82] A notable caveat is that Trinidad and Tobago, for example, now has elements of a presidential structure.

contributed over time to the strengthening of that principle in the UK and the Caribbean?

The series of cases—*Hinds*, *Anderson*, *Mollison* and *Astaphan*—assist in dissecting the cyclical pattern and the issues it raises. Lord Diplock's statements on the separation of powers have influenced the UK House of Lords, as revealed in the *Anderson* judgment in which attorneys on both sides cited *Hinds* in their submissions and *Hinds* was cited in the judgment of Lord Steyn, who maintained that:

> The relationship between the legislature and the executive is close. On the other hand, the separation of powers between the judiciary and the legislative and executive branches of government is a strong principle of our system of government. The House of Lords and the Privy Council have so stated: Attorney General for Australia v The Queen [1957] AC 288, 315; Liyanage v The Queen [1967] 1 AC 259, 291; Hinds v The Queen [1977] AC 195; Duport Steels Ltd v Sirs [1980] 1 WLR 142, 157b.[83]

The first notable feature of this quotation is the invocation of foreign law in supporting Lord Steyn's description of the application of the separation of powers. Secondly, most of the sources cited by Lord Steyn are Privy Council judgments emanating from former colonies. Thirdly, it was the less controversial aspect of Lord Diplock's assessment—that focussing on the separation of the judiciary from the other branches—which was expressly adopted in this case.

The *Mollison* case subsequently shows the full cycle of the use of implied constitutional principles to invoke foreign law. The courts in *Hinds*, *Anderson*, and *Mollison* were all faced with similar questions of the constitutionality or rights consistency of the exercise of sentencing powers by the executive. As we have seen, the *Hinds* panel found that the separation of powers principle prevented the legislature from transferring sentencing powers away from the judiciary. This judgment was cited by the House of Lords in *Anderson* in its application of the separation of powers principle as an aid in the interpretation of Article 6(1) of the ECHR. Both the *Hinds* judgment and *Anderson* were influential in the landmark decision in *Mollison*, revealing a continued cross-jurisdictional conversation on the separation of powers principle and its impact on the right to liberty. The impact of reasoning by principle and comparativism was central in *Mollison* as the court's decision effectively bypassed express provisions of the Constitution in question. In holding that a sentence of detention during the Governor General's pleasure was inconsistent with the implied principle of the separation of powers, the Privy Council evaded the savings law clause of the Constitution, which prevented the court from invalidating a statute for inconsistency with

[83] *R (Anderson) v Secretary of State for the Home Department* [2002] UKHL 46, [2003] 1 AC 837 [39].

the Constitution's fundamental rights provisions. In delivering the judgment of the Board, Lord Bingham referred to Lord Steyn's statement in *Anderson* that the separation of the exercise of judicial power from the other two branches, 'based on the rule of law', was 'a characteristic feature of democracies'. Lord Steyn in turn, had referred to Lord Diplock's judgment in *Hinds* in arriving at the decision in *Anderson*. There was a progression whereby the implied constitutional principle was used along with the constitutional provisions in *Hinds* and again in *Anderson*, while in *Mollison*, the implied principle arguably displaced the text of the Constitution.

What emerges is that reasoning by principles and the use of principles to incorporate foreign law reflects an attempt to develop solutions to similar problems. This factor, in combination with the similarity of personnel between the uppermost echelons of the judicial branch in the UK and the Caribbean (and formerly, Australia)[84], contributes to the cyclical borrowing pattern. It is, on the one hand, a cyclical pattern, but on the other hand, not entirely reciprocal, because in one sense, the judges of the House of Lords/UK Supreme Court are referring to the words of members of their own bench, despite the fact that the law being adjudicated is foreign.

Lord Diplock's description of the separation of powers principle in *Hinds* also influenced the judgment in *Astaphan*, which was discussed in detail in chapter seven. The Eastern Caribbean Court of Appeal held that unrestricted delegation of the legislative power of taxation to the executive constituted an abdication of the powers of the legislature which was inconsistent with the separation of powers doctrine.[85] In arriving at this conclusion, the court endorsed in totality Lord Diplock's assessment that the separation of powers was an implicit principle in Westminster model constitutions. Unlike *Anderson*, *Astaphan* showed a wider application of this principle, extending beyond the more broadly accepted separation of the judiciary from the other branches, to an understanding that there is also a meaningful—and judicially enforceable—separation between the executive and legislative branches. Accordingly, to the extent that Lord Diplock was mistaken or painted with too broad a brush in *Hinds*, this error was repeated, with concrete consequences in *Astaphan*. Alternatively, the *Hinds* assessment may have been applicable to Westminster-*style* constitutions, even if not to the Westminster system itself as practised in the UK. This distinction partly explains the difference between *Astaphan* and *Anderson*, in which Lord Steyn said of the UK constitution, that '*[o]ur* constitution has, however, never embraced a rigid doctrine of separation of powers.'[86]

[84] See *Attorney General for Australia v The Queen* [1957] AC 288 (JCPC, Australia), cited in *Anderson* (ibid) [39].

[85] *Astaphan & Co (1970) Ltd v Comptroller of Customs of Dominica* (1996) 54 WIR 153 (Eastern Caribbean CA, Dominica) 153.

[86] *Anderson* (n 83 above) [39] (emphasis added).

VII. CONCLUSION

Jeremy Waldron has articulated a defence of comparative judicial analysis premised on the belief that citation of foreign law takes account of the consensus developed in the *ius gentium*—a body of legal principles recognised in the legal world; within the *ius gentium* foreign law 'represents a legal consensus among the nations of the world'.[87] However, there must be more nuance in our assessment of the practice of using constitutional principles as a bridge to foreign law. There is an argument to be made that Waldron's thesis applies insofar as the implied constitutional principles are part of a consensus among nations that have adopted a form of democratic constitutionalism. However, as shown in this chapter, comparative analysis develops heavily within legal systems so that the jurisdictions cited by the courts referred to in this thesis are almost exclusively common law legal systems; there are some jurisdictions that are more frequently cited than others; and with the exception of the areas in which we see cyclical borrowing, there does not exist an equal, reciprocal borrowing pattern.

This chapter examined not merely the borrowing or migration of doctrines or principles, but also the migration of a particular methodology. This methodology is on one level, the invocation of implied constitutional principles, and on further examination, a methodology of invoking implied constitutional principles which are then connected to foreign norms or to international standards. The main functions of this connected use of comparative analysis and the invocation of implied constitutional principles are to forge a connection between the present and the past, and between the domestic and the global. The cases show that there is a process of 'transnationalisation' taking place at a high level of abstraction but that the details of the applications of implied constitutional principles in each state are heavily influenced by the domestic constitution or rights text, the particular governmental structure adopted in the state, and the judges' own views and assessments.

Burgeoning comparativism, levels of abstraction and interaction with text are all factors that influence the normative desirability of the practice of employing implied principles as gateways to comparative legal analysis. These issues form the subject of the proceeding chapter, which addresses the legitimacy of the use of implied constitutional principles in fundamental rights adjudication.

[87] Waldron, *Partly Laws Common* (n 65 above).

8

The Legitimacy of Reliance on Implied Constitutional Principles in Fundamental Rights Adjudication

I. INTRODUCTION

THIS BOOK HAS been decidedly aimed at exploring the functions of implied constitutional principles in rights adjudication, rather than joining the normative debate whether courts ought to rely on such principles. Yet, emerging from reflections on the functions played by principles are dynamics and considerations that should quite properly influence the determination whether and in what circumstances judges are constitutionally justified in turning to implied principles. While this chapter is not designed to encompass exhaustive discourse on the normative issues, it seeks to connect functions played by implied principles and the themes uncovered in the foregoing chapters, to the question of legitimacy. The chapter therefore suggests a path forward for systematic normative analysis of the implied principle techniques. This analysis provides useful categories for organising the normative critique and creating critical distinctions which clarify that the normative question may yield a multiplicity of answers, depending on factors discussed below. This discussion can thus be considered as a prolegomenon to normative analysis.

There are four factors that are likely to influence the normative question of whether judges ought to use implied constitutional principles in adjudication. These factors identify the main philosophical, institutional, and textual narratives that should influence an appraisal of the legitimacy of reasoning by implied principles in fundamental rights cases in a constitutional democracy. First among these is the process and source of implication of the constitutional principle, such as, for instance, implication from the preamble. Secondly, the specific use for which the implied constitutional principle is employed—as an interpretative aid, as a gateway to foreign law, or as a ground for invalidating legislation—conditions any conclusion on the institutional legitimacy of the courts in reasoning by implied constitutional principles. Included in this analysis is the question whether one or all of these uses of implied principles operates to supplant bills of rights by unwritten principles.

Further to institutional concerns, the distinction between the nature of principles and rules engages the level of determinacy of the constitutional principle in question. Despite charges of vagueness or indeterminacy as a driving complaint against the use of principles, it will be shown that the level of determinacy is the least important of the four factors, because, as is discussed below, the charge of indeterminacy can also be laid at the feet of rules expressed in a constitution or bill of rights. Moreover, determinacy is not the ultimate objective of prescribing constitutional and fundamental rights norms. The fourth and final factor considered is the degree of similarity between reasoning by implied principles and adoption of a doctrine that allows for the defeat of 'unconstitutional constitutional amendments'.

II. PROCESS OF IMPLICATION OF THE IMPLIED CONSTITUTIONAL PRINCIPLE

Discourse on the legitimacy of such implied constitutional principles must primarily take account of the process of implication of these principles, which were outlined in chapter two. For ease of reference, the five main methods of implication are: (1) description of terms in the text as synonymous with the implied principle in question (the equivalence method); (2) description of terms in the text, such as the right to equality, as applications of the principle in question (the application method); (3) implication of principles from the structure of the text (the structuralist method); (4) implication from references to principles in parts of the constitution which are not expressly justiciable, such as the preamble (the preambular method); (5) adoption from the unwritten British constitution from which independent constitutions in question derive much of their inspiration (the historical method).[1]

As the judicial decisions examined throughout this study are products of a process of interpretation of a constitution, bill of rights, and/or other legislation, the method of implication may be perceived as more or less legitimate based on its conformity with the accepted purpose and nature of judicial interpretation of statutes. Aileen Kavanagh has observed that the accepted purpose of statutory interpretation is to determine the meaning of the text.[2] Yet, as she argues, determining the meaning of a statutory

[1] These methods of implication relate to four sources, as outlined in ch 2: substantive provisions in the Constitutions or rights text, preambles, the structure of the Constitution, and the 'unwritten English constitution'.

[2] Aileen Kavanagh, 'The Elusive Divide between Interpretation and Legislation under the Human Rights Act 1998' 24 *Oxford Journal of Legal Studies* 259, 262.

text is not limited to finding the literal meaning of the words used. There are terms which are 'linguistically irresolvable', for which a literal meaning is not helpful in determining the issue before the court.[3] To determine the meaning of such terms, it is necessary for judges to engage in substantive evaluation.[4] Lord Hoffmann, sitting in the Privy Council in *Matadeen v Pointu* expressed a similar sentiment in reference to constitutional interpretation, where he stated that while judges are not free from 'the task of interpreting the statutory language':

> The background of a constitution is an attempt, at a particular moment in history, to lay down an enduring scheme of government in accordance with certain moral and political values. Interpretation must take these purposes into account. Furthermore, the concepts used in a constitution … may expressly state moral and political principles to which judges are required to give effect in accordance with their own conscientiously held views of what such principles entail.[5]

For instance, the literal meaning of the term 'discrimination' would not have resolved the issue in *Ghaidan* regarding whether the exclusion of same-sex couples from the scheme for succession to rent-controlled tenancies was inconsistent with the Article 14 right to non-discrimination. Nor would a literal construction of the words used in the Tribunals Act 2007 have led to a determination in the *Cart* case of the extent of judicial supervision over the Upper Tribunal allowed or required by the law.

Accordingly, the starting point is that the objective of interpretation is to declare the meaning of the text. This is not identical to a claim that the meaning of the text can only be gleaned from the text itself to the exclusion of techniques involving external material, but it assumes that the text is the focal point of the techniques used and the reasons given, and that the ultimate purpose remains to determine the meaning of that text. By this metric, the implication of a principle through the equivalence method and the application method are fairly consistent with the objective of determining the meaning of a statutory term or the text as a whole. Conversely, implication from unstated assumptions of the constitution would lie at the other end of the spectrum, as it possesses less explicit connection to the text. It is more challenging to maintain that implying principles from unstated assumptions of the constitutional or rights document satisfies this metric; the activity of 'assumption' may have a focal point based in the philosophy of the judge in question, or based on the judge's assumptions of the constitution, the state and the institution which she represents. The text may indeed be lost or obscured in the process of assumption. In fact, the very notion of an 'unstated assumption' suggests a disconnection with the text, in the way

[3] ibid.
[4] ibid.
[5] *Matadeen v Pointu* [1998] 3 WLR 18 (JCPC, Mauritius) 25.

that an implication from the structure of the constitutional instrument, for instance, does not. Therefore, the argument from the purpose of interpretation presents more challenges for the unstated assumptions method of implication.

The importance of a 'textual anchor' was reflected in Justice Major's judgment in *Imperial Tobacco*. In rejecting the appellants' argument that the retroactivity of the Tobacco Damages and Health Care Costs Recovery Act 2000 was invalid for violation of the rule of law, Justice Major maintained that such an application of the rule of law would undermine the principles of constitutionalism and democracy, principles which 'very strongly favour upholding the validity of legislation that conforms to the express terms of the Constitution (and to the requirements, such as judicial independence, that flow by necessary implication from those terms).'[6] Vincent Kazmierski sees a contradiction between the rejection of independent force for implied principles such as the rule of law and the suggestion that legislation must conform to the requirements 'that flow by necessary implication' from the terms of the text.[7] However, this criticism misses the crux of Justice Major's position, which illuminated a fine point regarding the process of implication of a principle. A similar approach had been advanced by Robin Elliott and Patrick Monahan, who argued that courts ought to be more receptive to implied principles where the application of the principle is a 'necessary implication' from the text and structure of the Constitution.[8] Justice Major's distinction between the respective methods of implication for judicial independence and the rule of law suggests that he perceives a difference between the text of the substantive provisions ('the express terms of the Constitution') and the words of the preamble. Thus, he described judicial independence—and not the rule of law—as arising by necessary implication from the terms of the Charter, despite the preamble's reference to the rule of law. Of course, acceptance of the view that the preamble does not form part of the express substantive provisions of the Constitution does not lead to the conclusion that the preambular method cannot be justified as a legitimate method of implication. This is where we return to Kavanagh's argument that interpretation is often about 'substantive evaluation' and Lord Hoffman's statement that constitutional interpretation must assess a constitution as an attempt to lay down, 'at a particular moment in history' a 'scheme

[6] *British Columbia v Imperial Tobacco Canada Ltd* [2005] 2 SCR 473 [66]; Vincent Kazmierski, 'Draconian But Not Despotic: The 'Unwritten Limits of Parliamentary Sovereignty in Canada' (2010) 41 *Ottawa Law Review* 245, 274.

[7] Kazmierski (ibid) 274.

[8] Robin Elliot, 'References, Structural Argumentation and the Organizing Principles of Canada's Constitution' (2001) 80 *Canadian Bar Review* 67, 83–84; Patrick J Monahan, 'The Public Policy Role of the Supreme Court in the *Secession Reference*' (1999) 11 *National Journal of Constitutional Law* 65, 76–77; Kazmierski (n 6 above) at fn 101.

of government in accordance with certain moral and political values'. As seen in chapter two, preambles may play an explanatory role in informing readers of the history and objectives of the enactment of the constitution.[9] Judicial implication of principles via the preamble may therefore represent a genuine attempt to discover the characteristics of that moment in history and the moral and political values underlying the governmental scheme established by the constitution.

Further interpretative guidance can be gleaned from Lord Hoffman's reference in *Matadeen* to the special character of constitutions. Thus, even in cases where the method of implication may diverge from traditional understandings of the nature and methods of statutory interpretation, if the construction in question is that of a Constitution, the divergence can be justified on the basis of the special nature of the statute in question. A Constitution is 'sui generis', as explained by Lord Wilberforce in another Privy Council decision in *Minister of Home Affairs v Fisher*, and requires 'principles of interpretation of its own, suitable to its character'.[10] This special character partly derives from the fact that constitutions must 'endure over time'. Raz emphasises the feature of endurance and continuity of a constitution:

> it is, and is meant to be, of long duration: It is meant to serve as a stable framework for the political and legal institutions of the country, to be adjusted and amended from time to time, but basically to preserve stability and continuity in the legal and political structure, and the basic principles that guide its institutions.[11]

The necessity of endurance justifies techniques that ensure the Constitution's continued relevance and authority, including, for instance, techniques that enable judges to call upon constitutional principles to fill gaps in the text.

The objective of endurance is indicative of the pivotal position of history and tradition in appraising the legitimacy of a jurisprudence of implied constitutional principles. In fact, a historical outlook is part of the very nature of legal interpretation in general. Raz describes the process of interpretation as possessing a 'Janus-like' quality, 'that it faces both backward, aiming to elucidate the law as it is, and forward, aiming to develop and improve it'.[12] The backward-looking aspect takes into account, first, the historical context of the law of the state, and secondly, the desirability of stability and continuity as part of a constitution's source of authority. The historical context of the

[9] Liav Orgad, 'The Preamble in Constitutional Interpretation' (2010) 8 *International Journal of Constitutional Law* 714, 722. See also Eric Voegelin, *Published Essays, 1934–1939, vol 9 of The Collected Works of Eric Voegelin* (University of Missouri Press, 2001) 32.

[10] *Minister of Home Affairs v Fisher* [1980] AC 319 (JCPC, Bermuda) 329 (Lord Wilberforce).

[11] Joseph Raz, *Between Authority and Interpretation: on the Theory of Law and Practical Reason* (Oxford University Press, 2009) 324.

[12] ibid 354.

law proceeds along two tracks. The first may be loosely termed 'external' as it relates to the overall political and legal context in which the law was developed, while the second track is internal as it relates to precedent and previous interpretations of the text in question or similar texts. This internal track is unsurprising, given the central place of precedent in common law systems.

On the importance of the historical context of the law, Mark Walters contends that the theory of *lex non scripta* as fundamental law must, if it is to represent more than the mere application of political-moral sentiment, fit within the legal system's traditions, doctrines, and assumptions about what is 'law' and what it is not.'[13] Case law does reveal traditional acceptance by judges of the use of common law principles—including constitutional principles—in the interpretation and application of statutes. The archetypal example of the application of common law principles to statutory interpretation is *Dr Bonham's Case*, in which Coke uttered the famous words:

> And it appears in our books, that in many cases, the common law will controul Acts of Parliament, and sometimes adjudge them to be utterly void: for when an Act of Parliament is against common right and reason, or repugnant, or impossible to be performed, the common law will control it, and adjudge such Act to be void.[14]

The meaning of Coke's judgment in *Dr Bonham's Case* is contested; the two dominant interpretations proffered being, first, that Coke meant to indicate the power of judges to *declare a statute void* for incompatibility with a higher order law, and secondly, that Coke merely articulated a power of *interpretation*.[15] It has been said of Coke's comments on the relationship between the common law and statute, that 'scholarship may help us narrow the range and his possible meanings, but his language is so rich and ambiguous, and his writing so unsystematic, that he cannot be pinned down exactly.'[16] Without fully engaging in this debate, if one accepts, for the sake

[13] Mark Walters, 'The Common Law Constitution in Canada: The Return of Lex Non Scripta as Fundamental Law' (2001) 51 *University of Toronto Law Journal* 91, 136.

[14] *Dr Bonham's Case* (1610) 8 Co Rep 107a, 118a.

[15] Ian Williams, 'Dr Bonham's Case and "Void" Statutes' (2006) 27 *Journal of Legal History* 111. Commentators who have argued that the Coke advanced a position that statute could be invalidated by judges include Chijioke Dike [1976] *Public Law* 283, 284–87; Allen Dillar Boyer, '"Understanding, Authority, and Will": Sir Edward Coke and the Elizabethan Origins Of Judicial Review' (1997–1998) 39 *Boston College Law Review* 43; Laurence Peronne, 'The Fundamental and Natural Law 'Repugnant Review' Origins of Judicial Review: A Synergy of early English Corporate Law with Notions of Fundamental and Natural Law' (2008) 23 *Brigham Young University Journal of Public Law* 61. The opposing view is advanced in Samuel Thorne, 'Dr Bonham's case' (1938) *Law Quarterly Review* 543; RH Helmholz, 'Bonham's case, judicial review and the law of nature' [2009] *Journal of Legal Analysis* 325.

[16] JW Tubbs, The Common Law Mind: Medieval and Early Modern Conceptions (2000) 160, cited in David Jenkins, 'From Unwritten to Written: Transformation in The British Common-Law Constitution' (2003) 36 *Vanderbilt Journal of Transnational Law* 863, 887 and fn 179.

of argument, the 'voidness account' of Coke's passage, it presents an exceptional occurrence of a statute 'against common right and reason', in which the courts will take the exceptional step of finding that Act of Parliament void. The 'interpretation account' of the passage also articulates the notion that exceptional situations may lead the court to apply a strong power of interpretation to ensure that the statute conforms more closely to common law principles. Whichever interpretation of Coke's statement is most convincing, the Glorious Revolution of 1688 established that Parliament was the supreme law-making authority and subsequently, legislation has been generally viewed as a source of law superior to the common law.[17] Accordingly, I will not belabour the point about *Dr Bonham's case* but Coke's judgment offers clear evidence in support of implied principles from the perspective of the backward-looking aspect of interpretation.

The need to secure continuity and stability, identified by Raz as a rationale for the backward-looking aspect of interpretation, has also received judicial acknowledgement, the Canadian Supreme Court having observed that judicial interpretation involves 'methods that ... ensure continuity, stability and legal order.'[18] In fact, judicial application of implied constitutional principles in interpretation does evince an attempt to maintain stability and continuity within the constitutional order of the state. The judges' anchoring of their interpretive techniques and interpretive reasoning in the history of the state and the desirability of continuity was a defining feature of *Manitoba* and *Hinds*, and Lord Diplock characterised continuity as an element of the intent of the framers of the Constitution.[19] As such, the desire for continuity which permeates the use of implied principles was presented as the result of the framers' intent, another common—and perhaps more orthodox—constitutional interpretive technique. These methods of reasoning represent the historical aspect of the nature of interpretation, which Raz correctly identifies as part of the core of the nature of interpretation.

III. THE TYPE OF USE INVOLVED

In a sceptical article on the use of implied constitutional principles by the Canadian Supreme Court, Jean Leclair acknowledged that the legitimacy of that use depends on the function of the principles in the court's reasoning.[20] However, the work of methodically classifying these functions

[17] Ian Loveland, *Constitutional law, Administrative Law, and Human Rights: A Critical Introduction*, 6th edn (Oxford University Press, 2012) 24–29.

[18] *Reference re Secession of Quebec* [1998] 2 SCR 217 (SC, Canada) [33].

[19] *Hinds v R* [1977] AC 195 (JCPC, Jamaica) 212.

[20] Jean Leclair, 'Canada's Unfathomable Unwritten Constitutional Principles' (2002) 27 *Queen's Law Journal* 389, 431.

and constructing a normative analysis that reflects the different functions has not been undertaken, until now. Further, the analysis of each function is, in turn, affected by the institutional and textual context of the constitutional law of the jurisdiction. The current section of this chapter begins this necessary analysis by indicating the key considerations that factor into the normative analysis of the legitimacy of the respective functions played by implied constitutional principles in fundamental rights adjudication in the respective contexts of the common law jurisdictions examined.

A. Implied Principles as Interpretative Aids

The use of implied constitutional principles as interpretative aids is more easily defensible as a legitimate exercise of the court's constitutional jurisdiction in a state without a constitution or bill of rights. Accordingly, in the UK which lacked both instruments prior to the HRA 1998, there is a particularly strong argument that it was the responsibility of the common law to produce the principles necessary for the protection of individual rights. The articulation of this role of the common law was a cornerstone of Dicey's conceptualisation of the rule of law. In fact, the capacity of the common law to protect individual rights was manifested in *Entick v Carrington*, in which the common law tort of trespass and the rule that there must be legal authority for the powers asserted and exercised by the executive were employed to protect the individual's property from invasion and confiscation by the state.[21]

The extent to which judges ought to have recourse to implied constitutional principles to resolve rights issues in the UK subsequent to the implementation of the HRA 1998 on 2 October 2000 remains a live issue. A useful factor to consider in resolving this question is the evidence that UK judges have largely accepted that the common law continues to be operative as a source of rights protection in the post-HRA era. First, this position was foreshadowed in cases (prior and subsequent to the HRA) establishing what the judges referred to as 'constitutional rights'. For instance, in *Leech*, Steyn LJ (as he then was) held that 'the principle of our law that every citizen has a right of unimpeded access to the court … must rank as a constitutional right'.[22] The use of the term 'constitutional' is evidence of something fundamental and of a higher order than ordinary law. Secondly, as we saw in chapters three and five, the principle of legality has emerged as a formidable venue for the application of constitutional principles to the interpretation

[21] *Entick v Carrington* (1765) 19 Str 1029, (1558–1774) All ER 41.
[22] *R v SSHD, ex p Leech (No 2)* [1994] QB 198 (CA) 210.

of legislation and this principle has seen continued application beyond the HRA 1998.[23] Beyond the HRA 1998, the courts continue to acknowledge the importance of common law principles of rights protection. Hence, the House of Lords held in *A v SSHD (No 2)* that:

> The principles of the common law ... compel the exclusion of third party torture evidence as unreliable, unfair, offensive to ordinary standards of humanity and decency and incompatible with the principles which should animate a tribunal seeking to administer justice.[24]

Further evidence of the continued acceptance of the role of the common law beyond the HRA 1998 in this field can be found in *Rabone v Pennine Care NHS Foundation Trust*. In *Rabone* the issue arose whether UK courts have an obligation or a discretion to develop Convention rights applied through the HRA 1998 beyond the definition provided by decisions of the European Court of Human Rights.[25] Lord Brown concluded that UK courts could develop the common law to protect rights, despite the absence of a consistent line of case law from the Strasbourg Court, but that in so doing, the UK courts must clarify that they are developing the common law and not providing a definition of Convention rights.[26] This admonition rests upon the premise that the common law continues to be a source of rights concurrent with the HRA 1998.

Most compelling however, is the common law resurgence in both rights issues and broader constitutional questions represented most vividly in *Osborn v Parole Board* and *HS2*. Lord Reed's admonition in *Osborn* that while the importance of the Human Rights Act is unquestionable, it does not supersede the protection of human rights under the common law or statute, signalled a renaissance of pre-HRA common law rights.[27] Moreover, specific reliance on common law doctrines of due process or procedural fairness as the first port of call before calling upon Convention rights, reinforced not only the worth of domestic law, but also that of the common law. Through *HS2*, the UK Supreme Court recognised the existence and potency of constitutional principles, proclaiming that in addition to constitutional statutes such as the European Communities Act 1972 and the HRA 1998, 'the common law itself also recognises certain principles as fundamental to the rule of law' and that 'there may be fundamental principles, whether contained in other constitutional instruments or recognised at common law, of which Parliament when it enacted the European Communities Act 1972

[23] *R v SSHD, ex p Simms* [2000] 2 AC 115 (HL) 132; *R v SSHD, ex parte Pierson* [1997] UKHL 37, [1998] AC 539 (HL) 577–78.

[24] [2005] UKHL 71, [2006] 2 AC 221 (HL).

[25] [2012] UKSC 2, [2012] 2 AC 72 (UKSC).

[26] ibid [113].

[27] *Osborn v Parole Board* [2013] UKSC 61, [2014] 1 All ER 369 [57].

did not either contemplate or authorise the abrogation.'[28] Thus, despite the impact of Europe through the European Convention on Human Rights and the European Community, common law constitutional principle is seen to retain a pride of place that stands alongside European norms.

Criticism of the interpretative function gains more credence where there is a codified Constitution as is the case in the Commonwealth Caribbean and Canada, where there is a written Constitution containing a Bill of Rights, and in Australia where there is a written Constitution (without a Bill of Rights). In states with a codified Constitution, the criticism is spurred by two factors. The first is the legal effect of the Constitution as a representation of the higher order law of the state; these Constitutions either expressly establish themselves as supreme in the hierarchy of legal sources in the state or have been interpreted as such by the courts. The second factor is the source of the special normative force of this written instrument, that is, the view that the constitution embodies the expression of the constituent power of the state. The constituent power has been described as 'the power that represents the regime's foundational enactment' and thus helps to account for the special status of a written constitution at the foundation of a state.[29]

These characteristics of the written constitution must contribute to normative critiques of the use of implied constitutional principles. However, the central point in the normative discourse surrounding the legitimacy of the use of implied principles in states with a written constitution is the legitimacy of particular interpretative techniques. Accordingly, the reflections on the nature of interpretation in general and of constitutional interpretation specifically, which were outlined in Part II of this chapter, are equally applicable to the current discussion. Consistently with those reflections, it is legitimate for judges to appeal to non-textual aids in interpretation as the constitution comprises much more than the text. Even in jurisdictions with a codified constitution, it has been repeatedly observed that the written constitution does not—indeed cannot—contain all rules and principles which are constitutional in the sense of operating as a restraint on the exercise of state power.[30] Accordingly, the Canadian Supreme Court observed that while the texts have a 'primary place' in determining the law of the Constitution, 'they are not exhaustive'.[31] Further, in using implied constitutional principles in interpretation, courts are acting consistently with precedent and tradition within the common law system.

[28] *R (on the application of HS2 Action Alliance Ltd) v Secretary of State for Transport* [2014] UKSC 3, [2014] 1 WLR 324 [207].

[29] Gary J Jacobsohn, *Constitutional Identity* (Harvard University Press, 2010) 38.

[30] This is the sense of the terms 'constitutional' and 'constitutionalism' that were established in ch 2 above.

[31] *Secession Reference* (n 18 above) [32].

Those are the factors that obtain in the face of codified constitutions but where does the HRA 1998 lie within this analysis? The starting point is that the HRA 1998 constitutes a bill of rights due to both its substantive provisions and their legal effect[32] and that it is a 'constitutional statute'. There are customarily two routes for claiming that the HRA 1998 is a constitutional statute: a procedural route and a substantive route. On the procedural side, the argument is that the HRA 1998 is a constitutional statute by virtue of its insulation from implied repeal. Constitutional orthodoxy holds that the doctrine of implied repeal applies to ordinary statutes, so that if there is a conflict between an earlier statute and a later one, the latter statute impliedly repeals the earlier statute to the extent of the inconsistency.[33] Section 3 of the HRA 1998 challenges this standard rule by requiring courts to interpret all statutes (whether preceding or postdating the entry into force of the HRA 1998) 'so far as it is possible to do so' to achieve consistency with the ECHR rights scheduled to the HRA 1998. By virtue of section 3, legislation enacted subsequent to 2 October 2000 is limited by the HRA to the extent of any inconsistency, rather than the HRA being qualified by the latter statute.[34] 'Proceduralists' therefore maintain that, by virtue of section 3 of the HRA 1998, the doctrine of implied repeal is inapplicable to the HRA 1998, and consequently removes it from the realm of ordinary statute. The substantive approach, on the other hand, maintains that the HRA 1998 does not attain constitutional status by virtue of its resistance to repeal' but by virtue of the fact that it 'purports to protect fundamental rights and freedoms' and does so 'by establishing such rights and freedoms as general norms, that apply to all legislation and all conduct of public authorities.'[35] The definition of constitutional statutes provided by Laws LJ in *Thoburn* is more consistent with the substantive approach, as the learned judge classified as 'constitutional' those statutes that enlarge or diminish fundamental constitutional rights[36] and in the view of Laws LJ, '[t]he special status of constitutional statutes follows the special status of constitutional rights'.[37] Moreover, the procedural argument can hardly stand on its own and ultimately derives sustenance from the substantive changes and substantive import of the statute; it is the substantive effect of the Act that largely contributes (in conjunction with the terms of section 3 itself) to the procedural impact. Whichever sense of

[32] Francesca Klug, 'The Human Rights Act—a "Third Way" or "Third Wave" Bill of Rights' [2001] *European Human Rights Law Review* 361; Aileen Kavanagh, 'Constitutional Review under the UK Human Rights' (Cambridge University Press, 2009) 307.

[33] *Thoburn v Sunderland City Council* [2002] EWHC 195 (Admin), [2003] QB 151 at [62].

[34] See challenge to the position that the HRA 1998 cannot be impliedly repealed in Alison Young, *Parliamentary Sovereignty and the Human Rights Act* (Hart Publishing, 2009) 52–54; Tom Hickman, *Public Law after the Human Rights Act* (Oxford University Press, 2010) 46–47.

[35] Hickman (ibid) 48.

[36] *Thoburn v Sunderland City Council* (n 33 above) [60]–[63].

[37] ibid [62].

the term 'constitutional statute' is used as a means of characterising the HRA 1998, it is clear that it does not function as a 'Constitution' in the way that the bills of rights that form parts of written or codified constitutions do. Despite that the HRA 1998 would be regarded as a constitutional statute under Laws LJ's characterisation of such statutes in *Thoburn*, it is not treated in the way a Constitution is treated. As Alison Young explains, unlike entrenched constitutions, the HRA 1998 can be expressly repealed by ordinary legislation.[38]

B. Implied Principles as Gateways to Comparative Judicial Analysis

The main objections to the legitimacy of the use of implied constitutional principles as gateways to comparative judicial analysis largely mirror those raised in the debate on comparativism in judicial constitutional and rights interpretation more generally. The main arguments can be categorised into three groups: the textual objection, the argument from democracy, and the nationalist or localist critique.[39] The textual objection maintains that judges must observe fidelity to the text of the constitution and to the extent that references to foreign law constitute an illegitimate reliance on a non-textual source. This objection is connected to the second critique—the argument from democracy—which objects to judicial comparativism on the ground that foreign laws have not been democratically approved by the state in question and that neither local judges nor foreign judges issuing foreign judgments are democratically accountable to the state in question. The nationalist critique maintains, as Cheryl Saunders explains, that the constitution is a 'quintessentially national instrument' which responds to 'national perceptions, national needs, and national values.'[40] The localist approach to constitutional interpretation therefore insists that the interpretation and application of the constitution must reflect the constitutional, legal, and political culture of the state as expressed in the founding document. In short, it states that interpretation of the constitution must respect the national identity of the state as expressed in the constitution. Thus, it is part of a drive to restrict epistemological openness in adjudication in order to respect the specific national identity of the state which the court serves.

A useful starting point for assessing the force of these objections in the context of the use of implied principles as a bridge to foreign law is an

[38] Young, *Parliamentary Sovereignty and the HRA* (n 34 above), ch 2.

[39] These are legitimacy-based objections to judicial comparativism; there also exist methodology-based objections to the practice. See Cheryl Saunders, 'The Use and Misuse of Comparative Constitutional Law' (2006) 13 *Indiana Journal of Global Legal Studies* 37; Robert Reed, 'Foreign precedents and judicial reasoning: the American debate and British practice' (2008) 124 *Law Quarterly Review* 253.

[40] Saunders, 'Use and Misuse' (ibid) 50.

observation made by Jeffrey Goldsworthy in his analysis of the migration of constitutional ideas that '[c]onstitutions rarely if ever prescribe a particular interpretive or analytical methodology.'[41] This provides ample space to judges to develop techniques that supply the methodology that has not been prescribed in the text of the constitution. This argument goes some distance towards answering textual objections to both comparative methodology and the use of devices such as implied principles to incorporate foreign law in judicial reasoning. Further, even where there are express rules of interpretation applicable to the constitution, 'the law of interpretation … cannot contain all that can and need be said in an account of legal or constitutional interpretation.'[42] Thus, valuable methodological space remains available to judges.

Moreover, in response to the nationalist complaint against using principles to incorporate foreign law, it must be observed that judicial use of implied constitutional principles inexorably bears a connection to foreign law and foreign or global doctrines. This is because, conceptually, implied constitutional principles are part of a model of constitutionalism[43] and, empirically, the principles are often borrowed or developed from experiences and law in other countries, as is sometimes reflected in preambles to the constitutions and bills of rights. It is these considerations which lie at the base of Gary Jacobsohn's response to localist objectors, which is that where 'courts attempt to interpret and apply 'the principles of democracy' … they are likely to benefit from, or at least not to be undermined by, consideration of how others have addressed these aspirations in the various structural and interpretive choices that define their unique constitutional identities.'[44] It is this argument which is at the crux of the response to originalist and localist objections to the use of the implied constitutional principles. The common law states examined in this study all lay claim to observance of, and 'constitutional commitment' to the rule of law and separation of powers. Despite that their precise application may vary according to local circumstances, the observance and recognition of these principles are not exclusive to any one state, and indeed, as argued in chapter two, they are foundational to the very edifice of democratic constitutionalism.

In considering attacks on the legitimacy of comparative judicial methodology, it is important to recognise and distinguish between comparativism

[41] Jeffrey Goldsworthy, 'Questioning the Migration of Constitutional Ideas: Rights, Constitutionalism and the Limits of Convergence' in Sujit Choudhry, *The Migration of Constitutional Ideas* (Cambridge University Press, 2006) 127, 137–40.

[42] Joseph Raz, *Between Authority and Interpretation* (n 11 above) 356.

[43] Goldsworthy, 'Questioning the Migration of Constitutional Ideas' (n 41 above) 116.

[44] Gary Jacobsohn, 'Constitutional Values and Principles' in Michel Rosenfeld and András Sajó (eds), *The Oxford Handbook of Comparative Constitutional Law* (Oxford University Press, 2012) 790.

at different stages of the life of the constitution. As with the use of implied principles, comparative methodology may occur at the legislative stage as well as at the interpretative stage. This is reflected in the use of foreign law by legislative drafters and the legislature on the one hand, and the citation of foreign law by judges, on the other. The invocation of comparative material by legislators is viewed by critics such as Justice Antonin Scalia as possessing a stronger claim to legitimacy than invocation of comparative law by members of the bench.[45] Thus, to the extent that complaints against the comparative function involve claims related to the argument from democracy and institutional legitimacy, a reasonable response to this critique is that it can be legitimate for courts to embrace methodology that has been embraced by the legislature. This is particularly so if, as shown in chapter seven, courts refer to laws from countries similar to those used in the drafting process.

C. Implied Principles as Grounds for Invalidating Legislation

Where the use of implied principles goes further than the interpretive or comparative functions, and extends to use of the implied principles as grounds for directly invalidating legislation, it can be argued that challenges to legitimacy arise acutely for all the jurisdictions examined, with some challenges applying to all the jurisdictions. However, the significance of particular challenges depends on the institutional and textual arrangements in each respective jurisdiction.

In each jurisdiction, the argument from democracy looms large as a challenge to the use of implied principles as independent grounds for invalidating legislation. The democratic challenge posits that the use of principles as independent grounds for invalidation undermines respect for the will of the people as expressed through their elected representatives in the legislature. The democracy-based objection contains two components. In the first, the complaint is that arguments against pieces of legislation should be settled through the democratic mechanism of voting, rather than the judicial process. Of course, this objection could just as easily be raised (and is often raised) in complaints against judicial review of legislation in general. Accordingly, there is a second component of the democracy-based objection, which is that if legislation is to be defeated through the judicial process, this defeat must be suffered through the weapon of the text of the constitution or bill of rights, rather than through an implied principle exterior to the particular sections of the constitutional or rights instrument. This component of the

[45] Vlad Perju, 'Constitutional Transplants, Borrowing, and Migrations' in Michel Rosenfeld and András Sajó (eds), *The Oxford Handbook of Comparative Constitutional Law* (Oxford University Press, 2012) 1317.

democracy argument views the text of the constitution as an expression of the democratic will. Justice Major expressed the argument from democracy in the following terms in the *Imperial Tobacco* case:

> the appellants' arguments ... fail to recognize that in a constitutional democracy such as ours, protection from legislation that some might view as unjust or unfair properly lies not in the amorphous underlying principles of our Constitution, but in its text and the ballot box.'[46]

Supplementary to the argument from democratic legitimacy is the objection based on the particular constitutive role of the constitution. The constitutive character of a constitution, which has been raised in debates regarding the legitimacy of comparativism in constitutional interpretation, has been explained in the following terms:

> Constitutions have a symbolic power that arises from their constitutive role. Precisely because they provide a framework for government, they are also seen as a repository of important values. Put at its highest, this view has it that constitutions are expressive of national identity.[47]

A meaningful discussion of the force of the democratic-constitutive critique must explore the following threads of argument. The first thread is temporal, raising the question whether the constitutive role of the constitution operates as a 'Big Bang', expressed at the point of enactment of the document and therefore resistant to change overtime. In this sense, the conversation must involve a discussion of the concept of the constituent power, which represents the state's foundational enactment.[48] The concept of the constituent power as a 'profound manifestation of democratic power' may be invoked to mount an acutely strong objection to limitations on legislative power which are not expressed in the text of the founding document. However, the implications of the idea of constituent power remain contested. Therefore, the idea may be marshalled by advocates of reasoning by implied constitutional principles by wielding the argument that as the constituent power was expressed at the founding, the principles derived from the constituent document should prevail over subsequent enactments which are not the product of the constituent assembly. At the base of this conflict over the constituent power are the complex, related questions regarding the definition of the exercise of constituent power and the composition of the constituent assembly. These debates become particularly significant in the discourse on 'unconstitutional' constitutional amendments, which is addressed in Part V of this chapter.

[46] *Imperial Tobacco* (n 6 above) [66].

[47] Adrienne Stone, 'Comparativism in Constitutional Interpretation' [2009] *University of Melbourne Law School* Series 15.

[48] Jacobsohn, *Constitutional Identity* (n 29 above) 38.

The second thread of argument related to the democratic-constitutive critique is textual and seeks to explore the connection between the written constitution and unwritten constitutionalism. The underpinning idea is that the written constitution is enacted, not in isolation, but against a background of implied principles that form the common law Constitution. Thus, Walters has suggested two ways of conceptualising the relationship between written and 'unwritten constitutionalism',[49] which emerge following the enactment of the constitution. The first is to perceive a formal distinction between the written constitution and unwritten constitutional norms. This conceptualisation is useful in common law jurisdictions with no written constitution or with an incomprehensive written constitution, which, for example, does not include a Bill of Rights. On the other hand, in jurisdictions with a comprehensive–rights inclusive–constitution, the second conceptualisation becomes relevant. On the second view, the written constitution is an abstract expression of unwritten norms. What this means, however, is that, in Walters' words, 'this constitution can no more break loose from the unwritten constitution of legality than an island can separate from the seabed that lies beneath the waters that surround it.'[50] Unfortunately, Walters' analysis does not distinguish between distinct functions of implied principles, but it is useful in discussing the critique of the invalidation function by highlighting the inexorable symbiosis between written and unwritten constitutional norms. If these types of norms are intertwined and 'the value of made-law is interdependent upon implicit law', this goes some distance towards establishing that in using implied principles, even as grounds of invalidation, courts are giving effect to the implicit norms that are intimately connected to the written instrument.

The third thread of reasoning to be explored through the lens of the democracy objection centres on the relative institutional legitimacy of organs of the state. As noted in chapter six, where the court concludes that implied constitutional principles can serve as invalidating grounds, the application of the principle in question is usually one related to the separation of the institutional powers of the state and almost exclusively in defence of the court's jurisdictional sphere and institutional power. This generates a 'conflict of interest' perception which may serve to undermine faith in the court's activity as impartial legal decision-making. From a theoretical perspective, this pattern in the judgments can be seen to fall neatly within the framework of rational choice theory or institutional theory. The judges' reasoning could be accounted for as representations of personal self-interest or the interests of the institution of the judiciary. Leclair perceives great danger for the very

[49] See ch 2.

[50] Mark Walters, 'Written Constitutions and Unwritten Constitutionalism' in Grant Huscroft (ed), *Expounding the Constitution: Essays in Constitutional Theory* (Cambridge University Press, 2008) 273.

legitimacy of the court in the use of the implied principles in defence of the judicial sphere, arguing with respect to Canada, that 'in some cases, while the unwritten principle of judicial independence was praised, others, such as the principle of democracy or the rule of law, were clearly neglected' and that '[d]ecisions in which legislation was impugned on the basis of the unwritten principle of judicial independence have all had to do with judicial remuneration, and were all initiated by judges.'[51] Leclair maintains that as '[t]he credibility of the judiciary requires that judges not initiate recourse to law', the initiation of such actions by judges is highly problematic.[52] However, this criticism is, with respect, overblown. There must be, and indeed have been, in various jurisdictions, occasions that judges have recourse to the law. Apart from the *Remuneration Reference*, judges have also had recourse to the law in Trinidad and Tobago, where a judge made a claim challenging his removal from office[53] and the United States of America, where judges have challenged the constitutionality of reductions of their salaries.[54] Further, a purely rational choice model that explains the trend as solely a matter of judicial self-interest is overly simplistic. It is also critical to account for the judges' belief in the suitability and necessity of the institutional processes of the court to do justice to the individual. Such belief in the institutional virtues of the court, and their utility in mediating between the individual and the state, was expressed by judges in the *Remuneration Reference*, *Jackson*, and *White v DPP*.[55]

A final feature of the debate on the legitimacy of the use of implied principles as grounds of invalidation is the impact of parliamentary supremacy. The potency of the challenge posed by the argument from parliamentary supremacy operates on a sliding scale in relation to the extent of the power conferred upon the court to review and strike down legislation. For the UK, there is a particularly strong challenge arising from the orthodox view that the doctrine of parliamentary sovereignty is the controlling principle in the UK Constitution. The upshot is that the substantive limitation on legislative power has not been prescribed or permitted by Act of Parliament, and, secondly, from the institutional point of view, courts do not possess the power to invalidate legislation. While remaining a recognised principle of

[51] Leclair (n 20 above) 432.

[52] ibid.

[53] *Rees v Crane* [1994] 2 AC 173 (JCPC, Trinidad and Tobago).

[54] *Williams v United States* 53 SCt 751, 289 US 553 (1933); *O'Donoghue v United States* 53 SCt 740, 289 US 516 (1933); MK 'Constitutional Law-Court of Claims-Legislative Courts-Reducing Judge's Salary' (1934) 9 *Indiana Law Journal* 318.

[55] *Reference Re Remuneration of Judges of the Provincial Court of Prince Edward Island [1997] 3 SCR 3 (SC, Canada) (Provincial Judges Reference* or *Remuneration Reference)* (Lamer CJ) [124–25]; *R (Jackson) v AG* [2005] UKHL 56, [2006] 1 AC 262 [102] (Lord Steyn), [107] (Lord Hope), [159] (Lady Hale); *White v DPP* (2007) 81 ALJR 1259 (HC, Australia) [189]–[198] (Kirby J, dissenting).

the Australian Commonwealth Constitution, parliamentary supremacy has been diluted by the Constitution's conferral—as interpreted by the courts—of judicial authority to strike down inconsistent statutes. The parliamentary supremacy critique is accordingly less compelling in Australia than in the institutional context of the UK. What does provide significant force for the parliamentary supremacy argument in Australia is that the Constitution does not include a bill of rights and does not expressly confer jurisdiction on the courts to invalidate legislation for violation of rights. Therefore, the use of implied principles to incorporate rights protections and thereby invalidate legislation is in tension with the wide berth provided to Parliament by the Constitution.

In the other states, the supremacy of Parliament as it is understood in the UK or Australia is not the dominant issue, as the courts are accorded the power to invalidate legislation on the ground of rights violations. In the Commonwealth Caribbean the Constitutions are expressly declared to be the supreme law[56] while Canada embraces neither complete parliamentary supremacy nor constitutional supremacy. As discussed in chapter two, in Canada there is an interplay between clauses asserting constitutional supremacy and providing for enforcement of the Charter of Rights on the one hand, and the notwithstanding clause on the other, resulting in two characterisations of Canada's constitutional structure: the dialogue model and the 'new Commonwealth' model.[57] The dialogue model seeks to identify the distinctiveness of the Canadian system of constitutional review from the US system of 'strong' constitutional review. The 'new constitutionalism' model is broader in focus and seeks to identify the distinctions between 'strong-form systems' operating in the US and in countries that form part of the post-World War II paradigm of constitutional review and a new intermediate model which provides a mechanism which permits the legislature to take the final decision away from the courts.[58] What is common to both models is the emphasis on meaningful legislative involvement in the contouring and protection of rights.

From such descriptive analysis of the involvement of the Canadian judicial and legislative branches in the articulation and protection of rights, there has developed a normative discourse requiring the rejection of 'judicial

[56] See, eg, s 1, Constitution of Barbados 1966, which states that the Constitution 'is the supreme law'. Section 2 of the Constitution of Jamaica 1962 does not expressly state that the Constitution is the 'supreme law' but is to the same effect, providing that 'if any other law is inconsistent with this Constitution, this Constitution shall prevail and the other law shall, to the extent of the inconsistency, be void.'

[57] Peter Hogg and Alison Bushell, 'The Charter Dialogue between Courts and Legislatures' (Or Perhaps The Charter of Rights Isn't Such a Bad Thing After All)' (1997) 35 *Osgoode Hall Law Journal* 75; Stephen Gardbaum, *The New Commonwealth Model of Constitutionalism: Theory and Practice* (Cambridge University Press, 2013) 2.

[58] Gardbaum (ibid) 111–21.

supremacy' in Canadian constitutional law. This normative condition is represented in Leclair's critique of the Supreme Court's decisions incorporating implied constitutional principles. For Leclair, the court's decision-making in constitutional cases must evince 'respect for the dialogical dimension of law-making'.[59] A significant part of Leclair's concern that using implied principles erodes the dialogic interplay arises from the observation that, because implied principles are not part of the 'particular sections' of the Charter, they are not subject to the notwithstanding clause.[60] There is therefore, acute apprehension that the use of implied principles as independent grounds fails to maintain the ethos of 'joint responsibility of rights'.[61]

D. Implied Principles as Substitutes for Bills of Rights?

Leclair, while ultimately acknowledging that the legitimacy of using implied principles depends on the purpose they serve and the use courts make of them, expressed concern that '[c]ourts have latitude in the interpretation of a constitution, but they must not appeal to unwritten constitutional principles with the intent of rewriting it.'[62] Accordingly, an analysis of the legitimacy of reasoning by implied constitutional principles in adjudicating rights issues requires consideration whether this reasoning technique acts to supplant the constitutional rights specified in the constitutional or rights text.

Two main features of the courts' invocation of rule of law and separation of powers may prove threatening to the supremacy of the *text* of the constitution, and/or bill of rights. Most clearly, there is the possibility that the implied principles may be used to supply substantive limits against the legislature despite the absence of a bill of rights in the jurisdiction.[63] In Australia, this is arguably the dynamic that is developing through the use of the rule of law and separation of powers principles in rights cases. Through this route, despite the absence of a bill of rights in the Constitution, the courts have created judicially enforceable rights with an unwritten source. Accordingly, commentators on Australian constitutional law have observed that the Australian High Court has implied a bill of rights into the Constitution through implied rule of law and separation of powers principles.[64]

[59] Leclair (n 20 above) 428.
[60] ibid.
[61] The term 'joint responsibility for rights' is borrowed from Gardbaum (n 57 above) 7.
[62] Leclair (n 20 above) 431.
[63] Walters, 'Common Law Constitution' (n 13 above) 91.
[64] George Winterton, 'The Separation of Judicial Power as an Implied Bill of Rights' in Geoffrey Lindell (ed), *Future Directions in Australian Constitutional Law* (Federation Press, 1994); Fiona Wheeler, 'Due Process, Judicial Power and Chapter III in the New High Court' (2004) 32 *Federal Law Review* 205.

This phenomenon has been most pronounced in the High Court's protection of due process rights through the implication of a separation of powers doctrine (particularly a separation of judicial power).[65] For instance, in a leading Australian case on this issue, *Leeth v Commonwealth of Australia*, it was stated that one consequence of respect for the separation of judicial power is that judicial power must be exercised consistently with rules of natural justice.[66] While natural justice requirements would be protected in administrative law, decisions such as *Leeth* have the effect of entrenching these requirements by elevating them to inclusion in the Constitution itself.[67]

A further potential impact of reasoning by implied principles could see implied constitutional principles applying regardless of (contradictory) written provisions in the constitution. Thus, in the UK there is the possibility that implied constitutional principles could provide a foothold for judicial exercise of a power that is wider in scope and greater in potency than that granted by the HRA 1998. The roots of this potential development can be seen from the perspective of Allan's theory on the fundamental pillars of British constitutionalism and the evolution of the British constitution. Allan maintains that it is essential for courts to accord due normative force to the rule of law along with parliamentary supremacy. This would involve courts acknowledging that they are bound by the rule of law to reject legislative breaches of the rule of law. On this view, it is unnecessary for a bill of rights to do this work of restraining legislative interference with rights, since the rule of law as part of the British constitution supplies the normative and institutional space for that restraint on legislative power.[68] This line of argument provides both theoretical foundation and constitutional justification for the potential impact of reasoning by implied constitutional principles.

The application of the implied principles in a manner that seemingly contradicts the constitution or bill of rights could produce both conservative and activist effects. The activist effect in the sense used here refers to the application of the implied principles in support of invalidation of a legislative or executive act. A vivid example of the activist impact is presented by the decision in *Mollison*, in which the Privy Council invalidated legislation on the ground of the implied principle of the separation of powers in order to evade the savings law clause, which saves pre-independence laws from declarations of inconsistency with the Bill of Rights.[69] The conservative

[65] Wheeler, 'Due Process, Judicial Power' (ibid).

[66] (1992) 174 CLR 455 (HC, Australia) 470, 487.

[67] Fiona Wheeler, 'The Doctrine of Separation of Powers and Constitutionally Entrenched Due Process in Australia' (1997) 23 *Monash University Law Review* 248.

[68] TRS Allan, 'Legislative Supremacy and the Rule of Law: Democracy and Constitutionalism' (1985) 44 *Cambridge Law Journal* 111.

[69] *DPP of Jamaica v Mollison* (2003) 64 WIR 140 (JCPC, Jamaica).

effect occurs where the principles provide a basis on which a court declines to invalidate a governmental act or to otherwise exercise restraint in its review of governmental acts. The use of the rule of law in *Reference re Manitoba Language Rights* provides a useful precedent for this conservative effect. The grant of temporary validity to unconstitutional Manitoba statutes, to comply with the 'constitutional guarantee of the rule of law', was fundamentally a preservative act. The novelty and constitutional significance of this decision was signalled by Jean LeClair who observed that '[p]reviously, such principles were never held capable of counteracting the explicit provisions of the Constitution.'[70] Nevertheless, it will be apparent to the reader that the application of the rule of law in the *Manitoba* case, though of substantial normative force, temporarily salvaged the validity of legislation. Thus, a complete appraisal of the decision must account for the fact that the use of the implied principles was conservative in the sense used in this section, and moreover, was applied as a temporary remedial measure.

Where the Canadian Supreme Court has been invited to invalidate legislation using constitutional principles as independent grounds, the Court has been more reticent. *Babcock v Attorney General Canada* provides a useful example.[71] The case arose out of a claim by lawyers at the Vancouver branch of the federal Department of Justice against the federal government for breach of fiduciary duty and breach of contract following the Department of Justice's decision to increase the pay of lawyers in the Toronto branch but not in the other branches. In the course of the case the government objected to the disclosure of 51 documents on the ground that they contained confidential information of the Queen's Privy Council for Canada under section 39 of the Canada Evidence Act 1985. The Vancouver lawyers argued, inter alia, that section 39 was unconstitutional for violation of the implied principles of the rule of law, the independence of the judiciary, and the separation of powers. The Supreme Court rejected these arguments, finding that it is not within the power of the judges to invoke the rule of law and the separation of powers to control legislative power which is not restricted by the terms of the Charter. For McLachlin CJ:

> [i]t is well within the power of the legislature to enact laws, even laws which some would consider draconian, as long as it does not fundamentally alter or interfere with the relationship between the courts and the other branches of government.[72]

The Court's reluctance to apply implied constitutional principles in preference to the terms of the Constitution and Bill of Rights was mirrored in the more recent case of *Imperial Tobacco*, which saw a rejection of submissions that the rule of law could be applied to enforce substantive limitations on

[70] Leclair (n 20 above) 391.
[71] [2002] 3 SCR 3 (SC, Canada).
[72] ibid [57] (McLachlin CJ).

legislation and as a ground on which to invalidate legislation. Major J stated that 'the appellants' conception of the unwritten constitutional principle of the rule of law would render many of our written constitutional rights redundant and, in doing so, undermine the delimitation of those rights chosen by our constitutional framers.'[73]

Overall then, there is some evidence of implied principles emerging as substitutes for bills of rights where such principles supply rights protections in the absence of textual rights provisions for the jurisdiction in question and where the principles apply contrary to contradictory stipulations in the relevant text. Nonetheless, it is also critical to take account of the variation in results that can be produced when principles are applied in a manner that seemingly contradict the constitutional or rights text.

E. Exceptional Cases

A final question to consider before departing from the topic of the type of use involved is the question whether to treat exceptional cases differently in an assessment of the legitimacy of the use of implied constitutional principles. As noted in previous chapters, the concept of 'exceptional circumstances' has been referred to by Lord Steyn in the *Jackson* case, and adopted by Lord Hope in *AXA*, but its lineage is much older. In fact, exceptional cases have long formed part of the discourse in constitutional law. The nature of the exception can refer to the facts that arise in the case before the court, as well as the powers exercised by the court to resolve the dispute in the case.

There are two sets of cases in which the character of exceptionality is claimed. The first category contains cases where the constitution does not permit judicial invalidation of legislation (a jurisdiction whose Constitution includes the principle of parliamentary supremacy) yet judges lay a claim to common law or judicial control of statute in exceptional cases. In this category, we may place *Dr Bonham's case* and the *obiter dicta* in the *Jackson* case. This category involves two propositions. The first proposition is that there is a source of law, that, in at least 'exceptional circumstances', may be superior to parliamentary legislation. The second proposition is that the courts have a residual power to enforce that higher law as against legislation. In the second category are the necessity cases, which usually arise from questions regarding the validity of legislation passed and institutions constituted in a manner and form that contradict the formal requirements of the constitution. Within this category we can place cases arising out of the aftermath of a revolution. The quintessential examples of this category occurred in cases in post-revolution cases in Pakistan and Cyprus, which

[73] *Imperial Tobacco* (n 6 above) [65].

were cited by the Canadian Supreme Court in the *Manitoba Language Rights* case. However, a notable example arose subsequent to the revolution in the Caribbean jurisdiction of Grenada, which was addressed in *Mitchell v DPP of Grenada*.[74] This category also includes cases arising from the rescue of unconstitutional statutes passed in ordinary social and political circumstances (unlike the revolution cases) but which failed to comply with constitutional manner and form requirements, as in the *Manitoba* case.

The parallels between the revolution cases (some of which use the doctrine of necessity) and the *Manitoba* case (which relied on the rule of law) reveal that the implied constitutional principles can lead to the same results as other unwritten doctrines which have been applied in constitutional law and in other fields of law in common law jurisdictions. The discussion of these cases is also meant to demonstrate the complexities of the circumstances which are sometimes presented to judges, to emphasise that even in the hardest of hard cases the judge has a duty to decide the case, and that in exceptional cases, there is a strong argument to be made for judges basing their decisions on non-textual material in order to arrive at a sensible decision.

The unprecedented action of the Canadian Supreme Court to avoid a legal vacuum was premised on the preservation of law and order and this impetus has influenced judges in other jurisdictions to rely on non-textual sources and arrive at a result similar to that reached by the Supreme Court in the *Manitoba* case. Such was the case in *Mitchell v DPP*, the facts of which it is useful to set out in some detail. The circumstances of the *Mitchell* case arose in the aftermath of a revolution in Grenada, a usually peaceful 'small island in the Eastern Caribbean'.[75] A 'bloodless revolution' was staged in March 1979, which led to the establishment of the People's Revolutionary Government (PRG) in 1979, led by Maurice Bishop, who assumed the position of Prime Minister of Grenada. The PRG suspended the Constitution of Grenada 1973 and abolished existing local courts as well as appeals to the Privy Council. A set of People's Laws were enacted, including People's Laws Nos 4 and 14 which created a new Supreme Court consisting of a High Court and a Court of Appeal. The PRG was overthrown in October 1983, when Maurice Bishop and several of his Ministers were murdered. Following the murders, a Revolutionary Military Council assumed power, until their reign was terminated by invasion from foreign forces led by the USA. The Governor General proclaimed a state of emergency, declaring that he would exercise executive authority until a government was elected pursuant to the Constitution. Pursuant to

[74] [1986] LRC (Const) 35 (CA, Grenada). See also discussion of *Mitchell* in Se-shauna Wheatle, 'Comparative Law and the Ius Gentium' (2014) 3 *Cambridge Journal of International and Comparative Law* 1065, 1066–68.

[75] ibid (Haynes P) 41.

the proclamation, the 'existing laws' (including People's Laws Nos 4, 14, and 84, which established the new judicial system) would continue in force. Constitutional government returned when the Constitution of Grenada Order 1984 was published, which provided that the Constitution of 1973 was in force with the exception of specified provisions, and a new Parliament was elected in December of 1984. The first Act passed by this new parliament in 1985 confirmed the validity of PRG laws passed during the suspension of the Constitution.

Mitchell and others were charged with the murders of Maurice Bishop and other PRG ministers, under an indictment filed in September 1984, prior to the resumption of government under the Constitution. They applied to the High Court challenging the High Court's competence to hear the charge, on the ground that the Court was established under the PRG by People's Laws No 4 and No 14 and that the invalidity of the PRG rendered those laws invalid, and hence the High Court itself as it was then constituted was invalid. Nedd CJ, sitting on the bench of the High Court, dismissed the application, holding that while the PRG was not the *de jure* government, the laws passed by it validly established the Supreme Court.[76]

The Court of Appeal subsequently held that while there was insufficient evidence before it to decide whether the PRG had achieved *de jure* status, People's Laws Nos 4 and 14 were validated under the law of necessity, and therefore the Supreme Court (including the Court of Appeal itself) was validly constituted.[77] Haynes, P identified one of the maxims from which the doctrine of necessity is derived as that expressed by Bacon: 'that the preservation of the state is the supreme law (*salus populi suprema lex*)'.[78] This led Haynes to list five conditions for the operation of the doctrine of necessity, the primary condition requiring an imperative necessity that arises from exceptional circumstances not provided for in the Constitution, for immediate action to preserve a vital state function. Simeon McIntosh objected to the application of the necessity doctrine to the facts of the case, arguing that the doctrine applied exclusively to unconstitutional acts of a constitutional state.[79] McIntosh also maintained that 'it is only a court that is itself already validly constituted that would have jurisdiction' in the case.[80] The latter criticism, regarding the validity of the court, certainly indicates a logical flaw in the decision. However, a court that is asked to resolve such a crucial constitutional issue must issue a decision; such is the distinction between legal (and judicial) practice and legal theory.

[76] The Chief Justice's decision was given ten days after the Constitution of Grenada Order 1984, which reinstated the Constitution of 1973.

[77] *Mitchell* (n 74 above) 73–74, 88–94, 120.

[78] ibid 76.

[79] Simeon McIntosh, *Kelsen in the 'Grenada court': Essays on Revolutionary Legality* (Ian Randle Publishers, 2008) 28.

[80] ibid 37.

Despite its potential for substantial effect on the legal, political, and social structures of the state, the doctrine of necessity has generally been recognised as one of ancient vintage and, in fact, was relied upon by an English court as early as 1672.[81] Indeed, Glanville Williams identified twelve maxims underpinning the doctrine of necessity,[82] noting that:

> 'The law' is not a body of systematised rules enacted as a whole and fixed for all time. Judges have always exercised the power of developing the law, and this is now recognized to be a proper part of their function. 'The law', in a word, includes the doctrine of necessity; the defence of necessity is an implied exception to particular rules of law.[83]

In a similar vein, Mark Stavsky has commented on the use of the doctrine of necessity in Pakistan that 'if narrowly and carefully applied, the doctrine constitutes an affirmation of the rule of law'.[84] Notably, McIntosh's critique of the *Mitchell* decision was centred on a perceived judicial misconstruction of the necessity doctrine[85] and not on the ground that the doctrine itself was an improper ground for judicial decision-making. The Supreme Court of Canada stated in the *Manitoba* case that 'the doctrine of necessity is not used in these cases to support some law which is above the Constitution; it is, instead, used to ensure the unwritten but inherent principle of rule of law which must provide the foundation of any constitution.'[86] Thus, this brief discussion on the use of the doctrine of necessity in constitutional law cases was intended to show that similar effects can be achieved through the use of constitutional principles such as the rule of law and the use of common law doctrines such as that of necessity, and that necessity can be viewed as affiliated with the rule of law itself.

The 'exception' category combines aspects of the legitimising function of implied principles while possessing attributes that answer many of the charges against the use of implied principles. On the legitimising side, the use of constitutional principles in exceptional cases do appear to be attempts to identify and glean the *core* elements of the state and the constitution by 'dig[ging] down to the level of constitutional theory'[87] to find and apply the *core* of foundational principles of the constitution. So, for instance, if in an exceptional case, the implied constitutional principle is used to ensure the

[81] *Manby v Scott* (1672) 1 Lev 4; Mark Stavsky, 'The Doctrine of State Necessity in Pakistan' (1983) 16 *Cornell International Law Journal* 341, 342.

[82] Glanville Williams, 'Defence of Necessity' (1953) 6 *Current Legal Problems* 216.

[83] ibid 224.

[84] Stavsky (n 81 above) 344.

[85] McIntosh (n 79 above) 28.

[86] ibid; *Reference re Language Rights Under s 23 of Manitoba Act, 1870 and s 133 of Constitution Act, 1867* (*Manitoba Language Rights Reference* or *Reference re Manitoba Language Rights*) [1985] 1 SCR 721 [105].

[87] *Pierson* (n 23 above) 584.

maintenance of laws in a jurisdiction, this is a core application of the rule of law, universally accepted, that the rule of law requires that there must be laws. This was the application of the rule of law in the *Manitoba* case. Hence, while there may be controversy surrounding the court's resolution of the facts of the case, it is unlikely that there would be debate surrounding the particular application of the implied constitutional principle, that is, that the rule of law demands that there must be laws. In the framework of legitimisation, the exceptions category not only uses principles that have been accepted throughout constitutional democracies, it also taps into the elemental human, institutional, and state and institutional propensity towards stability and continuity. The necessity for continuity and stability is so fundamental and obvious in exception cases (particularly in the latter two categories) that it would generate broad cross-jurisdictional support.[88] This cross-jurisdictional consensus is evident cases from jurisdictions as diverse as Pakistan, Canada,[89] and Grenada. This elemental need has traditionally been recognised through constitutional provision for the exercise of executive and legislative powers during times of emergency and in justifications for exceptional state action taken in exceptional situations. Thus, John Ferejohn and Pascale Pasquino correctly observe that emergency powers 'have long been thought to be a vital and, perhaps, even an essential component of a liberal constitutional—that is, a rights-protecting—government.'[90] The objective of this power is 'fundamentally *conservative*', to resolve the threat to the system in a manner that restores the legal and constitutional system to its prior relatively stable condition.[91] The necessity of providing for exceptional or emergency situations is well-acknowledged, even if there are disagreements on the tools to be used to respond to such situations.[92]

Such exceptional cases evade many of the complaints made by sceptics of implied principle techniques. For instance, in the jurisdictions in which parliamentary supremacy remains an influential doctrine, restriction of the use of implied principles to exceptional circumstances accords more respect to parliamentary supremacy by excluding overturn of legislation in 'ordinary' circumstances. Expanding this argument, it is not simply that the exceptional cases category reduces the number of instances of use of implied principles to invalidate legislation. The category may also rest on deeper normative claims regarding the justification for parliamentary supremacy;

[88] See further Wheatle (n 74 above).

[89] See discussion in the *Manitoba* case (n 86 above): [84]–[107].

[90] John Ferejohn and Pascale Pasquino, 'The Law of the Exception: A Typology of Emergency Powers' (2004) 2 *International Journal of Constitutional Law* 210.

[91] ibid 210.

[92] For a recent proposal on the best responses to emergency situations, see David Dyzenhaus, *The Constitution of Law: Legality in a Time of Emergency* (Cambridge University Press, 2006).

this is consistent with the view—advanced by Craig—that parliamentary supremacy must be underpinned by normative arguments justifying that principle.[93] As part of Craig's rejection of the ultra vires justification of judicial review, he contends that the formalist approach adopted by ultra vires theorists and modern defenders of parliamentary supremacy is flawed for failure to advance a normative claim in support of parliamentary supremacy. As Craig documents, while the orthodox defence of parliamentary supremacy tends to rely heavily on Blackstone and Dicey, its defenders fail to account for the context in which those writers developed their theories and the underlying normative claims that supported their account of parliamentary supremacy. The traditional approach used by Dicey and Blackstone, as well as by venerated judges such as Coke was to support their account of the legal hierarchy with normative claims.[94]

Vincent Kazmierski uses the premise of Craig's rejection of formalism in the context of the debate over substantive limitations on legislative power by implied constitutional principles. Kazmierski argues that if the court accepts a normative claim in favour of parliamentary supremacy (for instance, that parliamentary supremacy upholds parliamentary democracy), this normative argument can simultaneously provide the tools for rejection of the use of implied principles in ordinary cases while permitting the use of such principles in 'exceptional circumstances' to defeat legislation that would undermine the very normative basis of parliamentary supremacy. This line of argument provides a clarifying lens through which to view the Canadian Supreme Court's application of implied constitutional principles. Thus, the Canadian Supreme Court attaches weight to parliamentary supremacy so despite the Court's exploration of implied principles in constitutional cases, it has sought to respect the principle of parliamentary supremacy by rejecting arguments that other constitutional principles should be used to invalidate legislation.[95] On the other hand, accepting—as Kazmierski argues—that the judicially accepted source of parliamentary supremacy is the 'representative function of democracy', when presented with legislation that erodes representative democracy, the Court is entitled to reject such legislation on the ground of other implied constitutional principles.

Despite the fact that permitting the use of implied principles in the exception category avoids many of the strong complaints of implied principle sceptics, there are conceptual questions that must be answered. First among these is the primary question of what must be considered exceptional: the factual context or the legal issue arising. The view proposed by the case law that the label 'exceptional' must be a reference to the factual context and

[93] Paul Craig, 'Public law, Political Theory and Legal Theory' [2000] *Public Law* 211.
[94] ibid 212–22.
[95] Kazmierski (n 6 above) 251.

it is this factual context that gives rise to exceptional legal issues. Second, what is the result of the characterisation of circumstances as exceptional and does this characterisation affect the interpretive style of the court or does it transform the (hierarchy of) the sources of law in the state? In the *Manitoba* case, there was an undoubtedly an impact on the interpretive style of the court whereas *Jackson* suggested that in exceptional circumstances, the very hierarchy of sources in the state is altered. Thus, in *Manitoba*, the Canadian Supreme Court reasoned on the basis that the rule of law has always been a fundamental principle of the Canadian Constitution and that the court must seek to observe the principles and rules of the Constitution by acknowledging the unconstitutionality of the unilingual legislation while avoiding a legal vacuum. By contrast, Lord Steyn in *Jackson* envisioned a more profound legal and constitutional impact by suggesting a qualification of the doctrine of parliamentary supremacy 'established on a different hypothesis of constitutionalism' in exceptional circumstances.[96]

This section opened with the observation that there are two types of exceptional cases: one in which judicial control of statutes is claimed in a jurisdiction that observes parliamentary supremacy and the second in which it is claimed that statutes which were not validly enacted in accordance with the formal requirements of the constitution should be accorded validity by the court. A fundamental distinction between these two forms of exceptionalities is that while in the second form, the court plays a secondary role in ascribing validity to legislation under an understanding that it is 'necessary' to do so, under the first form, the court plays a primary role in validating to judicial control and, consequently, judicial invalidation, of legislation. Most of the literature defending special legal treatment of exceptional cases in constitutional law speaks to exceptional acts of the legislature and executive and the necessity of recognising the validity of such acts, rather than the court invalidating legislation in exceptional circumstances. Accordingly, the distinction made here between these two classes of exceptional cases would, undoubtedly, enhance assessments of the legitimacy of the use of the exceptionalities category.

IV. DETERMINACY

Leclair perceives persistent uncertainty in the meaning of an implied principle, arguing that there is an indeterminacy which exists in implied principles that exceeds that which exists with respect to written norms. Leclair's view is that while written norms may also be vague, the words do provide

[96] *Jackson* (n 55 above) [102].

some guidance which does not exist for unwritten norms.[97] Therefore, the fear expressed is that reasoning by implied principles potentially opens the door for judges to import values into the Constitution and supply their own meaning to such values.

The vagueness complaint comprises two main components, the first being that the principle is vaguer for lack of textual expression. Textual objections are addressed earlier in the chapter, but it bears repeating that the 'unwritten' quality does not, on its own, automatically result in less determinacy than written norms. The charge of indeterminacy may also appropriately be laid at the feet of written provisions in constitutional and bill of rights texts. Indeterminacy occurs where the legal rule or principle in question provides no single solution or single right answer to the question of how the court should decide the dispute at hand.[98] As Kavanagh writes in the context of the indeterminacy of the terms in the HRA 1998:

> [t]he task of the interpreting judge is to redress this, ie to make clear something which is not clear on the face of the legislation. … This view seems to be supported by Lord Bingham of Cornhill when he stated in *Brown v Stott* that 'the language of the Convention is so general that some implication of terms is necessary, and the case law of the European Court shows that the court has been willing to imply terms into the Convention when it has judged necessary or plainly right to do so'. It follows that the meaning of legislative provisions is not contained within the text of those provisions, waiting to be 'discovered' by the interpreting judge. The justifying reasons, which constitute the interpretation, will necessarily be drawn (in part) from evaluations not contained within the legislation.[99]

The Privy Council has also spoken to the generality of constitutional rights provisions, noting that:

> the terms in which these provisions of the Constitution are expressed necessarily co-opts future generations of judges to the enterprise of giving life to the abstract statements of fundamental rights. The judges are the mediators between the high generalities of the constitutional text and the messy detail of their application to concrete problems.[100]

Indeed, there is an inevitable degree of indeterminacy in many constitutional (rights and non-rights) provisions, requiring judges to supply substantive evaluative content even where they purport to rely on norms expressed in

[97] Leclair (n 20 above) 431; Ronald Dworkin, *Taking Rights Seriously* (Harvard University Press, 1978) 109.

[98] Kavanagh, 'Elusive Divide' (n 2 above) 264. See also Joseph Raz, *The Authority of Law: Essays on Law and Morality* (Clarendon Press 1979) 70–72, 181–82; Timothy Endicott, 'Linguistic Indeterminacy' (1996) 16 *Oxford Journal of Legal Studies* 667, 669.

[99] Kavanagh, 'Elusive Divide' (n 2 above) 264.

[100] *Boyce v R* [2004] UPKC 32, [2005] 1 AC 400 (JCPC, Barbados) [28] (Lord Hoffmann).

the text.[101] The near ubiquity of indeterminacy in constitutional and rights interpretation suggests that, if we assume acceptance of the legitimacy of constitutional and rights interpretation by courts, the standard by which to judge the epistemological choice to use implied constitutional principles ought not to be a standard of determinacy. Thus, as argued by James Kelly and Michael Murphy, the 'standard of certainty is the error',[102] and the inquiry must be more nuanced.

The second component of the vagueness objection is that principles are inherently vaguer than rules. Accordingly, the argument from determinacy has been made in resistance to the use of implied principles in constitutional adjudication but has also been made generally to the use of principles as legal norms. Thus, Raz objects that '[p]rinciples, because they prescribe highly unspecific acts, tend to be vaguer and less certain than rules.'[103] We can acknowledge that the rule of law and separation of powers do manifest a higher level of abstraction than *some* textual provisions and *some* rules. As has been noted in earlier chapters, it is in part their abstract quality that accounts for their appeal to judges (and, indeed, to other legal actors). However, as with the comparison between textual and non-textual norms, so between rules and principles, there is a level of generality and vagueness in both.[104]

These two components of the argument from determinacy should be disaggregated and each treated on its own merits. In addition, analysts of the legitimacy of implied principle techniques must query whether determinacy ought properly to be regarded as a sensible goal and appropriate standard for measuring the normative desirability of particular norms and interpretive techniques in fundamental rights cases. Again, it is suggested that certainty is a false standard and that the main focus of the legitimacy inquiry lies in the sources of, and institutional roles played by, and to be played by the courts and other organs of the state.

V. THE ROAD TO DEFEAT OF CONSTITUTIONAL AMENDMENTS?

The implications of the use of implied principles should also be considered alongside the notion of 'unconstitutional constitutional amendments', which

[101] James B Kelly and Michael Murphy, 'Confronting Judicial Supremacy: A Defence of Judicial Activism' (2001) 16 *Canadian Journal of Law & Society* 3, 10–12; Adrienne Stone, 'Judicial Review Without Rights: Some Problems for the Democratic Legitimacy of Structural Judicial Review' (2008) 28 *Oxford Journal of Legal Studies* 1, 8–15.

[102] Kelly and Murphy (ibid) 11.

[103] Joseph Raz, 'Legal Principles and the Limits of Law' (1972) 81 *Yale Law Journal* 823, 841.

[104] Robert Alexy, *A Theory of Constitutional Rights* (Julian Rivers tr, Oxford University Press, 2002) 58; Humberto Avila, *Theory of Legal Principles* (Law and Philosophy Library) (Springer, 2007) 638–39.

has been explored in jurisdictions from Latin America, India, and Africa.[105] Subsequently, Caribbean and Canadian constitutionalists have raised the possibility of implied principles operating as a substantive restraint on constitutional amendments, suggesting that 'certain constitutional amendments, such as those abolishing fundamental rights, might be precluded by the unwritten constitution.'[106]

A prominent model for the judicial rejection of constitutional amendments is the basic structure doctrine which was developed in India and has recently been applied in the Commonwealth Caribbean.[107] The basic structure doctrine holds that the constitution has fundamental features which cannot be destroyed by the legislature, meaning that both ordinary legislation and constitutional amendments must be measured against the basic features of the constitution. Consequently, under the doctrine, the constitution's express limits on legislative power are not exhaustive of the constitutional restraints on legislators; there are also implied limits on legislative power which must be met in order to achieve constitutional validity. Further, the limits on the power to amend the constitution are not purely manner and form restrictions; there are also substantive limits on the legislature's amendment power. This bold doctrine emerged as a result of a series of cases before the Supreme Court of India between 1951 and 1973 in which litigants mounted challenges to constitutional amendments related to far-reaching socio-economic reforms.[108] The development of the basic structure doctrine in *Kesavananda Bharati v State of Kerala* arose out of a series of land reform laws championed by the Government of India. When the constitutional validity of that legislation was challenged in the courts, the government amended the Constitution, including an amendment protecting the right to property by excluding its application to laws relating to land reform. Among the critical amendments was the 24th Amendment which sought to ensure that fundamental constitutional rights could be amended without restraint and provided that the Constitution granted no judicial power to review constitutional amendments. This was bolstered by the 29th Amendment, which sought to insert the land reform legislation into the Ninth Schedule to the Constitution, which meant that the legislation

[105] Jacobsohn, *Constitutional Identity* (n 29 above) 34–83.

[106] Walters, 'Common Law Constitution' (n 13 above) 140; Arif Bulkan, 'The Limits of Constitution (Re)-making in the Commonwealth Caribbean: Towards the "Perfect Nation"' (2013) 2 *Canadian Journal of Human Rights* 79; Richard Albert, 'The Theory and Doctrine of Unconstitutional Constitutional Amendment in Canada' (2016) *Queen's Law Journal* (forthcoming).

[107] *Kesavananda Bharati* v *State of Kerala* (1973) 4 SCC 225 (SC, India); *Bowen v AG* BZ 2009 SC 2 (13 February 2009) (SC, Belize).

[108] Sudhir Krishnaswamy, *Democracy And Constitutionalism In India: A Study Of The Basic Structure Doctrine* (Oxford University Press, 2009) 1–2.

would be immune from being adjudged void by virtue of inconsistency with the fundamental rights provisions in the Constitution.[109]

The basic structure doctrine has been adopted in the Commonwealth Caribbean by a judge at first instance in the Supreme Court of Belize, but has so far not been approved by an appellate court. The Government of Belize attempted to amend the Constitution of Belize 1981 by providing, in clause 2 of a Bill entitled 'Belize Constitution (Sixth Amendment) Act 2008', that the right to property in the Constitution does not apply to petroleum, minerals, and accompanying substances. After the Bill had passed both Houses of Parliament, but before it received Royal Assent, clause 2 was challenged by two landowners who sought a declaration that the provision was an unconstitutional attempt to amend the Belize Constitution and was likely to contravene the constitutional rights of the applicant, including the right to property and the right to seek redress for breach of constitutional rights,[110] and that the clause was in violation of the rule of law and the separation of powers. In *Bowen v AG* the Supreme Court of Belize[111] held that the challenged clause would be inconsistent with the structure of the Constitution 'regarding the principle of the separation of powers and its undoubted concomitant, the rule of law'.[112] Conteh CJ concluded that the clause was fatal due to its interference with individual access to courts and its inconsistency with fundamental constitutional principles. In so finding, he held that the clause would be unconstitutional despite its passage with the requisite super-majority specified in the Constitution for amendment of the constitutional rights provisions.

Despite the boldness of the decision, the breadth of its implications is limited by two factors. First, the decision was one of the lower court and the appellate courts did not take up the issue, finding alternate means of resolving the case.[113] The Court of Appeal referred to the fact that, subsequent to

[109] See Vivendra Kumar, 'Basic Structure of the Indian Constitution: Doctrine of Constitutionally Controlled Governance' (2007) 49 *Journal of the Indian Law Institute* 365.

[110] The applicants alleged breach of ss 1, 3, 6, 17, 20 and 95 of the Constitution. Section 1 of the Constitution of Belize 1981 provides that Belize shall be a democratic state; s 3 guarantees to the right to protection from arbitrary deprivation of property; s 6 enshrines the right to equal protection of the law; s 17 protects the right to property and forbids the compulsory acquisition of such without compensation; s 20 of the Constitution stipulates that any person who alleges that any of his constitutional rights is being or is likely to be infringed is entitled to apply to the Supreme Court for redress and s 95 stipulates that the Supreme Court shall have unlimited jurisdiction to hear and determine civil and criminal proceedings and such jurisdiction as the Constitution or any other law confers upon it.

[111] The Supreme Court of Belize is a court of first instance in constitutional claims.

[112] *Bowen* (n 107 above).

[113] *Attorney General v Bowen* BZ 2010 CA 1 (19 March 2010) (CA, Belize).

the Supreme Court decision, the Parliament amended the impugned clause in the Bill, to provide that:

> nothing in this subsection shall affect the right of the owner of any private land beneath which any petroleum deposits are located to receive royalty from the Government, as provided in the Petroleum Act and the regulations made there under, existing at the commencement of the Belize Constitution (Sixth Amendment) Act.

The Court of Appeal found that, as the Bill which was in issue before the lower court no longer existed, the issue of the accuracy of the Supreme Court's rulings had become moot.[114] Secondly, in the lower court, Conteh CJ did not undertake a sufficiently rigorous conceptual analysis that addressed the complex underlying theories, the textual and institutional foundations and implications of the decision, or the connection between reasoning by implied constitutional principles and the basic structure doctrine.

Assessment of the potential for the adoption of a form of basic structure doctrine as a consequence of the use of implied constitutional principles, requires recognition of the fact that the doctrine has been rejected by some jurisdictions that rely on implied constitutional principles. As Gary Jacobsohn explains, the Supreme Court of Ireland rebuffed the idea that the judiciary had the capacity to restrain the legislature's amendment power by implied substantive limits. In *State (Ryan and Others) v Lennon* the majority of the Irish Supreme Court found that the judiciary could not legitimately identify and distinguish the articles in the Constitution of the Irish Free State 1922 which were of fundamental importance and those which were not.[115] Further, in the *Secession Reference*, the Supreme Court of Canada considered and commented unfavourably upon the potential for invalidating constitutional amendments on the ground of inconsistency with implied constitutional principles:

> The amendments necessary to achieve a secession could be radical and extensive. Some commentators have suggested that secession could be a change of such a magnitude that it could not be considered to be merely an amendment to the Constitution. We are not persuaded by this contention. ... The fact that those changes would be profound, or that they would purport to have a significance with respect to international law, does not negate their nature as amendments to the Constitution of Canada.[116]

114 ibid [21].

115 *The State (Ryan and Others) v Lennon* [1935] IR 170 (SC, Republic of Ireland) 180 (Meredith J).

116 *Secession Reference* (n 18 above) [84]; Warren Newman, 'The Principles of the Rule of Law and Parliamentary Sovereignty in Constitutional Theory and Litigation' (2005) 16 *National Journal of Constitutional Law* 175, 295–96.

The history of the use of implied principles in the jurisdictions examined shows that the doctrine of reasoning by implied principles has not yet developed an analytical narrative that confronts constitutional amendments. Could the doctrine do so? It is possible, but this refinement would depend on the accepted theoretical and textual justification for the use of implied principles, including whether the principles are viewed as representing higher order law, as well as conclusions regarding the source of the principles and the process of implication.

The argument that implied constitutional principles may supply a basis for rejection of constitutional amendments would be strongest if implied principles are viewed as an expression of 'higher order' law, on which the text of the constitution itself is based. As noted above, Walters has written extensively on the perception of implied constitutional principles as an expression of higher law but this concept is not concretely developed in the case law so there would need to be more concrete articulation of this higher law analysis in the courts. Regarding the source and process of implication, if the source of the implied principles is the text of the constitution, this may lead to the conclusion that if legislation is validly passed according to the procedure for amendment specified in the constitution, the constitutional validity of that reform cannot be challenged on the basis of implied principles. On the other hand, if the source is conceived as a broader notion of the structure of the constitution, the argument could be made that the concept of constitutional 'structure' can sustain a wider interpretation and potentially provide greater scope for argument that implied principles could operate as a restraint on the legislative power of amendment. Yet, it remains unclear that the concept of the structure of the constitution as applied in cases using the structural method of implication could supply substantive limits to the amending power. For instance, in cases such as *Hinds* and the *Provincial Judges Reference* structural implication was applied as a reference to the manner in which the Constitution arranged its several chapters and to the structure of the institutions of government. Consequently, there are conceptual and precedential limits to the extent to which the structural basis of implication could supply grounds for substantive restrictions on the amending power in those jurisdictions. In summary, then, the current analysis in the case law does not offer sufficient support for a conclusion that reasoning by implied principles leads inexorably to judicial support for doctrines that would permit the judicial defeat of constitutional amendments. In fact, the highest court in one of the jurisdictions examined has expressed clear reluctance to adopt this suggestion.

VI. CONCLUSION

This chapter reveals a complex combination of challenges to the legitimacy of the use of implied constitutional principles, some of which fall within what Kazmierski would classify as a 'British approach' to the legitimacy question, an approach that 'recognizes the legitimacy of unwritten principles but favours the principle of parliamentary sovereignty above other principles'. Others fall within what Kazmierski would classify as an 'American approach' which focuses on 'the potential dangers to the legitimacy of judicial review which are raised by judges departing from the constitutional text to identify and apply constitutional principles as limits on legislation'.[117] Therefore, the challenges arise mainly from a combination of institutional and textual considerations. While this chapter did not purport to be an exhaustive treatment of these issues, it lays the groundwork for more accurate, fulsome discourse on the legitimacy of courts' use of implied constitutional principles.

Fundamentally, we must acknowledge that the use of implied constitutional principles, far from being monolithic, manifests in a variety of ways which must be accounted for in any normative analysis. Accordingly, a systematic examination of the normative question must include analysis of the impact of these factors along a spectrum of functions, ranging from the interpretative function to the invalidating function. Overall, in the assessment of the legitimacy of the use of implied constitutional principles, primacy should be accorded to the issues relating to the process of implication and the function played by the implied principles, along with the institutional contexts in which both of these factors emerge. Indeed, these factors—in particular the institutional context—are reflected in the pattern of functions adopted by varying jurisdictions. Thus, stronger normative force accompanies the use of principles in the Caribbean, where courts are imbued with more substantial enforcement powers, while there is much more of an interpretive (as opposed to independent) role accorded to principles in the United Kingdom. This pattern suggests an effort at—or least potential for—reconciliation of implied principle techniques within the existing constitutional order. Such scope for reconciliation and coherence with the overall frame of the constitution is central to the legitimacy of reliance on implied constitutional principles.

[117] Kazmierski (n 6 above) 245.

9

Conclusion

THE OVERARCHING OBJECTIVE of this study was to take a step back from the discourse on the legitimacy and desirability of judicial reliance on implied constitutional principles in fundamental rights adjudication. Immersion in the normative question can obscure variations in the sources, methods of implication, and functions of principles across a range of textual and institutional backgrounds. By engaging with the prior question of why judges appeal to implied principles and the functions played by such principles in the doctrinal, institutional, and legal historical frameworks of common law jurisdictions, this book has attempted to clarify the practice of reasoning by implied constitutional principles as well as provide analytical categories to inform and enhance the normative debate.

I. DECISIONAL FLEXIBILITY

The operation of the rule of law and the separation of powers as constitutional principles allow for an interaction of the substantive, the methodological, and the institutional. Within the substantive sphere, the flexibility occasioned by implied constitutional principles was seen to facilitate their applicability in cross-jurisdictional exchanges and across a range of issues. This flexibility was on display in the analysis of the applications of implied constitutional principles in chapter three, 'Judicial Conceptions of the Rule of Law', and chapter four, 'Applications of the Separation of Powers'. It is partly what has been described as the 'principled ambiguity'[1] of constitutional principles that make them so appealing in the process of development of the constitution of a state, both at the design stage and the adjudication stage. A feature of the decisional flexibility afforded by the principles is that their content and the results of their application are capable of significant evolution overtime. Thus, as observed in chapter three, the rule of law has been invoked to promote equality in ways that would not have been contemplated when Dicey penned his famous treatise.

[1] Heinz Klug, 'South Africa's Experience in Constitution-Building' available at http://papers.ssrn.com/sol3/papers.cfm?abstract_id=1808168 (accessed 23 June 2013) 31.

The generality of the content of the separation of powers and rule of law also serves other interpretive approaches such as purposive interpretation. Thus, chapter four set out how the separation of powers principle serves as a tool in the purposive interpretation of Constitutions and Bills of Rights in the common law jurisdictions examined. This process provides decisional flexibility to the judges in the case at hand while opening the door to flexible adoption and case specific application in subsequent cases. As such, the essential variability of the content and application of implied constitutional principles contribute to judicial engagement with these principles in adjudicating fundamental rights claims.

II. DISTANCING DEVICES AND INSTITUTIONAL DEFENCE

Implied constitutional principles play a critical function in operating as devices that purport to distance judges from the appearance of personal and political judgments. By appealing to principles that are foundational to the Constitution, there is an attempt to buttress the legitimacy of decisions on contested fundamental rights issues. This argument was advanced in chapter five, 'Implied Principles as Interpretative Aids'. It was maintained that in cases where judges invoke the implied principles in their judgments but yet do not use the principles as independent grounds for their decisions, the principles nonetheless play an important role as distancing devices.

Attempts to dismiss judicial invocation of constitutional principles as mere rhetoric must confront the reality that the rhetorical force and normative force of these principles are not mutually exclusive. The significant rhetorical power behind references to rule of law and separation of powers—owing in no small part to their wide acceptance not only as features of constitutional democracy, but also foundational to constitutionalism itself—is manifest. However, this fact does not exclude the possibility that the principles also have normative force. Further, the use of constitutional principles as legal norms is evident in judgments in which judges derive more specific norms and rules from the more general principles.

It is within the overlapping content of the rule of law and separation of powers principles—which sees the separation and independence of the judiciary from other branches of the state as well as the corresponding jurisdiction of the courts to adjudicate as an independent and impartial tribunal operating as applications of both principles—that we see much of the activity of employing the implied constitutional principles. It is also within this overlapping sphere that we see the strongest normative force of the implied constitutional principles. Several explanations for this occurrence are suggested in case law. The first is that the interlocking area represents the field of these principles that has gained most acceptance from constitutional actors, including judges and legal commentators. This acceptance argument was discussed in chapter three's examination of 'Judicial Conceptions of the Rule of Law', chapter four on 'Applications of the Separation of Powers', and chapter six regarding 'Implied Principles as Grounds for Invalidating Legislation'.

Chapter six highlighted cases which advanced the engagement of implied principles as grounds for invalidating legislation, independent of text, finding that such cases applied constitutional principles as jurisdictional grounds, which falls within the overlapping sphere of the rule of law and separation of powers. Further, underlying reliance on jurisdictional grounds allows for the presentation of the court's decision as one founded on structural argumentation rather than evaluative value-based argumentation. This is closely allied with the idea of principles acting as distancing devices in hard fundamental rights cases, and cements the appeal of principles as mechanisms directed at situating the judicial role within the constitutional order and legitimating judicial decisions, by seeking to divorce rights decisions from overtly moral and political value judgments. However, as explained in chapter six, the presentation of such jurisdictional arguments as exclusive of value judgments is ultimately unconvincing as such grounds may be influenced by evaluations of the role of institutions in rights protection, of competing conceptions of the separation of powers or the rule of law, as well as results-oriented comparisons of the decisions likely to proceed from each of branch of government. The overlapping application of the principles is at its peak when deployed in defence of a jurisdictional sphere of power, specifically, the court's sphere. It is in this sense that constitutional principles function not merely as discursive tools, but as weapons used to protect encroachments on the court's jurisdiction. Even in this decidedly more active role, the principles remain essentially reactive and defensive.

Nonetheless, the question must be posed whether courts achieve a Pyrrhic victory in such cases. Do they succeed at protecting their powers of review while sacrificing some of their institutional legitimacy in the eyes of other institutional actors in the state? The court's institutional legitimacy may be undermined by perceptions that the judges are motivated by institutional self-interest and not by legal reasoning and legal argumentation. It may also be undermined by criticisms that the tools used to preserve that power—in this study, the implication of principles—are imposed on the constitution by unelected and unaccountable judges in order to preserve or expand their power. Consequently, the complaint may be raised that lack of democratic accountability as a restraint on judicial power is exacerbated by the use in judicial decision-making of principles which have not been formally enacted as part of the constitution. These arguments were canvassed in chapter eight, where it was suggested that these institutional democratic considerations were generally more serious challenges to the legitimacy of judicial invocation of implied constitutional principles than were complaints of the vagueness or indeterminacy of the principles.

Finally, the institutional element of the practice of using implied principles also emerges as a significant theme in the analysis of the use of the implied principles as gateways to comparative judicial reasoning. Thus, the analysis in chapter seven highlights the function of implied principles and comparative adjudication as a means of legitimating institutions and institutional processes. The importance of methodological trends is thrown into sharp relief, demonstrating that while results may be divergent, there remains a strong similarity of methodology across the jurisdictions.

III. INVITATIONS

Current scholarly literature, including this book, focuses the spotlight on *judicial* reasoning by implied principles. However, judicial activity using the implied principle techniques only tells one part of the story. There are accompanying narratives surrounding the activity by legislatures and governments in invoking such principles in drafting, as evidenced by the fact that constitutional principles often feature in preambles to constitutions and bills of rights. A second accompanying narrative surrounds human rights lawyers' encouragement to judges to engage in reasoning by implied principles. Accordingly, there are 'grand entrance halls' to the judicial use of implied constitutional principles on a general level in the form of legislative deliberation and drafting, and on a specific level in parties' submissions before the court.

IV. CONTINUITY AND TRANSITION

To study the role of implied constitutional principles in fundamental rights adjudication is also to observe the role of continuity in the development of constitutions and rights protection. There are elements of continuity in modes of reasoning that have been adopted from the common law for application to the interpretation of codified constitutions and bills of rights, such connection having been recognised by Lord Hoffmann's reference in *Simms* to the continuity and strengthening of the principle of legality under the HRA 1998.[2] There is also ample evidence of common law modes of reasoning in the evolutionary impulses of judges in former colonial states and in the continued and sustained appeal to implied norms in interpreting their written constitutions.

[2] *R v Secretary of State for the Home Department, ex p Simms* [2000] 2 AC 115 (HL) 132.

V. AUTOCHTHONY

This leads to a final consideration that emerges from observations of the relationship between 'principled reasoning' and bills of rights. Reliance on implied constitutional principles has a differential impact on the autochthony of constitutional development in the jurisdictions examined. In former colonial states, the argument may quite sensibly be made that continued invocation of principles in the face of a domestic bill of rights or constitution—developed upon or subsequent to independence—undermines the autochthonous nature of the constitution or bill of rights. On the other hand, the dynamic is quite different in the UK, where reasoning by principles that do not derive their normative force from statutory enactment is quite natural and indigenous. This is where Dicey's description of the centrality of the common law as a source of rights protection in the English constitution is apposite. The common law mode of rights protection is traditional and understood as a continuation of English (if not British) modes of reasoning in cases concerning fundamental rights. On the contrary, the HRA 1998 is not widely perceived as autochthonous, as is observed in the report by the Commission on a Bill of Rights, which cited a lack of British public 'ownership' of the HRA 1998.[3] Therefore unwritten constitutional principles have a stronger claim to autochthonous belonging in the UK than does the current Bill of Rights. Indeed, the current resurgence of common law rights and reasoning in British public law—which is in part a reaction to concerns about the advance and perceived dominance of European norms—serves as a reassertion of home grown constitutional principle.[4]

VI. CONCLUDING THOUGHTS

The motivation for this study lay in part in the need to evaluate what judges actually say about the content and application of implied constitutional principles, particularly the rule of law and separation of powers. In so doing, the discussion in the chapters above takes stock of the institutional, historical, and doctrinal contexts in which the courts operate. These contexts influence the ways in which judges employ the principles and they ultimately influence any comprehensive analysis of the legitimacy of the use of these principles.

[3] The Commission on a Bill of Rights, 'A UK Bill of Rights? The Choice Before Us' (December 2012) http://webarchive.nationalarchives.gov.uk/20130128112038/http:/www.justice.gov.uk/downloads/about/cbr/uk-bill-rights-vol-1.pdf (accessed 3 September 2016), Overview at para 80 and ch 12 at para 12.7.

[4] Roger Masterman and Se-shauna Wheatle, 'A common law resurgence in rights protection?' [2015] *European Human Rights Law Review* 57, 61–63.

Reasoning by implied constitutional principles remains a significant force in rights adjudication, though the functions they play vary, depending on the factual circumstances before the court, the text in question, and the structural arrangements of the jurisdiction. They provide a route for courts to fill gaps in constitutional and rights instruments and thereby allow for a more comprehensive rights system. They also function as gateways to connect the court, the text, and the state to a transnational web of rights language and rights protection. Further, on a fundamental level, in the sense that these principles are central to the very foundation of constitutionalism, there is an immediate transnational connection, contributing to a dialogue that occurs not only between institutions in the same state, but also among institutions across national lines. However, the commonality of language masks divergences that occur across national lines and through the decades as the understandings and applications of constitutional principles evolve.

There are questions that remain to be answered and lines of argument that remain to be pursued, particularly in relation to the legitimacy of the various uses of the implied constitutional principles. However, it is hoped that the analysis explored in this book will contribute to—and enhance—debates regarding the continued utilisation of implied constitutional principles by providing a thematic account of the functions of these principles. Adopting this analytical structure offers a clearer understanding of their intrinsic appeal and of the work that they do in fundamental rights adjudication. This form of analysis also serves a broader constitutional purpose by developing our understanding of the courts' role in constitutional development and rights protection in common law jurisdictions.

Bibliography

HL Debate 04 February 1969, vol 299, col 55

'Judicial Independence', The Australian Judicial Conference, Australian National University, Canberra, 2 Nov 1996

Ackerman, B, 'The Rise of World Constitutionalism' (1997) 83 *Virginia Law Review* 771

Ackner, D and Sargant, E, 'Foreign Compensation Bill: Threat to the Rule of Law' *The Times* (London, 4 February 1969)

Akehurst, M, 'Parliamentary Sovereignty and the Supremacy of Community Law' (1989) 60 *British Yearbook of International Law* 351

Alexy, R, *A Theory of Constitutional Rights* (Julian Rivers tr, Oxford University Press, 2002)

Allan, J, 'Not In for a Pound—In for a Penny? Must a Majoritarian Democrat Treat All Constitutional Judicial Review as Equally Egregious?' (2010) 21 *King's Law Journal* 233

Allan, TRS, 'Legislative Supremacy and the Rule of Law: Democracy and Constitutionalism' [1985] *Cambridge Law Journal* 111

—— 'Parliamentary Sovereignty: Law, Politics, and Revolution' (1997) 113 *Law Quarterly Review* 443

—— *Constitutional Justice: A Liberal Theory of the Rule of Law* (Oxford University Press, 2001)

—— 'The Constitutional Foundations of Judicial Review' (2002) 61 *Cambridge Law Journal* 87

—— 'Constitutional Dialogue and the Justification of Judicial Review' (2003) 23 *Oxford Journal of Legal Studies* 563

—— 'Constitutional Justice and the Concept of Law' in G Huscroft (ed) *Expounding the Constitution: Essays in Constitutional Theory* (Cambridge University Press, 2008)

—— 'Questions of legality and legitimacy: Form and substance in British constitutionalism' (2011) *International Journal of Constitutional Law* 155

Avila, H, *Theory of Legal Principles (Law and Philosophy Library)* (Springer, 2007)

Bagaric, M, 'Editorial: The revived Kable doctrine as a constitutional protector of rights?' (2011) 35 *Crim L J* 197

Bamforth, N, 'Parliamentary Sovereignty and the Human Rights Act 1998' [1998] *Public Law* 572

Barak, A, 'Response to The Judge as Comparatist: Comparison in Public Law' (2005–2006) 80 *Tulane Law Review* 196

Barber, NW, 'Must Legalistic Conceptions of the Rule of Law Have a Social Dimension?' (2004) 17 *Ratio Juris* 474

Barnett, LG, *The Constitutional Law of Jamaica* (Oxford University Press, 1977)

Basten, J, 'The Supervisory Jurisdiction of the Supreme Courts' (2011) 85 *Australian Law Journal* 273

Beatson, J, 'Reforming an Unwritten Constitution' (2010) 126 *Law Quarterly Review* 48
Beetham, D, *The Legitimation of Power* (Macmillan Publishers, 1991)
Bellamy, R, *Political Constitutionalism: A Republican Defence of the Constitutionality of Democracy* (Cambridge University Press, 2007)
Bennion, FAR, *Bennion on Statutory Interpretation: A Code*, 5th edn (LexisNexis, 2008)
—— *Understanding Common Law Legislation: Drafting and Interpretation* (Oxford University Press, 2009)
Bingham, TH, *The Rule of Law* (Allen Lane, 2010)
—— *Widening Horizons: The Influence Of Comparative Law And International Law On Domestic Law* (Cambridge University Press, 2010)
Blom-Cooper, L, 'Bias on Appeal' [2005] *Public Law* 225
Bobbitt, P, *Constitutional Fate: Theory of the Constitution* (Oxford University Press, 1982)
Bognador, V, *The New British Constitution* (Hart Publishing, 2009)
Boyer, AD, '"Understanding, Authority, and Will": Sir Edward Coke and the Elizabethan Origins Of Judicial Review' (1997–1998) 39 *Boston College Law Review* 43
Bradley, AW and Ewing, KD, *Constitutional and Administrative Law*, 15th edn (Longman, Harlow, 2011)
Brooke, D, 'The Rule of Law and the British Empire—Part II' (2013) 8 *Irish Law Times* 121
Brooks, RE, 'The New Imperialism: Violence, Norms, and the Rule of Law' (2003) 101 *Michigan Law Review* 2275
Bulkan, A, 'The Limits of Constitution (Re)-making in the Commonwealth Caribbean: Towards the "Perfect Nation"' (2013) 2 *Canadian Journal of Human Rights* 79
Campbell, T, 'Incorporation through interpretation' in T Campbell and others (eds) *The Legal Protection of Human Rights: Sceptical Essays* (Oxford University Press, 2011)
Carnegie, AR, '*Floreat* the Westminster Model?' A Commonwealth Caribbean Perspective' (1996) 6 *Caribbean Law Review* 1
Carolan, E, *The New Separation of Powers: A Theory for the Modern State* (Oxford University Press, 2009)
Carroll, E, '*Woolworths Ltd v Pallas Newco Pty Ltd*: A case study in the application of the rule of law in Australia' (2006) 13 *Australian Journal of Administrative Law* 87
Carter, M, 'The Rule of Law, Legal Rights in the Charter and the Supreme Court's New Positivism' (2007) 33 *Queen's Law Journal* 453
Césaire, A, *Discourse on Colonialism* (Monthly Review Press, 1978)
Chang, W-C and Yeh, J-R, 'Internationalization of Constitutional Law' in M Rosenfeld and A Sajó (eds), *The Oxford Handbook of Comparative Constitutional Law* (Oxford University Press, 2012)
Cheng, B, *General Principles of Law as Applied by International Courts and Tribunals* (Repr edn, Cambridge University Press, 1994)
Craig, P, 'Formal and Substantive Conceptions of the Rule of Law: An Analytical Framework' [1997] *Public Law* 467

—— 'Public Law, Political Theory and Legal Theory' [2000] *Public Law* 211
—— 'Constitutional Foundations, the Rule of Law and Supremacy' [2003] *Public Law* 92
—— *Administrative Law*, 6th edn (Sweet & Maxwell, 2008)
—— *Administrative Law*, 7th edn (Sweet & Maxwell, 2012)
'Constitutionalising Constitutional Law: *HS2*' [2014] *Public Law* 373
DeCoste, FC, 'Smoked: Tradition and the Rule of Law in *British Columbia v Imperial Tobacco Canada Ltd*' (2006) *Windsor Yearbook of Access to Justice* 328
DeHart, P, *Uncovering the Constitution's Moral Design* (University of Missouri Press, 2007)
Demerieux, M, *Fundamental Rights in Commonwealth Caribbean Constitutions* (Faculty of Law Library, University of the West Indies, 1992)
Department of Constitutional Affairs, *Constitutional Reform: A New Supreme Court for the United Kingdom* (CP 11/03), July 2003
—— *Constitutional Reform: Reforming the Office of Lord Chancellor* (CP 13/03) September 2003
De Smith, SA, *Judicial Review of Administrative Action*, 6th edn (Woolf Lord, and others eds, Sweet & Maxwell, 2007)
Dicey, AV, *Introduction to the Study of the Law of the Constitution*, 10th edn (Macmillan, 1959)
Dike, C, [1976] *Public Law* 283
Dworkin, R, *Taking Rights Seriously* (Harvard University Press, 1978)
—— 'Rights as Trumps' in Jeremy Waldron (ed), *Theories of Rights* (Oxford University Press, 1984)
—— *A Matter of Principle* (Oxford University Press, 1985)
—— *Law's Empire* (Harvard University Press, 1986)
Dyzenhaus, D, *The Constitution of Law: Legality in a Time of Emergency* (Cambridge University Press, 2006)
Elliot, R, 'References, Structural Argumentation and the Organizing Principles of Canada's Constitution' (2001) *Canadian Bar Review* 67
Elliott, M, *The Constitutional Foundations of Judicial Review* (Hart Publishing, 2001)
—— 'The Sovereignty of Parliament, the Hunting Ban, and the Parliament Acts' (2006) 65 *Cambridge Law Journal* 1
Endicott, T, 'Linguistic Indeterminacy' (1996) 16 *Oxford Journal of Legal Studies* 667
Erdos, D, *Delegating Rights Protection: the rise of bills of rights in the Westminster World* (Oxford University Press, 2010)
Fallon, R, 'The "Rule of Law" as a Concept in Constitutional Discourse' (1997) 97 *Columbia Law Review* 1.
Fanon, F, *Black Skin, White Masks* (Paladin, 1970)
Ferejohn, J and Pasquino, P, 'The Law of the Exception: A Typology of Emergency Powers' (2004) 2 *International Journal of Constitutional Law* 210
Fiadjoe, A, 'Judicial Attitudes to Commonwealth Caribbean Constitutions' (1991) 20 *Anglo-American Law Review* 121
—— *Commonwealth Caribbean Public Law*, 3rd edn (Routledge-Cavendish, 2008)
Forsyth, C and Elliott, M, 'The Legitimacy of Judicial Review' [2003] *Public Law* 286

Foster, S, 'Anti-terrorism, Human Rights and the Constitutional Role of the Courts' (2005) 10 *Coventry Law Journal* 63

Fraser, S, 'Constitutional Protection of Fundamental Rights in Guyana' (25 November 2000), http://www.guyanalaw.net/index.php/8-news-events/41-constitutional-protection-of-fundamental-rights-in-guyana

Gardbaum, S, *The New Commonwealth Model of Constitutionalism: Theory and Practice* (Cambridge University Press, 2013)

Gedicks, FM, 'An Originalist Defence of Substantive Due Process: Magna Carta, Higher Law Constitutionalism and the Fifth Amendment' (2009) 58 *Emory Law Journal* 585

Gee, G and Webber, G, 'What is a Political Constitution' (2010) 30 *Oxford Journal of Legal Studies* 273

Gee, G and Webber, G, 'Rationalism in Public Law' (2013) 76 *Modern Law Review* 708

Gentili, G, 'Canada: protecting rights in a "worldwide rights culture", an empirical study of the use of foreign precedents by the Supreme Court of Canada (1982–2010)' in T Groppi and M Ponthoreau (eds), *Use of foreign precedents by constitutional judges* (Hart Publishing, 2013)

Gerangelos, P, *The Separation of Powers and Legislative Interference in Judicial Process: Constitutional Principles and Limitations* (Hart Publishing, 2009)

Goldsworthy, J, 'Questioning the migration of constitutional ideas: rights, constitutionalism and the limits of convergence' in S Choudry, *The Migration of Constitutional Ideas* (Cambridge University Press, 2006) 127

Greenberg D, (ed) *Craies on Legislation: A Practitioners' Guide to the Nature, Process, Effect and Interpretation of Legislation*, 10th edn (Sweet & Maxwell, 2012)

Griffith, JAG, 'The Political Constitution' (1979) 42 *Modern Law Review* 1

—— 'The Brave New World of Sir John Laws' (2000) 63 *Modern Law Review* 159

—— 'The Common Law and the Political Constitution (2001) 117 *Law Quarterly Review* 42

Grimm, D, 'The Achievement of Constitutionalism and its Prospects in a Changed World' in Dobner, P and Loughlin, M, *The Twilight of Constitutionalism* (Oxford University Press, 2010)

Groves M, 'Substantive Legitimate Expectations in Australian Administrative Law' (2008) 32 *Melbourne University Law Review* 470

Hamilton, A, *The Federalist Papers* (Michael A Genovese ed, Palgrave Macmillan, 2009)

Harris, S, 'Ideological exchanges in British magistrates courts' in J Gibbons (ed) *Language and the Law* (Longman Publishing Group, 1994)

Hartley, TC and Griffith, JAG, *Government and Law: An Introduction to the Working of the Constitution in Britain*, 2nd edn (Weidenfeld and Nicolson, 1981)

Helmholz, RH, 'Bonham's Case, Judicial Review, and the Law of Nature' (2009) 1 *Journal of Legal Analysis* 325

Hewart, G, *The New Despotism* (Ernest Benn, 1929)

Hickman, T, *Public Law after the Human Rights Act* (Hart Publishing, 2010)

Hirschl, R, 'On the Blurred Methodological Matrix' in S Choudry, *The Migration of Constitutional Ideas* (Cambridge University Press, 2006)

Hoffmann, Lord, 'The COMBAR Lecture 2001: Separation of Powers' (2002) *JR* 137
Hogg, P and Bushell, A, 'The Charter Dialogue between Courts and Legislatures' (Or Perhaps The Charter of Rights Isn't Such a Bad Thing After All)' (1997) 35 *Osgoode Hall Law Journal* 75
—— and Zwibel, CF, 'The Rule of Law in the Supreme Court of Canada' (2005) 55 *University of Toronto Law Journal* 715
——, Bushell Thornton, A, and Wright, W, 'Charter Dialogue Revisited—or "Much Ado About Metaphors"' (2007) 45 *Osgoode Hall Law Journal* 1
Inglis, CA, *Studies in Australian Constitutional Law* (Charles F Maxwell (G Partridge & Co, 1901))
Irvine of Lairg QC, Lord, 'The Impact of the Human Rights Act: Parliament, the Courts and the Executive' [2003] *Public Law* 308
Jackson, VC, 'Comparative Constitutional Law: Methodologies' in M Rosenfeld and A Sajó (eds), *The Oxford Handbook of Comparative Constitutional Law* (Oxford University Press, 2012)
Jacobsohn, GJ, *Constitutional Identity* (Harvard University Press, 2010)
—— 'Constitutional Values and Principles' in M Rosenfeld and A Sajó (eds), *The Oxford Handbook of Comparative Constitutional Law* (Oxford University Press, 2012)
Jennings, I, *The Law and the Constitution*, 5th edn (University of London Press, 1963)
Jones, TH, 'Case Comment: Judicial Bias and Disqualification in the Pinochet case' [1999] *Public Law* 391
Jowell, J, 'Is Equality a Constitutional Principle' (1994) 47 *Current Legal Problems* 1
—— 'Beyond the Rule of Law: Towards Constitutional Judicial Review' [2000] *PL* 671
—— 'Of Vires and Vacuums: the Constitutional Context of Judicial Review' in C Forsyth (ed) *Judicial Review and the Constitution* (Hart, 2000)
—— 'Judicial Deference: Servility, Civility or Institutional Capacity?' [2003] *PL* 592
—— 'The Rule of Law's Long Arm: Uncommunicated Decisions' [2004] *PL* 246
—— 'Parliamentary Sovereignty under the New Hypothesis' [2006] *Public Law* 562
—— 'The Rule of Law and Its Underlying Values' in J Jowell and D Oliver (eds), *The Changing Constitution*, 6th edn (Oxford, OUP, 2007)
—— 'The Rule of Law and Its Underlying Values' in J Jowell and D Oliver (eds), *The Changing Constitution*, 7th edn (Oxford, OUP, 2011)
—— 'The Rule of Law: Rhetoric or Universal Principle?' (2012) 20 *Asia Pacific Law Review* 3
Kavanagh, A, 'The Elusive Divide between Interpretation and Legislation under the Human Rights Act 1998' (2004) 24 *OJLS* 259
—— *Constitutional Review under the UK Human Rights* (Cambridge, CUP, 2009)
—— 'Defending Deference in Public Law and Constitutional Theory' [2010] *LQR* 222
—— 'The Irish Constitution at 75 Years: Natural law, Christian Values and The Ideal of Justice' (2012) 48 *Irish Jurist* 71

Kazmierski, V, 'Draconian But Not Despotic: The 'Unwritten Limits of Parliamentary Sovereignty in Canada' (2010) 41 *Ottawa Law Review* 245
Kelly, JB and Murphy, M, 'Confronting Judicial Supremacy: A Defence of Judicial Activism' (2001) 16 *Can JL & Soc* 3
Klug, F, 'The Human Rights Act—a "Third Way" or "Third Wave" Bill of Rights' [2001] *EHRLR* 361
Klug, H, 'South Africa's Experience in Constitution-Building' available at http://papers.ssrn.com/sol3/papers.cfm?abstract_id=1808168
Knight, J and Epstein, L, 'On the Struggle for Judicial Supremacy' (1996) 30 *Law & Society Review* 87
Krishnamurthy, V, 'Colonial Cousins: Explaining India and Canada's Unwritten Constitutional Principles' (2009) 34 *Yale J Int'l L* 207
Krishnaswamy, S, *Democracy And Constitutionalism In India: A Study Of The Basic Structure Doctrine* (OUP, 2009)
Kumar, V, 'Basic Structure of the Indian Constitution: Doctrine of Constitutionally Controlled Governance' (2007) 49 *Journal of the Indian Law Institute* 365
The Law Commission, *Simplification of Criminal Law: Public Nuisance and Outraging Public Decency* (Law Com No 193, 2010)
Laws, Sir J, 'Law and Democracy' [1995] *PL* 7292
—— 'The Constitution: Morals and Rights' [1996] *PL* 622
Lane, PH, 'Constitutional Implications and a Bill of Rights' (2001) 75 *ALJ* 469
Leclair, J, 'Canada's Unfathomable Unwritten Constitutional Principles' (2002) 27 *Queen's LJ* 389
Leslie, J, 'Vindicating Common Law Constitutionalism' (2010) 30 *Legal Studies* 301
Loomba, A, *Colonialism/Postcolonialism* (Routledge, 2005)
Loughlin, M and Walker, N, 'Introduction' in M Loughlin and N Walker, *The Paradox of Constitutionalism: Constituent Power and Constitutional Form* (Oxford University Press, 2008)
—— 'What is Constitutionalisation?' in P Dobner and M Loughlin, *The Twilight of Constitutionalism?* (Oxford University Press, 2010)
Loveland, I, *Constitutional law, Administrative Law, and Human Rights: A Critical Introduction*, 6th edn (Oxford University Press, 2012)
Lutz, D, *Principles of Constitutional Design* (Cambridge University Press, 2006)
Macklem, T, 'Entrenching Bills of Rights' (2006) 26 *Oxford Journal of Legal Studies* 107
Magen, A and Morlino, L, 'Hybrid regimes, the rule of law, and external influence on domestic change' in A Magen and L Morlino (eds), *International Actors, Democratization and the Rule of Law: Anchoring Democracy?* (Routledge, 2009)
Lord Mance, 'Constitutional reforms, the Supreme Court and the Law Lords' (2006) 25 *Civil Justice Quarterly* 155
Marshall, G, *Constitutional Theory* (Oxford University Press, 1971)
Masterman, R, 'Determinative in the abstract? Article 6(1) and the separation of powers' [2005] *European Human Rights Law Review* 628
—— *The Separation of Powers in the Contemporary Constitution: Judicial Competence and Independence in the United Kingdom* (Cambridge University Press, 2011)
—— and Wheatle, S, 'A common law resurgence in rights protection?' [2015] *European Human Rights Law Review* 57

McCrudden, C, 'A Common Law of Human Rights: Transnational Judicial Conversations on Constitutional Rights' (2000) 20 *Oxford Journal of Legal Studies* 499

—— 'Human Rights and Judicial Use of Comparative Law' in E Örücü (ed), *Judicial Comparativism in Human Rights* (Martinus Nijhoff Publishers, 2004)

—— 'Northern Ireland, and the British Constitution' in J Jowell and D Oliver (eds), *The Changing Constitution*, 6th edn (Oxford University Press, 2007)

—— and Gerald Chambers, 'Introduction: Human Rights in British Law' in C McCrudden and G Chambers (eds), *Individual Rights and the Law in Britain* (Clarendon Press, 1994)

McIntosh, S, *Kelsen in the "Grenada court": essays on revolutionary legality* (Ian Randle, 2008)

McKenna, M, Simpson, A and Williams, G, 'First Words: The Preamble to the Australian Constitution' (2001) 24 *University of New South Wales Law Journal* 382

McLachlin, B, 'Unwritten Constitutional Principles: What is Going On?' (2006) 4 *New Zealand Journal of Public & International Law* 147

Merrill, TW, 'The Constitutional Principle of the Separation of Powers' (1991) 7 *Supreme Court Review* 225

Mitchell, W and Simmons, R, 'Public Choice and the Judiciary: Introductory Notes' [1990] *Brigham Young University Law Review* 729

MK 'Constitutional Law-Court of Claims-Legislative Courts-Reducing Judge's Salary' (1934) 9 *Indiana Law Journal* 318

Möller, K, 'Balancing and the Structure of Constitutional Rights' (2007) 5 *International Journal of Constitutional Law* 453

Möllers, C, *The Three Branches: A Comparative Model of Separation of Powers Constitutionalism in Global Constitutionalisation* (Oxford University Press, 2013).

Monahan, PJ, 'The Public Policy Role of the Supreme Court in the *Secession Reference*' (1999) 11 *National Journal of Constitutional Law* 65

baron de Montesquieu, C, *The Spirit of Laws* (AM Cohler, ed and tr, Cambridge University Press, 1989)

Morgan, J, 'Amateur Operatics: The Realization of Parliamentary Protection of Civil Liberties' in T Campbell and others (eds) *The Legal Protection of Human Rights: Sceptical Essays* (Oxford University Press, 2011)

Newman, W, 'The Principles of the Rule of Law and Parliamentary Sovereignty in Constitutional Theory and Litigation' (2005) 16 *National Journal of Constitutional Law* 175

Noyes, H, 'Lords Attack Foreign Compensation Bill', *The Times* (5 February 1969)

O'Donoghue, A, *Constitutionalism in Global Constitutionalisation* (Cambridge University Press, 2014)

Oliver, D, 'Is the Ultra vires Doctrine the Basis of Judicial Review?' (1987) *Public Law* 543

—— *Constitutional Reform in the UK* (*Constitutionalism in Global Constitutionalisation* (Oxford University Press, 2003)

Orgad, L, 'The Preamble in Constitutional Interpretation' (2010) 8 *International Journal of Constitutional Law* 714

Örücü, E, 'Comparative Law in British Courts', in U Drobnig and S van Erp (eds), *The Use of Comparative Law by Courts* (Kluwer Law International, 1999)
—— 'Whither Comparativism in Human Rights Cases' in E Örücü (ed), *Judicial Comparativism in Human Rights* (Martinus Nijhoff Publishers, 2004)
Pennycook, A, *English and the Discourse of Colonialism* (Routledge, 1998)
Perju, V, 'Constitutional Transplants, Borrowing, and Migrations' in M Rosenfeld and A Sajó (eds), *The Oxford Handbook of Comparative Constitutional Law* (Oxford University Press, 2012)
Peronne, L, 'The Fundamental and Natural Law "Repugnant Review" Origins of Judicial Review: A Synergy of early English Corporate Law with Notions of Fundamental and Natural Law' (2008) 23 *Brigham Young University Journal of Public Law* 61
Phillips, OH, 'A Constitutional Myth: Separation of Powers' (1977) 93 *Law Quarterly Review* 11
Poole, T, 'Dogmatic Liberalism? TRS Allan and the Common Law Constitution' (2002) 65 *Modern Law Review* 463
—— 'Back to the Future? Unearthing the Theory of Common Law Constitutionalism' [2003] *Oxford Journal of Legal Studies* 435
Rawlings, R, 'Review, Revenge and Retreat' (2005) 68 *Modern Law Review* 378
Raz, J, 'Legal Principles and the Limits of Law' (1972) 81 *Yale Law Journal* 823
—— 'The Rule of Law and Its Virtue' (1977) 93 *Law Quarterly Review* 195
—— *The Authority of Law: Essays on Law and Morality* (Clarendon Press, 1979)
—— 'On the Authority and Interpretation of Constitutions' in Larry Alexander (ed) *Constitutionalism: Philosophical Foundations* (Cambridge University Press, 1998)
—— *Between Authority and Interpretation: On the Theory of Law and Practical Reason* (Oxford University Press, 2009)
Reed, R, 'Foreign precedents and judicial reasoning: the American debate and British practice' (2008) 124 *Law Quarterly Review* 253
Reynolds, NB, 'Grounding the Rule of Law' (1989) 2 *Ratio Juris* 1
Robinson, T, 'Gender, Nation and the Common Law Constitution' (2008) 28 *Oxford Journal of Legal Studies* 735
Russell, P, 'Constitutionalism' in Adam Kuper and Jessica Kuper, *The Social Science Encyclopedia*, 3rd edn (Routledge, 2009)
Sadurski, W, *Equality and Legitimacy* (Oxford University Press, 2008); Fabienne Peter *Democratic Legitimacy* (Routledge, 2011)
Saunders, C, 'The Use and Misuse of Comparative Constitutional Law' (2006) 13 *Indiana Journal of Global Legal Studies* 37
—— 'The Constitution of Australia: Contextual Analysis' (Hart Publishing, 2011)
Schønberg, S and Craig, P, 'Substantive Legitimate Expectations after Coughlan' [2000] *Public Law* 684
Selznick, P, *The Moral Commonwealth: Social Theory and the Promise of Community* (University of California Press, 1992)
Slaughter, A-M, 'A Typology of Transjudicial Communication' (1994) 29 *University Richmond Law Review* 99
—— 'Judicial Globalization' (1999–2000) 40 *Virginia Journal of International Law* 1103
Smith, A, 'Internationalisation and Constitutional Borrowing In Drafting Bills Of Rights' (2011) 60 *International and Comparative Law Quarterly* 867

Smith, R, 'Rights And Wrongs: Asylum Star Chamber' (2004) *Legal Studies Gazette*, 15 Jan, 16

Hon, JJ, Spigelman, AC, 'Principle of Legality and the Clear Statement Principle' (2005) 79 *Australian Law Journal* 769

Stavsky, M, 'The Doctrine of State Necessity in Pakistan' (1983) 16 *Cornell International Law Journal* 341

Steyn, Lord, 'Democracy through law' (2002) 6 *European Human Rights Law Review* 723

—— 'Democracy, the rule of law and the role of judges' (2006) *European Human Rights Law* Review 243

Stone, A, 'Judicial Review Without Rights: Some Problems for the Democratic Legitimacy of Structural Judicial Review' (2008) 28 *Oxford Journal of Legal Studies* 1

—— 'Comparativism in Constitutional Interpretation' [2009] *University of Melbourne Law Research Series* 15

Stoner, JR, 'Natural Law, Common Law and the Constitution' in Douglas E Edlin (ed) *Common Law Theory* (Cambridge University Press, 2007)

Sunstein, C, 'Constitutionalism after the New Deal' (1987) 101 *Harvard Law Review* 421

Taiwo, O, 'The Rule of Law: The New Leviathan?' (1999) 12 *Canadian Journal of Law & Jurisprudence* 151

Tamanaha, BZ, *On the Rule of Law: History, Politics, Theory* (Cambridge University Press, 2004)

Taylor, J, 'Human Rights Protection in Australia: Interpretation Provisions and Parliamentary Supremacy' (2004) 32 *Federal Law Review* 57

The Commission on a Bill of Rights, 'A UK Bill of Rights? The Choice Before Us' (December 2012) http://webarchive.nationalarchives.gov.uk/20130128112038/ http://www.justice.gov.uk/about/cbr

Thomas, EW, *The Judicial Process: Realism, Pragmatism, Practical Reasoning and Principles* (Cambridge University Press, 2005)

Thorne, S, 'Dr Bonham's case' (1938) *Law Quarterly Review* 543

Tomkins, A, 'In Defence of the Political Constitution' (2002) 22 *Oxford Journal of Legal Studies* 157

—— 'The Rule of Law in Blair's Britain' (2007) 27 *University of Queensland Law Journal* 255

Tremblay, L, *The Rule of Law, Justice and Interpretation* (McGill-Queen's Univeristy Press, 1997)

Twomey, A, 'Constitutional Recognition of Indigenous Australians in a Preamble' (Constitutional Reform Unit, Sydney Law School, 2011)

Vayda, P, 'Chipping Away at Cost Barriers: A Comment on the Supreme Court of Canada's Trial Lawyers Decision' (2015) 36 *Windsor Review of Legal and Social Issues* 207

Verkuil, PR, 'Separation of Powers, the Rule of Law and the Idea of Independence' (1989) 30 *William & Mary Law Review* 301

Vile, MJC, *Constitutionalism and the separation of powers*, 2nd edn (Liberty Fund, 1998)

Voegelin, E, Published Essays, 1934–1939, vol 9 of *The Collected Works of Eric Voegelin* (University of Missouri Press, 2001)

Waldron, J, 'The Rule of Law as a Theater of Debate' in Justine Burley (ed) *Dworkin and His Critics: With Replies by Dworkin* (Blackwell Publishing, 2004)
—— 'The Core of the Case Against Judicial Review' (2006) 115 *Yale Law Journal* 1346
—— 'Constitutionalism—A Sceptical View' (2012) NYU School of Law, Public Law Research Paper No 10–87 http://ssrn.com/abstract=1722771
—— *Partly Laws Common to All Mankind': Foreign Law in American Courts* (Yale UP, 2012)
Walters, M, 'The Common Law Constitution in Canada: The Return of Lex Non Scripta as Fundamental Law' (2001) 51 *University of Toronto Law Journal* 91
—— 'Written Constitutions and Unwritten Constitutionalism' in Grant Huscroft (ed), *Expounding the Constitution: Essays in Constitutional Theory* (Cambridge University Press, 2008)
Waluchow, WJ, *A Common Law Theory of Judicial Review: The Living Tree* (Cambridge University Press, 2007)
Wheatle, S, 'Comparative Law and the Ius Gentium' (2014) 3 *Cambridge Journal of International and Comparative Law* 1065
Wheeler, F, 'The Doctrine of Separation of Powers and Constitutionally Entrenched Due Process in Australia' (1997) 23 *Monash Law Review* 248
—— 'Due Process, Judicial Power and Chapter III in the New High Court' (2004) 32 *Federal Law Review* 205
White, R, 'Separation of powers and legislative supremacy' (2011) 127 *Law Quarterly Review* 456
Williams, G, 'Defence of Necessity' (1953) 6 *Current Legal Problems* 216
Williams, I, 'Dr Bonham's Case and "Void" Statutes' (2006) 27(2) *Journal of Legal History* 111
Winterton, G, 'The Separation of Judicial Power as an Implied Bill of Rights' in Geoffrey Lindell (ed), *Future Directions in Australian Constitutional Law* (Federation Press, 1994)
Woodhouse, D, 'Law and Politics: More Power to the Judges—and to the People?' (2001) 54 *Parliamentary Affairs* 223
—— 'The English judges, politics and the balance of power' (2003) 22 *Modern Law Review* 920
Woolf, Lord, 'The rule of law and a change in the constitution' (2004) 63 *Cambridge Law Journal* 317
Wormuth, FD, *The Origins of Modern Constitutionalism* (Harper, 1949)
Young, A, *Parliamentary Sovereignty and the Human Rights Act* (Hart Publishing, 2008)
—— 'The Rule of Law in the United Kingdom: Formal or Substantive?' (2012) 6 *Vienna Journal on International Constitutional Law* 259
Zagrebelsky, G, 'Ronald Dworkin's principle based constitutionalism: An Italian point of view' (2003) *International Journal of Constitutional Law* 621
Zaum, D, 'International Organisations, Legitimacy, and Legitimation' in D Zaum, *Legitimating International Organizations* (Oxford University Press, 2013)
Zines, L, *The High Court and the constitution*, 5th edn (The Federation Press, 2008)

Index

www.ingramcontent.com/pod-product-compliance
Ingram Content Group UK Ltd.
Pitfield, Milton Keynes, MK11 3LW, UK
UKHW020138290926
15471UKWH00003B/570

9 781509 931323